GLOBAL LEADERSHIP

Portraits of the Past, Visions for the Future

Michael Harvey and
JoAnn Danelo Barbour, Editors

a volume in the International Leadership Association series
Building Leadership Bridges

THE INTERNATIONAL LEADERSHIP ASSOCIATION (ILA) is a global network for all those who practice, study, and teach leadership. The ILA promotes a deeper understanding of leadership knowledge and practices for the greater good of individuals and communities worldwide. The principal means by which this mission is accomplished is through the synergy that occurs by bringing together public- and private-sector leaders, scholars, educators, consultants, and students from many disciplines and many nations. For more information, please visit www.ila-net.org.

The ILA was founded by and is based at The James MacGregor Burns Academy of Leadership at the University of Maryland. The Burns Academy of Leadership fosters leadership through scholarship, education, and training, with special attention to advancing the leadership of groups historically underrepresented in public life. For more information, please visit www.academy.umd.edu.

The ILA partnered with the Center for Creative Leadership (CCL®) to produce this publication. CCL is a top-ranked, global provider of executive education that develops better leaders through its exclusive focus on leadership education and research. Founded in 1970 as a nonprofit, educational institution, CCL helps clients worldwide cultivate creative leadership—the capacity to achieve more than imagined by thinking and acting beyond boundaries—through an array of programs, products, and other services. CCL is headquartered in North America with campuses in Brussels and Singapore. For more information, visit www.ccl.org.

For additional copies of this book, please contact the publisher:

THE JAMES MACGREGOR BURNS ACADEMY OF LEADERSHIP
University of Maryland
College Park, MD 20742-7715 USA
Phone: 301-405-5218
Fax: 301-405-6402
E-mail: ila@ila-net.org
Web: www.ila-net.org

Library of Congress ISBN: 978-1-891464-05-8

Production: Center for Creative Leadership
Production Editor: Joanne Ferguson

Table of Contents

GLOBAL LEADERSHIP:
PORTRAITS OF THE PAST, VISIONS FOR THE FUTURE

Introduction

"What's past is prologue," Antonio argues in Shakespeare's *Tempest*, suggesting that learning the right lessons from the past can help us shape the future. This year the International Leadership Association is pleased to offer *Global Leadership: Portraits of the Past, Visions for the Future*, the newest volume in the *Building Leadership Bridges (BLB)* series, as our own bridge from the past to the future of leadership. As ILA celebrates its tenth anniversary, we offer the baker's-dozen pieces assembled here as some of the best contemporary thinking in the leadership arena.

In keeping with the mission of the ILA, *BLB* connects ways of studying, imagining, and experiencing leadership across cultures, over time, and around the world. In this year's volume we begin with reflections on portraits, art, and leadership—a "subjective self-portrait," as she calls it, from the longtime editor of *BLB*, Nancy S. Huber. Nancy's own artwork uses evocative watercolor landscapes—portraits of the natural past, if you will—to encourage us to explore our own inner visions and dreams.

Following Huber, Marjorie E. Blum presents a tool for leadership development based on the concept of the genogram, a kind of self-portrait of one's family. By learning about and documenting one's family story, Blum suggests, the leader gains a truer sense of his or her identity—and thus can become more effective working with others. Kurt Takamine presents another take on developing an authentic portrait of oneself as a leader: the concept of the existential leader. He helps us understand the relationship and importance of the existential themes of essence, freedom and choice, meaning and value, existential anxiety, and spiritual attributes to the leader's self-awareness and efficacy.

Did you hear the one about the leader and the follower? Peter M. Jonas reminds us that some portraits are funny, contributing a most unusual and insightful piece on using humor to reshape and reflect on leadership. His thoughtful exploration of humor will actually make you laugh as you read it! After Jonas, Mark Bagshaw broadens the discussion by analyzing the GLOBE Project, an international study about leadership traits and behaviors, and concluding that painting leadership with the brush of American universals is inappropriate. Challenging the "one portrait fits all" picture of leadership, Bagshaw holds that a cultural approach to leadership is important for a global understanding and a global conversation. Karen Lokkesmoe continues the global turn by demonstrating the potential for leadership development of an intercultural inventory; then Sharon Turnbull lets us hear from global master's students—all working leaders—on the importance of a worldly mind-set for effective leadership in a globalizing world.

One major concept for those who study leadership is resistance to leadership; Kevin Baker and James Warn explore this important aspect of leader-follower relations from a military perspective, looking at significant twentieth-century mutinies. Their cautionary portraits of how leadership failed in these instances can serve as an important lesson for the future.

Liz Barber and colleagues then bring us a student perspective, describing and synthesizing the experience of a cohort of college students who traveled to Malawi in the summer of 2007 to help ordinary Malawians with development projects. The students, from historically black college North Carolina A&T, not only learned about Malawi but about themselves and their connection to others. Next, Nicola De Paul and colleagues discuss the Population Leadership Program, a nine-month residential program in which professionals from selected developing countries are partnered with each other for leadership development and management training. From relationships built through the program, the professionals partner with each other and the university instructors to create and implement their visions for change in the areas of population, family planning, and reproductive health.

In the next entries, the authors examine particular national cultures, those of Lithuania and China. From their studies of Lithuanian organizations, Dail Fields and colleagues conclude that the traditional view of Lithuanian employee needs and preferences is obsolete. The use of leadership approaches that assure employees of just treatment and active concern for employee welfare and development may be needed for organizational commitment and employee loyalty in the future. Then, Joanne Barnes and Sharon Drury offer voices of women leaders in China, and help us navigate the complex interconnections of dynamic capitalism, politics, and traditional culture in their lives and leadership journeys.

Finally, we close with what is very much both a portrait of the past and a vision of the future: Suheil Bushrui's evocative exploration of the role of the poet in shaping our imaginings about leaders and leadership. Bushrui, a noted Arab scholar and poet, draws on a rich vein of world literary traditions to suggest what it is that poets have to contribute to our own vision of leadership.

While this volume would not be possible without the contributions of the authors, we would especially like to express our appreciation to others who partner with us in this effort. We are grateful to the Center for Creative Leadership for the expertise they provide in the production of a quality publication. Special thanks go to CCL's Joanne Ferguson, whose diligence makes us all look good! Thank you also to the ILA Board of Directors for their continuing support and encouragement of our attempts to evolve in ways we hope will better serve all of you who study, practice, teach, and care about leadership in the world. Let us take the portraits of our past to use for our futures, for what has already transpired has merely prepared the scene for the *really* important stuff, the stuff of our visions.

Michael Harvey and JoAnn Danelo Barbour
Editors

Leadership and Art: A Subjective Self-Portrait

By Nancy S. Huber

CALLING MYSELF "LEADER" WAS INITIALLY A VERY DIFFICULT THING to do. It seemed an arrogant proclamation. It was many years ago and I had moved halfway across the country and determined that I was going to survive . . . and realized that simply surviving wasn't good enough. I was a single mother in graduate school and involved in the design and implementation of the first Wisconsin Rural Leadership Program seminar series. I stood before a group of young men and women and proclaimed myself a leader. More presumptuous than the leader label was the fact that I was involved in leadership development!

Fast forward 25 years. I've moved beyond survival to a successful career in academia. Not wanting to wait until I retire to take up a hobby that has intrigued me for many years, I began taking watercolor lessons with my oldest grandson. Writing an artist statement to accompany my first foray into exhibiting one of my watercolor paintings in a public show was, for me, a daunting task. Again, I asked myself just who I thought I was kidding. After all, I'd only been painting for a little more than a year. An artist statement indeed . . . people would laugh, I was sure. Even more embarrassing, I was expected to put a price on my work because all of the paintings in the show would be for sale.

It seems that, in both instances, the title might be subjective. Who decides who leads anyway? Who's to say what art is in this day and age? In Wisconsin, I didn't have a title, but I was leading anyway . . . I had a reason for leading and I was passionate about what I was learning and doing. When I first entered a watercolor show, I didn't even have a studio but I was painting anyway . . . I had a reason for painting and I was excited about what I was learning and creating. Over time, I've grown comfortable with the subjective nature of these titles.

When Michael Harvey asked me to contribute a reflection piece for this year's *Building Leadership Bridges* volume that explored and linked these two elements of my life, I began to think about the parallels and intersections. Earlier, I had responded to a similar invitation from cohorts at Ohio State University to write a newsletter item that spoke to the similarities evident in the language employed by one of my early watercolor instructors and the words I use often in my teaching of leadership. Now I'll take that a bit further and mingle what I know of learning, doing, and teaching leadership with my current understanding of learning, doing, and teaching watercolor.

Learning . . .
Both artists and leaders need to acquire the basic skills necessary to accomplish their goals. However, in both cases, the tool box of skills is not enough. One cannot expect success to follow automatically once a skill set is mastered. In fact, both leaders and artists must continually hone their skills. I've never known an effective leader or a successful artist who does not actively work on learning new techniques and trying different approaches.

A key skill for both leaders and artists is communication. Leaders must be able to communicate effectively, to organize their thoughts and deliver a coherent message that encourages others to become involved. Artists must be able to communicate effectively through visual media, to create art that engages the viewer and invites interpretation or simple enjoyment. It goes without saying that the required communication abilities are quite different and, further, they vary with the nature and purpose of the leader as well as with the type of artistic endeavor. Collaborative leadership employs a communication style that might not be useful at all in a military leadership setting. Some of the skills and techniques used by a watercolorist simply don't work for those who paint with oils.

> **❝ I'VE NEVER KNOWN AN EFFECTIVE LEADER OR A SUCCESSFUL ARTIST WHO DOES NOT ACTIVELY WORK ON LEARNING NEW TECHNIQUES AND TRYING DIFFERENT APPROACHES. ❞**

Decision making is a skill that takes time and experience to develop fully. Whether leadership is practiced collaboratively in a community or monopolistically at the top of an organizational chart, decisions must be made. Small decisions are often made quickly and without angst, while larger decisions that may be absolutely critical are more apt to be pondered and carefully scrutinized prior to making the final choice. Some decisions can be revisited with no harm done while others become permanent immediately.

Artists occasionally approach decision making collaboratively if, for example, they participate in a small group of watercolorists who paint together and critique each other's work. However, it is more likely that decisions will be made individually—whether the format will be tall and narrow or square, whether the approach will be soft and transparent or bold and abstract, or whether to tear up a painting and start over or try to save it. As is the case with decisions made by leaders, some artistic decisions can be revisited with no harm done while others become permanent immediately.

In addition to learning the skills required to be effective as a leader or proficient as an artist, becoming familiar with the concepts contributing to a successful outcome is essential. Consider the notion of ambiguity and its converse, predictability. Ambiguity is certainly present in the process of leadership (probably even for those who govern by Roberts' Rules of Order) as well as in the development of a painting (with the possible exception of those who do the paint-by-number kits). Without an understanding of the need for tolerance for ambiguity, leaders' expectations when dealing with a diverse group will be sorely tested. After all, moving a group of people forward is not a simple linear process but fraught with stops and starts and changes in both speed and direction. People just don't always behave as expected.

The watercolorist who expects paint and paper to behave in predictable fashion will experience frustration because mixing water with pigment and then applying it to paper presents a wide range of possible options. Too much water and a back run is produced or pigment runs off the paper. An interruption takes the artist away from the painting briefly and, lo and behold, there's a hard edge that was totally unexpected. If the slant of the work surface is too great, the colors can run together and make an unattractive muddy splotch. Because it is the nature of watercolor as a medium to produce surprises, it is important for the artist to develop a tolerance for ambiguity.

Composition is a concept that is important to both artist and leader. A leader will need to consider who is included in a project group and how the people are organized to do the work when designing team-building activities and developing a successful organization. Paying attention to compositional elements will assure that the structure of an organization suits its vision and mission. Care must also be taken to design teams in a manner that will produce results on assigned tasks. One needs only a rudimentary understanding of personality typologies to recognize the need for balance in team composition.

There are design elements to consider in the composition of a watercolor. Certainly, the artist's vision as well as the purpose of the painting play into the composition. Structure and balance are important, but I would hasten to add that balance is not necessarily synonymous with symmetry. Instead, the focal point will almost always be away from the center of the painting but will be balanced by means of other design elements. For example, repetition of a shape can help to harmonize a painting while careful attention to values (light to dark) adds interest and draws attention to that aspect of the creative piece the artist wishes to emphasize.

Doing . . .

Leaders must deal with an array of problems that are associated with group dynamics, organizational issues, and specific events. This is where both the learned skill set and a knowledge of leadership concepts comes to the fore . . . an understanding of people and how they interact, the ability to clarify (and simplify) the key aspects of a complex issue, and a willingness to explore alternatives and consequences of actions taken before making a decision. Artists deal with a whole different set of problems that need to be solved, but like leaders, they must employ skills they have developed over time as well as draw upon their knowledge of artistic concepts . . . an understanding of pigments and how they interact, the ability to clarify (and simplify) the elements of a complex design issue, and a willingness to anticipate consequences of brush strokes and application of paint to paper as they make decisions in the development of a watercolor painting.

Both leaders and artists make decisions in the process of implementing a plan or creating a watercolor and they do so drawing on both acquired knowledge and personal experience. However, I would posit that both artists and leaders rely on a deeper level of knowing that resides in the subconscious. Mackenzie (1999) makes this point quite earnestly when he says to aspiring watercolorists:

> Put intuition in control. Let your imagination and intuitive sense of composition assume control. The hardest part about this is believing in your ability to do it. The second-hardest part is shutting off that little left-brain voice that says, "this is stupid. It won't work." It takes courage to step into the unknown and trust what you find, particularly when the unknown is within you. (p. 114)

In *Leading from Within* (1999), I make a similar case for intuition in a discussion that differentiates leadership and management, saying that leaders may engage in a change process without a clear picture of what the outcome will be, but knowing intuitively that they are on the right path. When one learns to tap . . . and trust . . . intuition, it becomes a valued resource. It is difficult to call up insight and intuition at will. However, as leaders and artists engage their work with an eager sense of openness and possibility, the flow of ideas increases as innate wisdom and creativity come into play.

Both leaders and artists tend to develop a particular style over time. For most people, it is a function of both time and experience as well as a predisposition to approach the process in a way suited to individual personality and to the anticipated outcome. Another influencing factor is the context within which leadership happens or painting evolves. As examples, military leadership operates in a context that is not the same as rural community leadership. Similarly, studio artists approach their art in a way that can not readily be duplicated when painting *en plein air* as outdoor conditions may vary widely, even in the same day.

Another element that shapes the approach taken either by leader or artist has to do with control. Some leaders are not comfortable with minimal control and might be thought of as micro-managers while others are more collaborative as they deal with solving problems and charting a course for the future. In like manner, one does not need to be an art expert to recognize painting styles that are more controlled and iterative, easily differentiating them from those that are impressionistic and suggestive in their content.

From my own work, compare the two paintings that follow. The subject matter is the Sonoran desert sentinel, the saguaro. "Saguaro Solo" is a carefully crafted representation of a single cactus bloom. "Sonoran Snow Mist" is more of an impression of a sunny morning following a rare Tucson snowstorm and depicts a pair of saguaros against a misty background and the Catalina mountains appearing as a "sky island."

The realistic painting perhaps reflects my need to be more in control because of my insecurity as a novice watercolorist while the free-flowing rendition represents an increasing comfort level with the process . . . letting the pigment and water do its own thing to some extent. From my own leadership, I would have to say that those times when I have felt the need to try to be in control were uncomfortable for me but were good learning experiences . . . just as a more controlled, precise painting provides an important learning opportunity. However, I am much more at ease in a less structured and spontaneous environment as both leader and artist!

Teaching . . .

There is a significant element of subjectivity in how I understand both leadership and art. Long ago, I struggled with trying to define leadership and concluded that leadership has a personal (subjective) meaning for all of us. I leave the struggle for a universally acceptable definition of the term to others. For me, leadership is a shared responsibility for creating a better world in which to live and work. It manifests in our passion to engage others in bringing about purposeful change (Huber, 1999). More recently, I've thought about art in terms of its personal meaning. For me, watercolor provides an avenue to explore and express beauty and meaning in the world. It manifests in my passion to engage with others in learning and creating artistic interpretations of what I see and seek to understand more fully.

In large measure, my approach to teaching leadership is grounded in what it means to me although I take my responsibility for broadening the students' perspective quite seriously. That is why I purposely encourage them to come up with their own definition and develop a personal philosophy of leadership. Additionally, I teach leadership as a process, one that is collaborative and driven by a purpose—leadership for what reason and with whom because it doesn't happen in a vacuum. To that end, my lectures are brief if they occur at all! Just as one cannot learn to paint expressive watercolors without actually getting involved in the process, I believe it is impossible for one to truly learn to exercise effective leadership without actually "doing" leadership.

Over the years, I have come to realize that there are some aspects of leadership that I can teach people about, but that is no guarantee that the knowledge will be incorporated into the way they lead. I believe that being passionate, authentic, credible, and ethical are essential characteristics of effective leadership and so they are frequent topics in my teaching. However, I do not view these as skills to be learned; they are attributes and they represent choices to be made. For example, I can teach *about* ethics, but that doesn't guarantee that my students will *be* ethical unless they make that choice and act accordingly.

As for teaching a watercolor workshop, I really am not qualified to do so after just a three-year learning process! But I can say a bit about some of the teaching I have experienced. The Southern Arizona Watercolor Guild, of which I am a member, sponsors several workshops each year and offers demonstrations at the monthly meetings. The demonstrations are interesting and get the creative juices flowing. However, gaining hands-on experience in a workshop setting is much more valuable. I am an advocate of experiential education as a professor and, as a learner, I am very much predisposed to experiential learning.

To date, I have studied with a half dozen different artists, developing painting skills while becoming more familiar with watercolor approaches and concepts. One instructor has exhorted me to paint what I am most passionate about while another says that there's no point in painting unless you have something to say. Much to my dismay, I have been told that I can't be successful as an artist unless I learn to draw first (it's not something that comes easily to me). More encouraging is another teacher who tells her students to just play—to explore and have fun. The workshops have been very much hands-on and I have toted my palette to Mackinac Island, Michigan, as well as to several workshops here in Arizona. I confess that I still hesitate to call myself an artist, but it is not as embarrassing a proclamation as it once was!

Living up to the title of either artist or leader is, for me, much less daunting if I employ an adjective in each case. I know myself to be a collaborative leader and feel no embarrassment saying so. For me, it is very much in keeping with my belief that leadership is a shared responsibility and often only marginally related to carrying a title. I know that I am becoming a watercolor artist and that I will become more proficient with time. Clarifying that watercolor is the medium I choose for artistic expression relieves me of having to be competent in the many avenues open to those who pursue art professionally or as a fulfilling hobby. Both leadership and painting are important in my life, but the balance is beginning to shift as I approach that point when my career in academia is past and retirement is what the future holds.

REFERENCES

Huber, N. S. (1999). *Leading from within: Developing personal direction.* Malabar, FL: Krieger Publishing.

MacKenzie, G. (1999). *The watercolorist's essential notebook.* Cincinnati, OH: North Light Books.

NANCY S. HUBER is the Faculty Associate to the Vice President for Instruction at the University of Arizona. In the early 1980s, she left rural Maine and began a graduate program at the University of Wisconsin studying volunteer management. However, she came to realize that "volunteer" is often another word for "leader," and so began her career as a leadership educator/scholar. In addition to the book *Leading from Within* that she authored to use with her teaching, she has been involved with editing the *Building Leadership Bridges* series for ILA since 2003. As she approaches the possibility of retirement, her interest in painting with watercolor is growing!

Self-Defined Leadership: Exploring Family History to Enhance Future Leadership

By Marjorie E. Blum

One faces the future with one's past.—Pearl S. Buck

It is in the family that we first develop a sense of our identity, our values, our aspirations and our expectations for life. It is in our families that we have the *least* examined and *most* determining experiences. Because our family life was so powerful in influencing our views of leadership and because we often maintain an unconscious barrier to recognizing its impact, it is difficult to uncover the lessons we learned and the messages we received. (Bennis & Goldsmith, 1997, p. 61)

MOST MAJOR WORKS IN THE LEADERSHIP FIELD, REGARDLESS OF theoretical orientation or focus on public or private systems, emphasize the importance of self-knowledge necessary to be a healthy leader and to lead effectively (Bennis, 1994; Gergen, 2000; Heifetz, 1994; Heifetz & Linsky, 2002; Kets de Vries, 2001; Senge, 1990). Increased knowledge of self yields greater personal development and maturity, translating into a capacity to be a more emotionally stable and interpersonally effective leader. Current practices in professional coaching and leadership development curricula commonly include measures of who we are, typified by the Myers-Briggs Type Indicator®; how we are perceived by others, as with a 360-degree feedback instrument; and our capacity for interpersonal interaction and impact, for example, emotional intelligence. These measures provide the individual with a contemporary self-knowledge in order to develop plans for personal growth. However, this contemporary self-knowledge does not give leaders a view into their past, so critical for self-understanding. In integrating family psychology and leadership literature, there is compelling support and call for programs offering family exploration and understanding of self-in-systems in leadership development programs. Uncovering our psychological family history is not only possible, but powerful.

Foundation for Family Exploration in Leadership Development

One would never presume to lead an organization or a country without exploring its culture and history over decades. It is equally essential for the leader to understand his/her own legacies and history. Looking at self-in-family generates a view of one-self within a relational system, not solely as an individual. While the definition and composition of family may vary from culture to culture, the dynamics of families and human relationships are virtually the same across the globe.

> **66 LOOKING AT SELF-IN-FAMILY GENERATES A VIEW OF ONESELF WITHIN A RELATIONAL SYSTEM, NOT SOLELY AS AN INDIVIDUAL. 99**

Family exploration is routinely offered for family psychology trainees, clergy and pastoral candidates, physicians and residents. This author has spent many years guiding pediatric residents in the exploration of family. These physicians deliver more effective care as a result of understanding their own family history and understanding the dynamics of the families with whom they work. Medicine and ministry may appear to require more interpersonal focus; however, the success of every leader depends on interpersonal relationships. Understanding oneself systemically, of self within family or self within organization, enhances leadership effectiveness as well (Friedman, 1996).

This author suggests that methodical exploration of one's experience and development within a multigenerational family context enhances leadership development. This exploration invites an active process, allowing the person to develop a foundation for continuous self-defining in one's family and other systems such as political and business organizations. As will be discussed in more detail through this paper, the concept of self definition essentially refers to an individual's capacity to be less reactive to emotional stress and triggers in the system. Self definition allows the leader, with internal conviction and self-understanding, to remain objective, creative, and thoughtful. Additionally, the creation of a family genogram, a graphic documentation of psychological family history, provides a method of compiling the complex and copious family information gathered throughout the discovery process.

Using the genogram as a portrait in time, the leader can use it as a basis for learning about and documenting his/her emerging family narrative.

An additional benefit to examining one's family-of-origin is the understanding of systems in general. The basic concepts of family systems are applicable to all systems—social, work, and family. It is valuable to not only know one's family but to understand that all human organizations—whether corporations, government agencies, or small businesses—all operate on the same dynamics and principles as families. (1. The whole is more than the sum of parts. 2. Every system repeats its patterns of sensitivities, relationship styles, and structure over time. 3. Systems are homeostatic, resisting change.) Knowing these dynamics offers a framework for understanding any organization. A leader can use this knowledge proactively, increasing his/her capacity to be effective and have impact. Learning about systems and systemic concepts, coupled with increasing understanding of family-of-origin, provides one with the tools to step back and analyze any variety of contexts. Such analyses enhance one's ability to stay aware of and, therefore, independent of the system's historic patterns, expectations, and emotional reactivity. We can also learn to be sensitized to consider others' behaviors and beliefs within context. This exercise of identifying the original context for these "inheritances" can not only help us make grown-up decisions for ourselves, but has an additional benefit of promoting greater tolerance for our colleagues' differences. Our partners, customers, and colleagues grew up in their own family as well. While our general stance is to advocate for respect for cultural diversity, we also need to stay aware that each of us grew up in a unique micro-culture—the family. This appreciation and acknowledgement of our differences is the next level of diversity training.

Leadership and Family History: We Continue to Act Out Predictable But Unexamined Life Patterns—For Better or Worse

Systemic theories of human organization guide us to understand that individuals are inextricably interconnected with the groups within which we live and work. Viewing individual functioning within the context of the family system and devising systemic interventions for psychological health was first conceived by Murray Bowen in the 1950s. Bowen's seminal work is the basis of many forms of family therapies that have developed over the past 50 years (Bowen, 1978). One's family-of-origin, including extended family, the family within which one grew up, is the primary and most powerful social-emotional system to which one is historically, socioculturally, and psychologically deeply bound. Each of us is innately and deeply loyal to family. The family provides standards and expectations that influence our path throughout life. The leader might well benefit from family values and experiences which promote his/

her success; however, families also can be resistant to change, limiting opportunity for change and growth.

Despite later life experiences, automatic responses to others, even in the workplace, are often based on lessons learned from family history and experiences. Family psychologists have observed that we often re-create our family roles within work and social spheres. We find ourselves in similar dilemmas and struggles, facing similar limitations, as in our family-of-origin. We tend to migrate to familiar contexts and familiar roles (Bowen, 1978; Marlin, 1989; McGoldrick, Gerson, & Shellenberger, 1999).

> **❝ ONE'S FAMILY-OF-ORIGIN . . . IS THE PRIMARY AND MOST POWERFUL SOCIAL-EMOTIONAL SYSTEM TO WHICH ONE IS HISTORICALLY, SOCIOCULTURALLY, AND PSYCHOLOGICALLY DEEPLY BOUND. ❞**

In addition, it can also become the role of the current generation to seek to fulfill unmet family dreams, complete unfinished business, compensate for losses, fill in for someone no longer around, or take on the family issues. These roles and tasks may be directly or indirectly assigned; the individual feels compelled to attain a family vision. For example, a son takes over a family business because his father designated him as the next leader. The siblings are resentful and the new figurehead may not be personally committed to the job. He is stepping into a position solely out of loyalty and is very likely the wrong person for the job. When confronted with emotional situations similar to those which challenged his/her family, a leader might lose the capacity to stay objective, creative, and thoughtful; rather the leader is caught up in his/her own emotionality or in the tensions and anxieties of the group or others. As Goleman (1995, p. 295) states, "The emotional mind reacts to the present as if it were the past."

As relationships and patterns reliably recur, the leader may be curious and ask, "How did I get here . . . again?!" Tichy asserts, "Leadership is autobiographical. If I don't know your life story, I don't know a thing about you as a leader" (cited in Collingwood, 2001, p. 38). This author proposes, you can't know where you're going if you don't know where you've been. When we examine the families of historic figures and leaders, it is clear that family profoundly influences leadership beliefs, values, styles, and behaviors (Gergen, 2000; Greenstein, 2000; McGoldrick et al., 1999). Without awareness of the impact of their family, many potentially successful leaders have been derailed through family-based and unconscious choices. We must not forget that the converse is true: experience and learning from family can also empower the leader to persist and succeed in challenging circumstances.

Collingwood (2001) defines "breakthrough leadership" as personal, requiring self-knowledge and openness to new ideas. He invited leaders in business, education, and the arts to recall powerful people, events, or literature that positively or negatively informed their personal development and leadership. A majority of respondents reported the power and influence of parents and family. These family events included observation not only of leadership behavior, but also of values informally conveyed through dinner table conversations, encouragement of "creative ideas and independent thinking," "tough standards and unconditional love," and demonstration of calmness and grace in the face of challenge. One's models of leadership and leadership behaviors are influenced by the leadership one experiences within the family and observes in family members. Tichy states, "The most effective leaders are those who are in touch with their leadership stories" (1997, p. 77). He adds that often leaders identify childhood as the context where ideas and values develop and "when they began to develop emotional energy and edge" (p. 59). If, however, we limit our contextual self-knowledge solely to learning about our family's leadership beliefs and styles, we lose the richness and depth of family influence in all spheres. Leadership entails a complex set of behaviors and beliefs; family influence on leadership derives from all family history and dynamics and is not readily accessed simply by focusing on leadership per se.

There Is Power in Becoming One's Own Personal Historian

Examining experiences in our family-of-origin allows us to consciously surface these influences, powerful legacies, and loyalties, to which we are often unconsciously bound (Boszormenyi-Nagy, 1987; Kerr & Bowen, 1988). Objective and deep family exploration enhances our capacity to be consciously responsive to current relationships and contexts. We can minimize self-limiting behaviors, retain useful behaviors, and fashion new, more adaptive patterns, which will lead us toward our personal and professional goals. In this way, awareness can lead to choice and positive change. In addition to awareness, questioning the inherent values and implicit expectations in family narratives gives us power to understand new possibilities, which can define potential for positive change. Tichy asserts, based on leaders' life stories, "We all have fundamental beliefs . . . . But most people don't consciously recognize these views and can't trace their origin. In my experience, winning leaders not only can, but do" (1997, p. 59). Tracing our family history empowers us to review previously unquestioned meanings and authority of family stories, and to expand possibilities for ourselves (Anderson, 1997; Watzlawick, 1984; White & Epston, 1990).

Leaders serve best when they can fully appreciate their original position in the family—the roles they were assigned and played (for example, the smart one, the rescuer, the peacemaker), the relationship dynamics, and long-standing family sensitivities. Reflecting on one's role in the multigenerational family saga, the leader can become more clear about defining him/herself in the present. As we consciously come to know our family narratives (interpretations of stories), scripts (prescribed roles), contracts (implied agreements about beliefs and behaviors), and legacies, we can assess which of these are productive for us in the present. We can choose to modify a role or relationship pattern which is a "generational anachronism," that is, one that was functional in either the family's past or our individual past, but is no longer useful in the present. Each family reacts to nodal events or situations (such as births, deaths, immense success, migration) based on its unique experiences and history across the generations. Meanings and patterns were established in response to events, often many generations ago. As time goes on, the family's anxieties are conveyed to family members through direct teaching or in subtle ways, that is, through stories, humor, ritual, and observed behavior.

> **❝ REFLECTING ON ONE'S ROLE IN THE MULTIGENERATIONAL FAMILY SAGA, THE LEADER CAN BECOME MORE CLEAR ABOUT DEFINING HIM/ HERSELF IN THE PRESENT. ❞**

Based on family experiences and history, there are relationships and situations to which we respond automatically and often in an exaggerated form. Our pockets of insanity—issues to which we are reactive, fearful, and vulnerable—are solidly grounded in family history. If we are unaware of our vulnerabilities, we can get into trouble. We are confused by our own emotional intensity and childlike behavior, but helpless to do anything about it. While a leader may have adaptive behaviors and strategies in his/her repertoire, the leader does not call on these more mature behaviors when stuck in old thinking and responding. Once we identify and understand the sources of knee-jerk emotional reactions in our unique family history, we can distinguish between the present and our past. Managing reactivity while calling on thoughtful, cognitive abilities enables the leader to try out new responses, call upon internal resources, and employ new strategies in situations that previously triggered intense emotional reactivity.

Methodically studying family promotes the development of hypotheses about family's issues, identifying in what contexts, and why, one is emotionally sensitive, and therefore less effective. Friedman (1996) states, "I have found that (exploration of family-of-origin) universally appears to have a positive effect on a leader's capacity to deal with anxiety in all other relationship systems" (p. 49). Developing conscious awareness of emotionally loaded family issues can help an individual become more differentiated, reducing emotional reactivity and increasing the capacity for thoughtful and emotionally intelligent actions.

Bennis (1994, p. 3) asserts that those who become good leaders "know who they are" and "are able to express themselves fully." He states that these individuals participate in lifelong self-learning and are thereby released from their "habits, practices, and rules that make us ineffectual" (p. 36). Exploration of family gives the leader a significant edge to act responsibly from his/her internal examined convictions and visions *and*, at the same time, in the best interests of the organization. Whether in individual coaching or in study groups, family exploration is regularly described by participants as "transformative and powerful." Individuals who have pursued family study consistently report that this effort "enhances accountability in professional roles," "improves self awareness," is "personally strengthening," and is also noted to "identify areas for personal development."

A Model of Family Exploration in Leadership Development

As noted earlier, for many years this author has worked with medical residents, guiding them to understand their families and family systems. In addition, over the past five years, this author has had the opportunity to convene and work with mid-career graduate students/emerging leaders from more than 20 countries around the globe. Each participant is able to explore his/her unique family from a common framework. Not only does this process enhance development of a leadership identity from a new perspective, but the conversation among participants promotes cross-cultural understanding and empathy. This is a win-win for enhancing global leadership.

These training formats have varied over time and from setting to setting. The depth of conceptual teaching and family exploration might vary from setting to setting. A program can be conducted over the course of hours, days, or months. Longer term study allows participants to interact with family members, time for reflection and experimentation with relationship and leadership behaviors. The process of interviewing and examining one's family can be empowering and exciting, but also unsettling. Workshops should be structured to allow participants ample time to both compile information and be reflective. Personal privacy and psychological safety must be respected. Case examples of contemporary and historic leaders woven throughout a workshop demonstrate the impact of family on well-known leaders' choices, values, and behaviors.

A leadership workshop would ideally be designed to meet the following objectives:

1. Systematic examination of dimensions and dynamics of participant's unique family

It might appear to be a daunting task to learn about the complexities of our extended and nuclear family. The good news is there are standard areas of exploration, common elements we look at to understand any organization—family or professional. Some common dimensions of family exploration are noted below.

Cultural history. This is important as background and basis for the family's identity. It is related to countries of origin, ethnicity, religion, and the associated values.

Rules. All families have expectations for appropriate values, beliefs, and behavior. For example, "The world is a fair place," "Always take care of others before yourself," "Don't be an open book." Because of loyalty to family patterns, these rules are internalized, leading one to become extreme and inflexible. Bringing these to our consciousness, a leader can see where these rules are valuable and where they are unnecessarily restrictive.

Pivotal events. These can be either positive or negative and can determine a family's beliefs about the world and themselves. During pivotal events, one can assume that the family is facing stress and challenge, even if the event is positive. It is useful to look beyond the event to understand how the family handled tension. Could the family adapt? Were there relationship disruptions? What changes did the family make to adapt to the event?

Roles and labels. Based on time of birth, appearance, gender, and other dimensions, individuals are assigned their place (role) in their family systems. Additionally, each person is attributed with characteristics or labels.

Hierarchy. A hierarchy describes the assignment of power and leadership. In the ideal family, members of the older generation take the lead, and as children grow older they are more often included in family discussions and decision making. An example is offered:

> A young female engineer with a Ph.D. is the fourth of four girls in her Asian family. Even in adulthood, she continues to be called "Baby Girl" by her family. She is currently in a powerful position as chief government engineer, overseeing land management projects on a national level. She has a great deal of difficulty "managing down"—as she only had to manage up in her family. Assuming her role as leader and asserting her influence is a challenge. After exploring her family history and context, she now knows that her task is to develop this skill with the help of colleagues and friends. She is also asserting her developmental status as an adult in her family.

Boundaries. Boundaries are reflected in communication patterns, physical proximity, and emotional and psychological connectedness. Families establish comfort zones regarding to whom we can talk, how much, and about what. Respecting one's own and others' expectations regarding boundaries smoothes our relationships and creates better leaders.

Relationship management. Relationship management is most critical when families are under stress. During stressful periods in organizations and relationships, emotion overrides thinking and boundaries can be distorted. Common patterns are: fusion (two become as one), cut off, and triangulation (two people or groups aligning against a third). Other areas related to relationships that might be examined are patterns in conflict management and intimacy.

2. Introduction of the genogram as a tool for integrated view of one's family

Creating a personal genogram, a three-generational family tree with psychological detail, allows participants to translate complex family information and history into a snapshot of family dynamics, patterns, and relationships with a minimum of text. The genogram depicts cultural history, rules and beliefs, role assignments, relationship expression, family response to challenge and change, resilience, themes, and stories. We traditionally learn information about our family one story at a time and without context. The process of creating a genogram organizes and integrates a complete and adult view of family information.

> **❝ CREATING A PERSONAL GENOGRAM ALLOWS PARTICIPANTS TO TRANSLATE COMPLEX FAMILY INFORMATION AND HISTORY INTO A SNAPSHOT OF FAMILY DYNAMICS, PATTERNS, AND RELATIONSHIPS WITH A MINIMUM OF TEXT. ❞**

The genogram process may also be focused on specific issues of critical interest to the participants' leadership style. When we apply our learnings about our family history and beliefs to answer questions about our current functioning, we are better able to understand our beliefs and behavior in the present. We learn more about why we do what we do, the (family's) beliefs that drive our behavior, why we are reactive, and our pressure points. Often simply knowing the origins of these issues allows us to enact more deliberate personal choices, in effect "write new contracts" with our families of origin.

Individual genogram sessions might also follow large group workshops. Having constructed a basic genogram, the family history could be discussed and explored with a trainer experienced in family systems work.

3. Application and analysis of discoveries to one's leadership values, styles, and behaviors

Each area of family that is explored is then examined for its influence on leadership styles, beliefs, and behaviors. Participants have a unique opportunity to reflect on the impact of family on their current leadership approaches and behaviors. For example, we know that how the family describes and ascribes roles to an individual strongly impacts his/her view of self as a leader. Family style of hierarchy influences one's definitions of leadership in general. Every area of family study can be examined for its effect on leadership.

4. Creation of a personal action plan

With a multigenerational perspective, a leader has greater opportunity to define oneself with respect for family while also honoring one's visions and convictions. As we would explore the family attic, we can value and hold on to what is valuable while discarding what is no longer useful. Guided by hypotheses derived from the genogram, a personal action plan is developed. Action plans might include conversations with family members in order to gather multiple perspectives, taking courses to develop new behaviors, experimenting with new behaviors, rethinking one's values and beliefs, learning and practicing self management, and emotional regulation. The leader might seek to understand complexity by interviewing family members, soliciting more detailed information about pivotal issues or moments in family history. Speaking with family members not only informs one about the origins of family functioning, but can improve family (as well as work) relationships. We may derive personal development plans from this process, for example, taking a conflict management course, pursuing personal coaching or therapy, training in gender sensitivity, anger management, and so on. Finally, we can choose to define strengths and limitations taught from family-of-origin and pursue pathways to expanding our repertoires of leadership behaviors.

Conclusion

All leaders have much to gain from the process of exploring their unique family dynamics and history. Self management is developed through studying one's personal history, considering new frameworks and novel responses to current leadership challenges. The wise leader would never choose to rely on outdated operating systems in the workplace. Family exploration promotes an update in one's internal operating system. Seeing oneself as part of the patterns in all larger systems (family and work) empowers the leader to develop his/her leadership style in context. Recognizing the principles and elements of systems gives us the advantage to analyze and understand how best to lead an organization to achieve its highest potential. The critical need for in-depth understanding of family systems and the impact of family influence cannot be overstated. The opportunity for this learning is critical for conscious, authentic, and effective leadership.

REFERENCES

Anderson, H. (1997). *Conversation, language, and possibilities: A postmodern approach to therapy.* New York: Basic Books.

Bennis, W. (1994). *On becoming a leader.* Cambridge: Perseus Books.

Bennis, W., & Goldsmith, J. (1997). *Learning to lead.* Cambridge: Perseus Books.

Bowen, M. (1978). *Family therapy in clinical practice.* New York: Jason Aronson.

Boszormenyi-Nagy, I. (1987). *Foundations of contextual therapy.* New York: Brunner/Mazel.

Collingwood, H. (2001). Personal histories: Leaders remember the moments and people that shaped them. *Harvard Business Review on Breakthrough Leadership* (pp. 1–23). Boston: Harvard Business School Publishing Corporation.

Friedman, E. H. (1996). *Reinventing leadership: Change in an age of anxiety* (videotape and discussion guide). New York: Guilford Publications.

Gergen, D. (2000). *Eyewitness to power.* New York: Simon & Schuster.

Goleman, D. (1995). *Emotional intelligence: Why it can matter more than IQ.* New York: Bantam.

Greenstein, F. (2000). *The presidential difference: Leadership style from FDR to Clinton.* Princeton and Oxford: Princeton University Press.

Heifetz, R. A. (1994). *Leadership without easy answers.* Cambridge, MA: The Belknap Press of Harvard University Press.

Heifetz, R. A., & Linsky, M. (2002). *Leadership on the line: Staying alive through the dangers of leading.* Boston: Harvard Business School Press.

Kerr, M. E., & Bowen, M. (1988). *Family evaluation: An approach based on Bowen theory.* New York: W. W. Norton & Co.

Kets de Vries, M. F. R. (2001). *The leadership mystique: An owner's manual.* London: Pearson Education.

Marlin, E. (1989). *Genograms: The new tool for exploring the personality, career, and love patterns you inherit.* Chicago: Contemporary Books.

McGoldrick, M., Gerson, R., & Shellenberger, S. (1999). *Genograms: Assessment and intervention.* New York: W. W. Norton & Co.

Senge, P. M. (1990). *The fifth discipline.* New York: Doubleday.

Tichy, N. M. (1997). *The leadership engine: How winning companies build leaders at every level.* New York: Harper Collins.

Watzlawick, P. (Ed.). (1984). *The invented reality.* New York: Norton.

White, M., & Epston, D. (1990). *Narrative means to therapeutic ends.* New York: Norton.

MARJORIE E. BLUM is a psychologist with a clinical and coaching practice in Atlanta. She has created a training model which uniquely integrates family psychology and leadership development, and advocates that understanding and reflecting on multigenerational family history and dynamics powerfully impact the capacity to lead effectively in any organization or system. Dr. Blum was appointed a fellow at the Center for Public Leadership (Harvard) in 2007, and is an adjunct faculty member at Georgia State University and Emory University School of Medicine. She holds a doctorate in psychology from Emory University.

Existential Leadership: Embracing the Past While Reformulating the Future

By Kurt Takamine

LEADERSHIP SCHOLARS ARE CURRENTLY ON AN IDEALISTIC QUEST to discover the attributes, traits, characteristics, and attitudes of the so-called *global leader*, with the hope that harnessing the competencies of such an individual would provide a distinct advantage for the company that hires this leader. Hofstede, GLOBE Study researchers, and others (Dorfman, Hanges, & Brodbeck, 2004; Hofstede, 1980, 1991; Rosen, Digh, Singer, & Phillips, 2000; Wurtz, 2005) have all compared and analyzed leaders from around the world. Yet as one studies these findings one becomes aware that there is more disparity than uniformity, which raises the possibility that a universal leadership prototype might not exist.

The difficulty in identifying a universal leader might be that these leadership descriptors focus on what leaders *do*, not on how they *are*. The challenge in designating a global leader is understandable, since examining someone's actions is much less subjective than conjecturing about a person's values, intrinsic motivations, or beliefs. Management science has a history of examining the quantitative traits of executives, basing its findings on empirical, unbiased observations. However, are these findings global in nature, or are they merely Westernized interpretations of leadership? In this paper, I will introduce a conceptual global leadership model that is built on psychological and philosophical existential ideas.

Challenges of Identifying the Universal Leader

Certain management scholars question the viability of searching for the perfect leadership paradigm, or the discovery of the universal organizational model. As far back as the 1960s, Odiorne had this to say about the management theory jungle:

Combatants, in the management theory in its jungle warfare, attempt to win victories by showing how classical management principles, behavioral science, or mathematical management can provide static and fixed, or perhaps systematic determinants . . . . Many of the situations which surround the existential manager resist theoretical analysis, are ever-present, and insurmountable. Research to find universals end up with "inconclusive evidence." (1966, p. 110)

The reason that some organizational scientists are challenging scientific positivism is that it does not take into consideration the near infinite organizational choices (that affect so many attributes of the leadership realm) for which the leader or follower must account. The complexity of any given culture, the divergence with ethics, ideologies, religions, and the like make theory development challenging, if not impossible, in a global context. Richter stated that

The enemy of true reality is ultrapracticality. The managerial class has long given its homage to pragmatism, the method of prior formulation, recurrent testing, and optimal decision making. Such scientism is inevitably impersonal, because models formulated for testing cannot encompass the complexities of people problems . . . . Hence, large-scale organizations tend to lose, both inside and outside, their rapport with people—that is, their objectivity. Those who would uphold people interests are dismissed as utopians, while decision making is delegated to experts. (1970, p. 418)

One should not infer that the theories of the past are to be discarded or downplayed. This scientific, positivistic methodology (or human behavioral approach) has provided an excellent conceptual portrait of leadership in the West. For instance, from trait theories emerged style theories, and task versus relationship approaches (for example, path-goal, situational leadership, LMX theory, and so on), to name a few. More recently, "new leadership" paradigms such as charismatic, transformational, values-based, ethical, servant-leadership, and others have emerged (Northouse, 2007). However, if Richter (1970) and Odiorne (1966) are correct in their assessment that people are more complex and unpredictable than scientism would like us to believe, can a system of study capture the salient points of global leadership?

One way to understand global leadership might be to describe the subjective nature of leadership studies by utilizing a more humanistic orientation. A definition of a humanistic approach is "the subjective nature of human knowledge and reality" (Motamedi, 1978, p. 355), particularly as it relates to leaders in other countries. However, subjectivity requires that the researcher be intimately familiar with the idiolectic and idiosyncratic aspects of the leaders under study. If the researchers do not have the depth of emic (culturally specific) attributes of leadership, these behavioral aspects may be misinterpreted or improperly contextualized (Dickson, Den Hartog, & Mitchelson, 2003). Researchers are becoming aware that one's worldview automatically brings a subjective element into any social research construct, including those that affect social theories (Chung & Alagaratnam, 2001). The primary question for discussion might be this: Is there a culturally relevant way to understand leadership from a basic human perspective? If there is a way to answer this question affirmatively, perhaps the topic of global leadership can at least agree upon some ontological (essential) descriptions of leaders.

> **❝ ONE WAY TO UNDERSTAND GLOBAL LEADERSHIP MIGHT BE TO DESCRIBE THE SUBJECTIVE NATURE OF LEADERSHIP STUDIES BY UTILIZING A MORE HUMANISTIC ORIENTATION. ❞**

What do leaders—all leaders—share in common with each other, whether they are located in various parts of the globe, across time dimensions, beyond political boundaries and philosophical ideologies? How can we make connections between Gen-Xers, Millennials, or Baby Boomers? The answer can be found in existentialism.

Existentialism in Brief

The existential perspective envisions the individual as being unique and self-determined in the actualization of his or her life (Butcher, Mineka, & Hooley, 2006). The individual (in this case, leader) strives to become self-actualized; that is, the leader only finds fulfillment in life when he or she discovers that meaning, the particular *sine qua non* for which he or she was created. Yalom (1980) noted that if individuals are unable or constricted from freely choosing their destiny, an anxiety would develop that would pervade their life, resulting in a fear that these individuals would live meaningless, inconsequential lives. The persons leading these unfulfilled lives would have to rediscover the essence of who they are, and what they were created to become. For the leader, the question might become, "How can I impact my people to make their lives richer, more fulfilling, and more liberated through my leadership?" Before delving into that key question, however, I will provide additional background on existentialism and its use in a leadership context in the next section.

Key existential concepts. Modern existentialism (circa 1900 to the present) is defined differently depending on one's school of thought. Currently, there are two major schools in Western ideology: European and American. The reason that these existential schools were given such prominence in the field of psychology was that these therapeutic communities were becoming disenchanted with "Freud's mechanistic, deterministic model of the mind" (Yalom, 1980, p. 17). The Freudian therapist assumed that the client could not decipher his or her subconscious (and certainly not the unconscious) issues of psychological dysfunction on their own, and must depend on the expertise of the clinician to eradicate a phobia or neuroses (Yalom, 1980). Modern existentialism rejected that dependency on the clinician; rather, existentialists believed that the clients were able (in all but a few severe cases) to determine a positive course of action for their personal lives through introspection and personal freedom of choice (Cline, n.d.-a).

The focus of European existentialism was on a predilection with "death, meaninglessness, isolation and freedom" (Klugman, 1997, p. 303). Literal death often was a revisited theme in European existential thought since these doctrines were developed in the midst of two world wars and numerous fatal epidemics, yet a more figurative death (that is, a life that does not live up to its potential) might be more applicable for most readers (Frankl, 1984; Yalom, 1980).

The focus of American existentialism, in contrast, was on "the individual's potential for actualization, peak experience, self-realization and higher stages of development" (Klugman, 1997, p. 303). There was clearly a more positive attribute to the American version of this idea than that held by its European counterpart. Carl Rogers, Abraham Maslow, Rollo May, and others rejected the objectivism of the behavioral and reinforcement approaches, much like some social researchers in leadership and management studies were recognizing that scientific positivism was limited in studying leadership (Odiorne, 1966; Richter, 1970). This opposition to objectivism was described by Klugman in this way:

> May and his European cohorts took up the banner of existentialism in protest against the psychoanalytic tendency to see patients "in forms tailored to our own preconceptions" (p. 8) . . . in America, Rogers embraced existentialism against the objective trends of behavior modification and reinforcement theory, claiming in opposition to the reigning psychological clichés of the day that "the way to do is to *be*. The way to understand is from within" (May, 1969, p. 87). . . . And Abraham Maslow (Maslow, 1971; Maslow, 1964; Maslow, 1968) believed that existential psychotherapy, unlike Freud's psychoanalysis, honored the "aspirations . . . realizable hopes [and] Godlike qualities" of the person. (Klugman, 1997, p. 303)

In this paper, I will emphasize the American existentialist approach, while not entirely rejecting the European themes. In Table 1, key prominent American existential themes and major authors are listed for comparison.

Table 1. Comparison Chart of American Existential Themes According to Various Writers.

Writer	Existence & Essence	Freedom & Choice	Meaning & Value	Existential Anxiety	Spiritual Attributes
Butcher et al. (2006)	Yes	Yes	Yes	Yes	Yes
Klugman (1997)	Yes	Yes	Yes	Yes	Yes
Yalom (1980)	Yes	Yes	Yes	Yes	No*
Frankl (1984)	Yes	Yes	Yes	Yes	Yes
Koes-tenbaum (2001)	Yes	Yes	Yes	Yes	Yes

*Note. While Yalom (1980) does discuss the perspective of other theorists' spiritual attributes in his writing, he does not disclose his own personal beliefs about God in his text. Therefore, a "No" is recorded for Yalom's particular spiritual aspect in this chart.

In the next section, I will expound on these themes and discuss their application to the workplace environment.

Existence and Essence. Each individual leader exists in a reality in which he or she is the center of his or her world, whether in a corporate setting, the political arena, or in a nonprofit environment; this is known as one's *existence* (Butcher et al., 2006). Every person has an existence. If leaders fulfill their potential by actualizing their existence successfully, then they have maximized their *essence*; that is, they affected their world positively with their potential existence. Essence is connected to the next theme: freedom and choice.

Freedom and Choice. A leader's choices determine his or her essence. When Chrysler was struggling to avoid bankruptcy in the 1970s, Iacocca chose to reduce his annual salary to $1. During that same period, United Airlines, American Airlines, and The Boeing Company cut 20,000–30,000 positions each while executives did nothing to reduce their executive pay (Thomasch, 2001). All of these executives had the freedom to make the choices that they did. Iacocca's pay cut, however, did create a sense of camaraderie with his workers, even if the pay cut could not prevent Chrysler's layoffs. These choices reflect the values of the leader.

Meaning and Value. Maslow indicated that individuals strive to find meaning in their lives, and that meaning emerges from the values on which one focuses (Burke, 2002). More basic needs, such as the need for survival or the need to belong, can motivate an individual for a time, but higher needs (that is, self-actualization) are values that ascribe true meaning to one's life. There are scholars (Caldwell & Hayes, 2007; Griffin, 2008; Kouzes & Posner, 2002; O'Toole, 1995) who would argue that values (for example trustworthiness, honesty, empathy, and so on) are the most critical attributes of a leader. While the values noted in this essay may bring meaning to the lives of the followers and leaders themselves, the fear of being insignificant, called *existential anxiety*, may be a very powerful motivator for bringing value and meaning into the workplace.

Existential Anxiety. This anxiety is "a deep concern over whether we are living meaningful and fulfilling lives" (Butcher et al., 2006, p. 73). If a leader is not living a meaningful life, and is not leaving a meaningful legacy, then existential anxiety may develop. In fact, a meaningless and unfulfilled leader may not just corrupt an individual; the meaningless and unfulfilled leader may denigrate an entire organization (Ramstad, 1987). The situation with Enron is one recent example of individual and corporate anxiety (Feeley, 2006). Enron Chair and CEO Kenneth Lay was indicted on ten counts of securities fraud. Although one will never know if Lay felt any remorse since he died before sentencing, one could safely surmise that this duplicity did not bring value or meaning to himself or to others. Most leaders would hope to avoid that type of notorious legacy.

> **❝ IF A LEADER IS NOT LIVING A MEANINGFUL LIFE, AND IS NOT LEAVING A MEANINGFUL LEGACY, THEN EXISTENTIAL ANXIETY MAY DEVELOP. ❞**

Spiritual Attributes. The last theme noted in Table 1, spiritual attributes, is embraced by some existentialists, but not all. Cline wrote:

There developed both religious and atheistic strands of existentialism. The two disagreed on the existence of God and the nature of religion, but they too agreed on other matters. For example, they agreed that traditional philosophy and theology had become too remote from normal human life to be of much use. (n.d.-b, ¶7)

It is certainly in keeping with existentialist thought that a leader can hold to his or her subjective truth of religion (or lack thereof). Kierkegaard, a Christian, could coexist with Nietzsche, an atheist, in their individual truth (Klugman, 1997). Frankl was Jewish, and could embrace much of the existential views of Yalom, a purported atheist. In fact, any individual of any religious or nonreligious persuasion could be an existentialist, which enables the researcher to embrace a global universality in studying spiritualism (Lewin, 2001). Businesses are even beginning to embrace spiritualism, whether thought of in terms of organized religion or personal ideology.

Griffin (2008) argues that leaders need to engage the mystical part of their existential self, the part that some people have disassociated themselves from at work. He calls the once taboo words the "S" words: "spirit, spirituality, or soul" (p. 91). Izzo and Klein (1998) also argue that without an engagement of the "S" words at work, there is a loss of "vitality, inspiration, meaning, and creativity" (Griffin, 2008, p. 91). The existential leader is able to maintain a consonance with his or her spiritual proclivities, or lack thereof.

In summary, then, the existential leader focuses on matters of essence, choice, meaning, value, existential anxiety, and spiritual attributes. These are not extrinsic traits or behaviors of leadership. Existentialism allows social scientists to concentrate on the intrinsic factors that govern a person's life, whether that life is studied within the context of the family, avocation, or workplace. These are not values that are bound by geography, ideology, generation, gender, culture, or ethnicity. Researching anything less leads to erroneous conclusions of leadership, over-compartmentalizing and segregating components of the leader while ignoring a totality of the executive. Ethics have as much import to leadership studies as does process management, and inspiration is likewise as critical to leadership development as is production.

The new challenge in leadership studies is to examine and evaluate new leadership paradigms (Northouse, 2007) within the context of existential leadership, which has implication for succession planning, leadership ethics, executive selection, leadership development, and other applications. Existential leadership provides a clear and practical analysis when utilized in concert with global studies that examine extrinsic characteristics of leaders. Here is the existential perspective in summary:

> Thus existential [researchers] focus on the importance of establishing values and acquiring a level of spiritual maturity worthy of the freedom and dignity bestowed by one's humanness. Avoiding such central issues creates corrupted, meaningless, and wasted lives. Much abnormal behavior, therefore, is seen as the product of a failure to deal constructively with existential despair and frustration. (Butcher et al., 2006, p. 73)

The next challenge, consequently, is to link existentialism with the new leadership approaches such as servant-leadership, transformational leadership, and other current models. The Existential Leader can bring these various ideologies and theories into the boardroom, executive suites, and human resource departments. The challenge of connecting these new leadership paradigms will be addressed in the following section.

❝ THE EXISTENTIAL LEADER FOCUSES ON MATTERS OF ESSENCE, CHOICE, MEANING, VALUE, EXISTENTIAL ANXIETY, AND SPIRITUAL ATTRIBUTES. ❞

Impact of Existential Leadership on Other Leadership Approaches

The Existential Leaders (ExL) of the past have asked the question of transforming lives in a variety of ways. In servant-leadership the existential question takes on the following form:

> The servant-leader is servant first. It begins with the natural feeling that one wants to serve. Then conscious choice brings one to aspire to lead. The best test is: *Do those served grow as persons; do they, while being served, become healthier, wiser, freer, more autonomous, more likely themselves to become servants?* (Spears & Lawrence, 2002, p. 1 [emphasis mine])

Specifically, the servant-leader is concerned with bringing healing, empathy, deep listening, awareness, persuasion, conceptualization, foresight, stewardship, and commitment to the growth of their people, and community building into the workplace (Spears & Lawrence, 2002). Many of these ten characteristics of servant-leadership are in alignment with the thematic aspects of existential leadership. It is interesting that many of the characteristics of the ExL previously mentioned (actualization, freedom, courage, obligation to one another, and so on) are either identified in the servant-leaders' manifesto explicitly or alluded to implicitly.

Another new leadership theory is transformational leadership (Northouse, 2007). Transformational leadership is "concerned with emotions, values, ethics, standards, and long-term goals and includes assessing followers' motives, satisfying their needs, and treating them as full human beings" (Northouse, 2007, p. 175). These factors are consistent with the five thematic concerns of American existential thought.

Other new leadership approaches such as ethical leadership, women in leadership, or cultural leadership (Bennis, 2003; Ciulla, 2003; Dickson, Den Hartog, & Mitchelson, 2003; Dorfman, Hanges, & Brodbeck, 2004; Eagly & Karau, 2002; Engen, Leeden, & Willemsen, 2001; Hofstede, 1980, 1991; Kanungo & Mendonca,

1996) can be subsumed under the Existential Leadership rubric, which is explicated in the next section.

The PIE Model of Existential Leadership

The PIE model of Existential Leadership was created by me to integrate the five themes of existentialism (see Table 1), new leadership theories (servant-leadership, ethical leadership, and the rest), and business metrics. I created the PIE model, noted in Figure 1 and so named because of the integration of several concepts beginning with the letters P, I, and E, for consultants to utilize in their organizational change efforts. As a practical concern, if people in the organization do not understand a model they will disregard it, and then it will have questionable worth. The PIE model, thus, is not cluttered with obfuscative pathways or confusing terminology. One of its limitations, however, is that it is simple; yet, ironically, simplicity is also one of the strengths of the PIE model.

The focus of the PIE model is on vital indicators that will help in assessing the effectiveness of the ExL and all the stakeholders working with him or her. To address practical concerns, the PIE model also identifies the other key stakeholders (supervisors, vendors, employees, and the rest) in the various organizational processes, assigning responsibility areas to all. In this way, strategic progress can be evaluated, important for organizational growth.

The "P's" in the acronym stand for *people, purpose, product*, and *process*. These are the components of the PIE model. As one can see in Figure 1, the "E's" in this model are *engagement, expertise, efficiency,* and *effectiveness*. These are the outcomes.

The four P's in the model affect the four E's, or stated differently, the components affect the outcomes. As one example, if human resources do not hire the right people and do not train their people for expertise, this will affect the processes. Without the proper human capital and intellectual capital in place, processes will suffer and there will be a breakdown in performance.

If people, on the other hand, are in alignment with the purpose—that is, the vision, mission, and direction of the organization—then they will experience engagement (Motamedi, 1978). When this engagement occurs, workers are more positive, productive, and cooperative (Coyle-Shapiro, 2002; Koys, 2001). Properly connecting products and processes will result in greater efficiency of output. In addition, when one positions the purpose and product of the organization, the company is effective in its operations. This synergy is critical for the overall health and success of the organization.

Figure 1. The Four P's and Four E's Depicted in the PIE Model.*

The PIE Model of Organizational Interactions

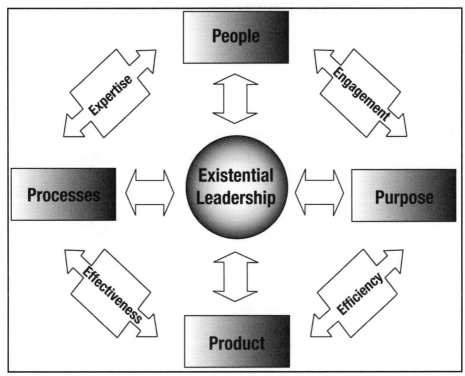

*Note. The four P's (People, Purpose, Product, and Processes) are all critical components of the company's structure. The four E's (Engagement, Expertise, Efficiency, and Effectiveness) are all impacted by the alignment and practice of the four P's. See text for more detail.

Figure 1 appears to depict a simple linear relationship between the P's and the E's. In reality, the P's and the E's should be three-dimensional in nature, with overlaps with all eight factors and interconnections and multidirectional arrows throughout the diagram. The P-E portion of the model has been simplified for illustrative purposes.

In Figure 2 (next page), one will note categorically the four "I's" of the ExL (that is, *innovation, integrity, inspiration,* and *integration).* The abstract skill that leaders must embrace to anticipate or create future trends in their industry is known as *innovation.* This quality is critical in separating the ordinary from the superlative leaders (Rosen et al., 2000; Senge, Scharmer, Jaworski, & Flowers, 2005; Spears, 2005). Much of this insight comes from internal reflection and inwardness, fully engaging one's being (Klugman, 1997). This experiential practice of being "present"

Figure 2. The Four I's Presented in the PIE Model.

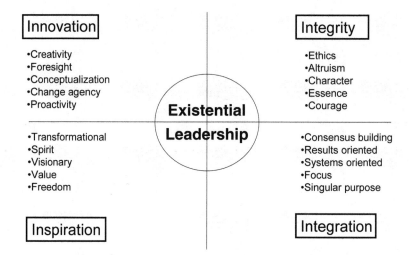

Leaders must demonstrate...

Innovation		Integrity
•Creativity		•Ethics
•Foresight		•Altruism
•Conceptualization		•Character
•Change agency	**Existential**	•Essence
•Proactivity		•Courage
•Transformational	**Leadership**	•Consensus building
•Spirit		•Results oriented
•Visionary		•Systems oriented
•Value		•Focus
•Freedom		•Singular purpose
Inspiration		Integration

has been studied by Senge and colleagues (2005), as well as Bennis (2003) and Spears and Lawrence (2002).

Existentialists identify *integrity* as the authenticity of one's life. This is the moral consciousness that people may accept or reject. With respect to the practice of leadership, those who reject authenticity become self-absorbed autocrats, and those who accept it become authentic existential leaders (Koestenbaum, 2001). Altruism, ethics, courage, essence, and character all testify to the existential leader's concern for personal integrity and service to others.

Inspiration includes those attributes that touch the human spirit, that develop followers through trust, vision, and creation of a transformational relationship. This relationship may involve spirituality and freedom of choice within this inspirational context.

Integration is the missing link in many models, where the ExL is held responsible for bringing every element of the organization together, whether that integration concerns consensus building, systems, financial and production results, evaluation of the vision/mission/strategic plans—in short, the operations part of business. A company can be the most freeing, supportive, encouraging organization in the world, but if it cannot turn a profit, it is doomed to failure. It is, after all, in the business of making money. But if the ExL can fulfill that drive in a humanitarian way, then it will be a win-win for everyone involved.

Now that the four P's (people, purpose, product, processes), four I's (innovation, integrity, inspiration, integration), and four E's (engagement, expertise, effectiveness, efficiency) have been identified, the responsibility areas must be determined, and the accountability assigned. In Table 2, I illustrate the responsibility areas under consideration, for example, product quality, and specify the accountable party (in this case the employees, vendor associates, and executives).

Table 2. The PIE Model's Accountability and Responsibility Areas.

PE Factors	Responsibility Areas	Accountability
People	•Hiring •Retention •Development	•HR •Executives •Supervisors
Purpose	•Vision & Mission	•Executives to Stakeholders
Process	•Technological support •Human Capital	•Supervisors •Employees
Product	•Quality control •Ethics •Brand recognition	•Executives •Vendor Associates •Employees
Expertise	•Intellectual capital •Training & Development	•Executives •Supervisors & HR
Engagement	•High Functioning Teams •Organizational culture	•Executives, Supervisors •Employees & HR
Efficiency	•Output •Customer satisfaction	•Supervisors •Employees
Effectiveness	•Return on investment •Utilization of resources	•Supervisors

An example to illustrate the use of Table 2: Chinese manufacturers recently used exceedingly high levels of lead paint in Mattel's products that led to a massive recall in America while these toys were pulled from the retail shelves. Yet, paradoxically, Thomas A. Debrowski, Executive Vice President for global operations, publicly apologized to China for damaging the reputation of the vendors in Asia

(Reuters, 2007). This public apology was necessary for Mattel's multi-billion dollar partnership to succeed in China, not only in maintaining an inexpensive labor force in Asia, but in establishing a $30 million Barbie store in Shanghai (Sy, Takamine, & Tram, 2008). In this case, the vendor, Chinese employees, and the Mattel executives were ultimately held responsible for the lead-paint debacle illustrating the areas of responsibility between vendor, executive, and Chinese employees, and the various levels of accountability in dealing with this situation. In Table 2, one sees this connection between areas of responsibility and levels of accountability with all of the P-I-E factors.

Conclusion

The current Holy Grail of contemporary leadership research is to identify and define the attributes of the global leader, an individual capable of transcending borders, cultures, generations, and ideologies. The salient question is this: Does such a leader exist? In this paper I explored the notion that perhaps such a leader is extant today, but he or she may not be easily identifiable utilizing positivistic (read quantitative) research methods alone.

In the past, leadership researchers have typically focused on what leaders *do*, not on how they *are*. This is understandable, since leadership studies emerged out of management science, which focused on traits, styles, and behaviors of executives in empirical terms. There are two concerns that arise. First, do the new leadership paradigms such as transformational leadership, servant-leadership, values-based leadership, for example, lend themselves to such an unyielding examination of extrinsic actions; second, are these aforementioned theories global in nature, or are they Westernized models of leadership? In this chapter, I addressed the first concern; future research would have to evaluate the second concern.

Since scientific positivistic methodology (or human behavioral approach) has provided an excellent conceptual portrait in the West, I do not infer that the theories of the past are to be discarded or downplayed. On the contrary, with this discussion, my intent was to add a more humanistic approach to the dialogue, which focuses on "the subjective nature of human knowledge and reality" (Motamedi, 1978, p. 355), particularly as it relates to leaders in other countries. The Existential Leader (ExL) model was introduced, looking at the intrinsic characteristics of leadership. This humanistic emphasis explores the "self-concept, self-understanding, insight, and self-orientation" of the executive (Motamedi, 1978, p. 355), whether that executive lives in Asia, South America, or New Zealand. This ExL easily embraces modern concepts such as emotional intelligence, servant-leadership, values-based leadership, transformational leadership, and the like.

The ExL is concerned with choice (or freedom), authenticity (character, identity, and attitude), and accountability (Agarwal & Malloy, 2000; Labarre, 2000). These virtues are universal, although there can be a gradient in how these virtues are expressed. For example, the manner in which a CEO wrestles with authenticity is not dependent on his or her cultural norms, generational upbringing, religious beliefs, or national ideology. Authenticity *does* have a great deal to do with the humanistic challenges and dilemmas that have faced humankind from time immemorial. Leaders in Oslo, Cairo, or Lagos all must encounter the same existential questions. What is the essence or meaning of their existence? Will they use their power for good or evil, for self-gain or for altruism? Will the executive live a values-centered life? How can the leader avoid living a meaningless life? Are employees impacted if the CEO brings spiritual beliefs into the workplace? These and other existential questions have a global perspective, rather than a localized or time-bound perspective, and provide a backdrop from which variant leadership approaches can be examined and understood.

The five major thematic emphases of American existentialism were presented, and the PIE model was explained. The PIE model depicts key components of organizational functions, roles and responsibilities, systemic accountability, and leadership of that corporation. Perhaps existentialism can provide the key to discovering global leadership—that it is not "out there somewhere," but that it has been "inside" all along.

REFERENCES

Agarwal, J., & Malloy, D. C. (2000). The role of existentialism in ethical business decision-making. *Business Ethics, A European Review, 9*(3), 143–154.

Bennis, W. (2003). *On becoming a leader.* New York: Basic Books.

Burke, W. W. (2002). *Organization change: Theory and practice.* Thousand Oaks, CA: Sage.

Butler, J. N., Mineka, S., & Hooley, J. M. (2006). *Abnormal psychology* (13th ed.). Boston: Pearson.

Caldwell, C., & Hayes, L. A. (2007). Leadership, trustworthiness, and the mediating lens. *Journal of Management Development, 25*(3), 261–281.

Ciulla, J. (2003). *The ethics of leadership.* Belmont, CA: Wadsworth/Thomson Learning.

Cline, A. (n.d.-a). Soren Kierkegaard biography. *About.com: Agnosticism/Atheism.* Retrieved on February 28, 2008, from http://atheism.about.com/od/existentialismphilosophers/a/kierkegaard.htm?p=1

Cline, A. (n.d.-b). What is existentialism? *About.com: Agnosticism/Atheism.* Retrieved on February 28, 2008, from http://atheism.about.com/od/existentialism/a/introduction_2.htm?p=1

Chung, E., & Alagaratnam, S. (2001). "Teach ten thousand stars how not to dance": A survey of alternative ontologies in marketing research. *Qualitative Market Research, 4*(4), 224–234.

Coyle-Shapiro, J. A. M. (2002). A psychological contract perspective on organizational citizenship behavior. *Journal of Organizational Behavior, 23,* 927–946.

Dickson, M. W., Den Hartog, D. N., & Mitchelson, J. K. (2003). Research on leadership in a cross-cultural context: Making progress, and raising new questions. *The Leadership Quarterly, 14,* 729–768.

Dorfman, P. W., Hanges, P. J., & Brodbeck, F. (2004). Leadership and cultural variation: The identification of culturally endorsed leadership profiles (pp. 669–720). In R. J. House, P. J. Hanges, M. Javidan, P. W. Dorfman, & V. Gupta (Eds.), *Leadership, culture, and organizations: The GLOBE study of 62 societies.* Thousand Oaks, CA: Sage.

Eagly, A. H., & Karau, S. J. (2002). Role congruity theory of prejudice toward female leaders. *Psychological Review, 109,* 573–598.

Engen, M. L. van, Leeden, R. van der, & Willemsen, T. M. (2001). Gender, context and leadership styles: A field study. *Journal of Occupational and Organizational Psychology, 74,* 581–598.

Feeley, D. (2006). Personality, environment, and the causes of white collar crime. *Law & Psychology Review, 30,* 201–213.

Frankl, V. E. (1984). *Man's search for meaning: Revised and updated.* New York: Washington Square Press.

Griffin, K. H. (2008). Metaphor, language, and organizational transformation. *Organizational Development Journal, 26*(1), 89–97.

Hofstede, G. (1980). *Culture's consequences: International differences in work-related values.* Beverly Hills, CA: Sage.

Hofstede, G. (1991). *Cultures and organizations: Software of the mind.* New York: McGraw-Hill.

Izzo, J. B., & Klein, E. (1998). *Awakening corporate soul.* Canada: Fairwinds Press.

Klugman, D. (1997). Existentialism and constructivism: A bi-polar model of subjectivity. *Clinical Social Work Journal, 25*(3), 297–313.

Koestenbaum, P. (2001). And looking to the future: The growing role of personal responsibility and accountability. *The Journal for Quality and Participation, 24*(4), 7–11.

Kanungo, R. N., & Mendonca, M. (1996). *Ethical dimensions of leadership.* Thousand Oaks, CA: Sage.

Kouzes, J. M., & Posner, B. Z. (2002). *The leadership challenge* (3rd ed.). San Francisco: Jossey-Bass.

Koys, D. J. (2001). The effects of employee satisfaction, organizational citizenship behavior, and turnover on organizational effectiveness: A unit-level, longitudinal study. *Personnel Psychology, 54,* 101–114.

Labarre, P. (2000). Do you have the will to lead? *Fast Company, 32,* 222–227.

Lewin, F. A. (2001). Gerotranscendence and different cultural settings. *Ageing and Society, 21,* 395–415.

Motamedi, K. K. (1978). Toward explicating philosophical orientations in organizational behavior (OB). *Academy of Management Review, 3*(2), 354–360.

Northouse, P. G. (2007). *Leadership: Theory and practice.* Thousand Oaks, CA: Sage.

Odiorne, G. S. (1966). The management theory jungle and the existential manager. *Academy of Management Journal, 9*(2), 109–116.

O'Toole, J. (1995). *Leading change: Overcoming the ideology of comfort and the tyranny of custom.* San Francisco: Jossey-Bass.

Ramstad, Y. (1987). Institutional existentialism: More on why John R. Commons has so few followers. *Journal of Economic Issues, 21*(2), 661–671.

Reuters. (2007, September 24). *China seizes on Mattel apology to emphasize safety.* Retrieved September 30, 2007, from http://www.reuters.com/article/healthNews/idUSPEK2141420070924

Richter, A. (1970). The existential executive. *Public Administration Review, 30*(4), 415–422.

Rosen, R., Digh, P., Singer, M., & Phillips, C. (2000). *Global literacies: Lessons on business leadership and national cultures.* New York: Simon & Schuster.

Senge, P., Scharmer, C. O., Jaworski, J., & Flowers, B. F. (2005). *Presence: Exploring profound change in people, organizations, and society.* New York: Currency Books.

Spears, L. C. (2005). The understanding and practice of servant-leadership. In S. Ferch (Ed.), *The International Journal of Servant-Leadership, 1*(1), 29–45.

Spears, L. C., & Lawrence, M. (2002). (Eds.). *Focus on leadership: Servant-leadership for the twenty-first century.* New York: John Wiley & Sons.

Sy, T., Takamine, K., & Tram, S. (2008). *Translators of profit (TOP): Developing Asian American TOP leaders to win in the Asian marketplace.* Manuscript submitted for publication.

Thomasch, P. (2001, September 22). CEOs slash jobs, but not their pay. *Reuters.* Retrieved March 17, 2008, from http://www.commondreams.org/cgi-bin/print.cgi?file=/headlines01/0922-03.htm

Würtz, E. (2005). A cross-cultural analysis of websites from high-context cultures and low-context cultures. *Journal of Computer-Mediated Communication, 11*(1), article 13. Retrieved on July 27, 2007, from http://jcmc.indiana.edu/vol11/issue1/wuertz.html

Yalom, I. D. (1980). *Existential psychotherapy.* New York: Basic Books.

KURT TAKAMINE is the interim Dean of Professional Studies at Chapman University College and Chair of the Organizational Leadership department. He has written *Servant-Leadership in the Real World: Re-Discovering Our Humanity in the Workplace* (2002), as well as articles addressing retention, Asian Pacific American leadership, the glass ceiling, leadership ethics, marketing strategies, succession planning, emotional intelligence, organization change, and leadership theory. He received his Ed.D. degree from Pepperdine University in organizational leadership.

How to Use Humor to Reshape Leadership

By Peter M. Jonas

A man piloting a hot-air balloon discovers he has wandered far off course and is hopelessly lost. He descends to a lower altitude and locates a man down on the ground. He lowers the balloon to within hearing distance and shouts, "Excuse me, can you tell me where I am?" The man below says: "Yes, you're in a hot-air balloon, about 30 feet above this field." "You must work in information technology," says the balloonist. "Yes, I do," replies the man. "And how did you know that?" "Well," says the balloonist, "what you told me is technically correct, but of no use to anyone." The man below says, "You must work in management." "I do," replies the balloonist. "How did you know?" "Well," says the man, "you don't know where you are, or where you're going, but you expect my immediate help, which I give to you. You're in the same position you were before we met, but now it's my fault!"

THERE IS AN AGE-OLD ARGUMENT ABOUT WHETHER LEADERS ARE born or made. This debate has gone on for some time, but the reality is that leadership can be developed. Leadership can be learned, if for no other reason than because I said so. (This argument works with my children so I thought I would try it here.) In fact, the environment that we are nurtured in has a remarkable impact on our learning, behavior, values, and humor. Infants are born with billions and billions of neural connections in the brain and the environment has a direct impact on their growth. In other words, the development of leadership is connected to the nurturing (teaching/learning) environment of the individual. The same is true for the nurturing of humor. You are neither a born leader nor born funny; these are traits learned through your environment and the neurological developments of the brain—and the connections may be more similar than you realize.

**" LEADERSHIP CAN BE LEARNED, IF FOR NO
OTHER REASON THAN BECAUSE I SAID SO. (THIS
ARGUMENT WORKS WITH MY CHILDREN SO I
THOUGHT I WOULD TRY IT HERE.) "**

Learning and the Brain

The brain is comprised of neurons (brain cells) with dendrites (tentacles of communication) that send impulses by chemical reactions through the synapses (gaps between dendrites). The brain is a complex organ, so in order to assist the learning process, the more connections that can be made to previous knowledge, the more efficient the learning process. Consequently, through occurrences that happen every day, the synapses in the brain make the connections that enhance leadership ability through the mistakes and the learning that takes place. All sensory input passes through the amygdala, which is the security part of the brain and which also determines emotional responses. It is the survival part of the brain, constantly asking the question: "Do I eat it, does it eat me, or do I mate with it?" The bottom line is that the brain needs to understand the content of the information to be learned, it must be deemed important, and then it has to be connected to some other relevant information already stored in memory. This is just one way we learn to be better leaders. The process is also how humor works to enhance leadership. Because humor is a universal language, the concept is common for most people, so leadership activities tied to humor can be connected in the brain and thereby more easily stored in memory.

Ultimately, the brain has three main functions: it is cognitive, reflective, and emotional. It is cognitive because people can learn—they can memorize facts and learn new material. The brain is reflective because individuals can analyze material. And finally, the brain is emotional. In order for the brain to operate at its most efficient level, individuals need to have their emotions in check. For example, a person learns best when his or her emotions are elevated but he or she is not too anxious or nervous. Humor helps provide the right level of emotional connection in establishing an atmosphere conducive to learning; consequently, we can become better leaders through the proper use of humor. Or said in another way, there is a connection between humor and emotional intelligence.

Facts and Myths about Humor

Let's start out with a few myths and facts about using humor as a teaching tool. Myth #1 is that everyone who writes about humor assumes that it is not a well-researched topic—incorrect. People who say that there is a lack of evidence are not looking hard enough. Myth #2 is that humor is not accepted into the mainstream of educators or researchers. This may be partially true, but a plethora of empirical studies have found that individuals use humor and it works. Myth #3, the process of humor needs to be dissected and analyzed to find the root cause. Definitely not true. Everyone writes about the Superiority Theory, Incongruity Theory, and Relief Theory of humor, blah, blah, blah. Remember, all theories are wrong, but some are useful. E. B. White wrote, "Humor can be dissected as a frog, but the thing dies in the process." Myth #4, there are mixed results about using humor in the classroom. This is more of a misinterpretation than a myth. Numerous research studies indicate that humor enhances academic achievement, while other studies do not indicate such academic gains. No studies suggest that humor used appropriately hinders learning; therefore, there is no controversy—the use of humor can only help or keep things the same, it cannot hurt.

66 THERE IS A CONNECTION BETWEEN HUMOR AND EMOTIONAL INTELLIGENCE. 99

Enough about myths, now here are a few facts about humor from research:

1. Women laugh more than men, but males use more humor in the classroom than females.

2. Speakers are 46 percent more likely to laugh than listeners at their own jokes.

3. You're 30 times more likely to laugh when you're with other people than you are when you're alone (Johnson & Foley, 2003, ¶14).

4. Laughing is a social function. People will laugh at things not funny, if they are in groups (Provine, 2000).

5. Males prefer aggressive humor more than females do.

6. To be perceived as effective, leaders should use humor that adds to the content of the speech (Edwards & Gibboney, 1992).

7. Over 80 percent of the executives in a 1998 study stated that lack of humor can be a sign that the company has a morale problem (Scriven & Hefferin, 1998, pp. 14–15).

The main points from the research are that if you get people laughing you can tell them almost anything and they will typically remember it longer and more efficiently. Leaders who use humor, even if it is not the best humor in the world, are still more appreciated than those who do not try humor. The research is clear that people understand and appreciate humor, so it serves as a universal language, a connecting point for building new information. However, the use of humor requires change. How many leaders does it take to change a light bulb? Change??????

Methodology

This article is a synthesis of the research concerning the effects of humor on leadership. Both qualitative and quantitative studies were reviewed. Because the conclusions are based on research, it is only appropriate to explain what is meant by the term. (Remember, a conclusion is the place where you got tired of thinking.) It must be noted that there really is a plethora of quality (quantitative and qualitative) studies on the positive effects of using humor, so the research had to be condensed. Listed below are the criteria used for selecting and using research studies.

1. Both qualitative and quantitative studies were considered, but they had to be empirical in nature, e.g., a solid research design followed with analysis and synthesis of the material.

2. The study directly, or indirectly, examined the relationship of humor and leadership.

3. The terms *humor* and *leadership* were broadly defined.

4. Studies that contained effect sizes were emphasized, but they may be estimates in some cases. Not every researcher calculates effect size, and they certainly do not do so with a standard formula.

5. There were many studies analyzed but not included because I found other studies that said the same thing but had a stronger research design, or were written in a more concise manner, or simply were of a higher quality.

There is one caveat to the criteria: if I thought it was funny, I included it; if I thought it made sense, I included it; and if it was just too good to leave out, I included it. Listed below are the eight strategies that surfaced from the research explaining how humor can reshape leadership. Along with each theory are practical examples on how to implement each strategy.

Research-based Theories and Practices

1. Humor Develops a Positive Culture
Theory

"Humor reinforces the absurdity of rigid, inflexible behavior and misunderstanding and helps us remember that mistakes are natural and widespread in all humanity" (Berger, 1993; Crawford, 1994, p. 31; Weinstein, 1986). The days of dictatorial leadership are gone. Humor breaks down the old industrial barriers of top-down leadership.

Ziegler, Boardman, and Thomas (1985) concluded through empirical research that educational leaders can use humor to increase their effectiveness. Their research demonstrates that there are significant relationships between certain humor factors and the school climate. These same relationships exist between certain humor factors and leadership styles of principals perceived by teachers. The logical consequence of this research would seem to provide principals an important reason for developing appropriate humor-related skills.

66 HUMOR BREAKS DOWN THE OLD INDUSTRIAL BARRIERS OF TOP-DOWN LEADERSHIP. 99

Now, it must be noted that numbers are just numbers. While these data may be scientifically calculated, humans are involved, and when humans are involved they will typically make mistakes. ["I always find that statistics are hard to follow and impossible to digest. The only one I can ever remember is that if all the people who go to sleep in church were laid end to end they would be a lot more comfortable."— Mrs. Robert A. Taft]. Nevertheless, the research does keep adding up.

Practice

Dickmeyer (1993) conducted a longitudinal content analysis of classroom studies from 1941 to 1991. He found that there are benefits of humor, but cautions against misuses. Here are a few guidelines:

1. Consider your skills (strengths and weaknesses) when planning the use of humor.

2. Consider the audience.

3. Consider the course material when planning to use humor—humor must be related directly to the content.

4. Practice the humor on colleagues or family members.

How many administrators does it take to screw in a light bulb? One this year, two next year, and we budgeted for three the following year.

2. Humor Creates Enthusiasm, Motivation, and Engagement
Theory

It seems like everyone likes a good joke and people certainly like to make others laugh. For example, Thompson (2000) notes that people remember information associated with jokes because they have to pay more attention to humorous items in order to "get" the joke. Remember, it is easy to be funny, but the main question is, can people take notes from the material or learn from it? After all, the point of using humor is to be a more effective leader. If individuals cannot take notes from your speech or meeting, than you have a content problem.

Before proceeding, there are three main guidelines to follow: practice, practice, practice. (I know this is an old joke, but it fits here.) Do not expect to be excellent the first time you use humor. Your comfort level will rise the more times you try humor. Integrating humor is like driving a car—you certainly were not great the first time you got behind the wheel; it takes practice. Remember:

1. Humor should never be used to embarrass, ridicule, or harm someone.

2. Humor needs to be kept appropriate to the ability level of the audience.

3. Humor should be intellectually challenging.

Practice

Before using humor, get to know your staff and colleagues. Listen to what they are saying and talking about. Remember, from listening comes wisdom and from speaking comes repentance. Give individuals a fun-quiz to find their likes, dislikes, what they do during their spare time. Do not be afraid to even ask people if something is funny. Use the information to provide humor in meetings, to connect with people. Lou Holtz said, "Motivation is simple. You eliminate those who are not motivated."

3. Humor Reduces Tension and Stress
Theory

On a scientific level (more brain stuff), research informs us that when a person laughs the body secretes endorphins, the brain's natural painkillers, into the body. "The connection between stress and high blood pressure, muscle tension, immunosuppression, and many other changes has been known for years. We now have proof that laughter creates the opposite effects. It appears to be the perfect antidote for stress" (Wooten, 1996, p. 2; see also, Berk, 2000).

Today's work environment is filled with stress for everyone. One of the most researched uses of humor is that it reduces stress. Humor has been found to be a coping mechanism for managing anxiety and embarrassment by diverting attention from the situation (Fink & Walker, 1997; Ziv, 1984). In fact, several empirical studies have found that the use of humor not only moderates the negative effects of stress, but it alleviates the negativity associated with stress in the environment (Humphreys, 1990; Rareshide, 1993; Wooten, 1996).

Practice

This means that as a leader you need to read about humor, study it, and even make it part of your research when developing leadership activities or training. Leaders need to use humor themselves, but also empower employees and allow them to create and explore new ways of using humor.

For example, during the introductions at a meeting, ask everyone to say something about their strengths, and then ask for an interesting, unique, or humorous story about themselves. You should go first and then the activity makes others more comfortable and, hopefully, more emotionally stable in a stressful environment. Get everyone involved. You might also have a joke board where individuals can post cartoons, websites, or jokes that relate to work material.

A prayer for the stressed: God, grant me the serenity to accept the things I cannot change, the courage to change the things I cannot accept, and the wisdom to hide from my boss. Help me to always give 100% at work: 12% on Monday, 23% on Tuesday, 10% on Wednesday, 20% on Thursday, and 5% on Friday.

66 HUMOR SHOULD BE INTELLECTUALLY CHALLENGING. 99

4. Use Humor to Improve Meetings

Theory

Meetings are like funerals—no one wants to go, but they have to. Everyone gets dressed up and is on their best behavior, but when the meeting is over and the lights go out, people try to forget the pain. Why not make the meetings more fun and effective? Research informs us that the use of humor increases the popularity of a speaker, so why not use this to your advantage? For example, Jennifer (2001) and Garner (2006) found that the use of humor increased memory and meta-cognition; that is, when humor is used, people remember the material longer. So, spice up your meetings with humor—people will enjoy them more and even remember the information longer.

Practice

Sheila Fiegelson (1998) and Ron Berk (2000) provide some of the best advice on how to use humor to improve meetings:

1. Use humorous material in your reports and in the announcements for meetings.

2. Use pretend cautions or warnings on the covers of handouts, such as DO NOT fold, mutilate, spindle, or close cover before striking. Put in funny clip art, cartoons, and clever sayings in the minutes—maybe someone will actually read them for once.

3. Use an opening joke or even challenge participants. Tell a joke and then have someone volunteer to tell a joke. Have the participants "vote" on whose joke was better. If you do not "win," give treats to everyone, or end the meeting early.

Remember, leading is mostly about listening. Learning is mostly about talking.

5. Humor Helps Build Relationships
Theory

Gunning (2001) found that purposeful humor reduces tension, entertains, builds rapport, and shares positive feelings. Provine (2000) experimented with laughter only to find that it is rarely a response to jokes. It is instead the quintessential human social signal, building relationships and pulling people into the fold. "Laughter seems intimately entwined with our physiology. It blocks a neural reflex that regulates muscle tone, proving the 'going weak with laughter' is more than a metaphor" (Begley, 2000, p. 76). More importantly, humor builds teamwork while helping new members assimilate into the groups (Brooks, 1992). Humor helps leaders gain approval; it reinforces group relationships and builds trust in teams. However, many leaders think that "teamwork is a lot of people doing what I say."

Teamwork and humor can be very contagious. Researchers found that kids under the age of five laugh 350 times per day, while people over 35 laugh five times per day. (I know one vice president who laughs once every five years, so he skews the average. Averages are misleading.) Why should the kids have all the fun? Humor develops teamwork, the teams become close and joke around more, which becomes infectious within the organization, and very soon the culture of the organization has changed. Humor can be learned and, therefore, it can be used to transform it into a less stressful environment by building teamwork. You will always do foolish things in life, so do them with enthusiasm.

To demonstrate these points, in 1985, Virginia Ziegler, Gerald Boardman, and M. Donald Thomas found in their research (with a .05 level of significance) that there was: (a) a significant positive correlation between neat, lighthearted humor and the leadership factor; and (b) a significant negative correlation between dullness humor and the leadership factor.

Practice

Listed are a few of my own related findings that may help to develop your own leadership:

1. Managers do the right thing, and leaders do things right.
2. You can always count on leaders to do the right thing after trying everything else.
3. Hark, there goes the crowd! I must hurry because I am their leader.
4. The squeeze is more important than the juice.
5. A leader is a person who knows when to hold someone up and when to push him or her down the stairs.

Here are a few ways to use humor in leadership positions:

1. Use humorous illustrations in presentations and meetings.
2. Videotape clever TV ads to be used as visual aids and inspiration.
3. Use cartoons that support your ideas.
4. Develop patterns of humor at work, for example, running gags.
5. Find one person to be the good humor man/woman. Look for him or her to supply humor.
6. Provide a positive reinforcement for using humor—for example, goofy awards or candy.

❝ RESEARCHERS FOUND THAT KIDS UNDER THE AGE OF FIVE LAUGH 350 TIMES PER DAY, WHILE PEOPLE OVER 35 LAUGH FIVE TIMES PER DAY. (I KNOW ONE VICE PRESIDENT WHO LAUGHS ONCE EVERY FIVE YEARS, SO HE SKEWS THE AVERAGE.) ❞

6. Humor Increases Communication

Theory

One of the most widely researched effects of humor is its enhancement of communication. Crawford (1994) noted in his research that humor is a communicative tactic used to engender support. Leaders can use humor to enhance communication, partially through the important symbolic realm to create a positive atmosphere.

There is little or no doubt (unless you read this article) that humor enhances communication, communication enhances leadership, and therefore humor enhances leadership. (This is true, if I have my logic correct from freshman-year philosophy class). Leaders use humor to communicate to colleagues, staff, and organizations by reinforcing positive behavior and discouraging negative behavior. Communication is probably the most important tool that can be used by leaders.

The analysis of humor, properly conducted, is a delicate dissection of uncertainties, a surgery of suppositions. ~ stolen from M. J. Moroney

Remember that:

- words are 7% effective
- tone of voice is 38% effective
- nonverbal cues are 55% effective

(Of course, statistics are like bikinis. What they reveal is suggestive, but what they conceal is vital. ~ Aaron Levenstein)

Humor can be the written word, the spoken word, or just silly gestures. What this means is that you need to paint a picture for the audience through humor using words, pictures, nonverbal cues, body language, and so forth. This can partially be accomplished by three simple concepts: refine, refine, and refine the joke. Less is always more with a joke. You should set up the joke appropriately, get into the story, tell the punch line, and get out. Moreover, body language is critical. People will be watching your eye movement, body language, etc., so you need to make your body work for you when using humor.

Practice

In education, pedagogy may be defined as the art, science, or profession of teaching. Obviously, there are numerous teaching styles and methods that have proven successful over the years, many of which serve as valuable lessons for leaders. Let me introduce to you the use of short videos—pedagogy plus videos or videagogy©. A key aspect of utilizing humor is to use visual effects. Communicating with the use of short videos is not only a fun way to integrate humor but it is a great way to integrate technology; it matches the learning style of many younger people, and even connects with Gardner's theory of multiple intelligences.

YouTube, collegehumor.com/video, MySpace, and video.google.com are sites filled with numerous videos that work great for enhancing communication. One of the best things is that these videos tend to run from 30 seconds to only a few minutes, which is long enough to get your point across but short enough not to bore the audience. Build a video library on a notebook computer that can be utilized at any time. Categorize the videos by main topic so you can find one for the main lessons. Show the humorous video and then discuss the lessons learned. Let me give you an example.

There is a commercial for the European lotto that has a taxi driver stopping in front of a crowd of people. Everyone wants a ride, but the driver is discerning. He turns on the radio and starts lip-syncing the song "Bar Room Blitz" by Sweet. Everyone on the curb seems confused except one individual who gets it. The individual starts lip-syncing the song, along with the taxi driver who ultimately offers the gentleman a ride and off they go—much to the dismay of everyone else waiting. The commercial fades out and says "Lotto millionaires are not like ordinary millionaires." Every time I show the commercial individuals always love it, plus it can then be used for discussions on topics such as why we do not have to follow the norm, or how there are topics that some people "get" and others simply do not understand. The bottom line with videagogy is that you find short videos that make people look, listen, think, and discuss—it is called critical thinking and analysis and is a great use of technology.

7. Leadership Starts at the Top, Making Organizations More Effective
Theory
To change the culture of an organization, humor has to start at the top. Leaders need to have a good sense of humor. While you do not have to hire only individuals who are funny, many organizations search specifically for leaders with a sense of humor; it helps build culture. Hire the humorous. This quality is often overlooked and certainly underrated. Humorous individuals tend to be more creative and apt to accept change.

Remember, "Individuals laugh because of the social context or their relationship with other individuals. This is the base for social theorists who insist that laughter is primarily a method of dealing with the environment" (Hudson, 1979, p. 18). It only makes sense that the more you promote laughter in your organization, the more connected individuals will become (Crawford, 1994; Dandridge, Mitroff, & Joyce, 1980). Humor also has been linked directly with improving the effectiveness of leaders (Avolio, Howell, & Soski, 1999; Crawford, 1994).

Practice
Do not reinvent the wheel. Save those "junk" e-mails with jokes, search the Internet, and use humorous websites. The Humor Project, www.humorProject.com, for example, celebrated its 30th anniversary in 2007 and is filled with presentations, conferences, research, resources, and many other humorous references.

If you take care of the little things, the larger problems disappear. Here are a few little things you can do to help change into a humor culture.

1. Give small awards, or candy, at every meeting for first to arrive, the best new idea, etc.

2. Add a timed "whine and cheese" item to the agenda. Use this time to celebrate accomplishments, or discuss upcoming events.

3. Use toys and props to loosen up people—the sillier the better. This sets the tone of the meeting.

4. Add a "rumor mill" to the end of each meeting to squash rumors and get issues and concerns on the table safely.

5. Instead of a meeting, watch an inspirational movie (Stephenson & Thibault, 2006, pp. 98–99).

8. Humor Helps Teachers Maintain Interest at Work
Theory

Priest and Swain (2002) used two different studies to find the "relation between leadership effectiveness and warm humorous style was a very strong one" while good leaders were rated higher in humor, even after controlling statistically for other attributes (p. 185). Leaders benefit by using self-deprecating humor, thereby creating a more positive climate. Ultimately, self-disparaging humor will enhance the leader's image, while self-promoting humor has the opposite effect (adapted from Gruner, 1985, p. 142).

Practice

You can consciously misuse terms or clichés, which will instill a sense of superiority in students and staff, and maybe even a feeling of empathy for you. Don't be afraid to laugh at your own mistakes.

Lists are a great way to integrate humor and leadership. Look at the success David Letterman has with his top ten lists. Allow individuals to decorate their offices anyway they want. I work with an advertising agency where they have a Ping-Pong table, complete with bleachers, in the middle of their meeting room. I actually have a six-foot-tall blow-up doll of the Incredible Hulk to look over me in my office.

You can also put humorous signs on doors. Daily cartoons or acceptable drawings lighten up the atmosphere. Have your staff read humorous books that have a message. Books like *Leadership Secrets by Attila the Hun* by Wes Roberts (1990) can be both clever and informative.

Cautions

Like using hazardous material, using humor should come with a few warnings and cautions that need to be addressed before trying to be funny without a net:

1. Humor should not be avoided, simply approach humor with respect for the fellow person.

2. Minimize the offensive nature of joking by avoiding jokes that discriminate against people (even lawyers).

3. Make sure that the humor reflects the interests and language of the followers.

4. Make the humor brief and conversational—no one likes to get lost in a joke or story and miss the punch line.

5. Take your message seriously, but don't take yourself too seriously (Gruner, 1970).

Conclusion: Ten Research-based, Practical Points to Use as a Leader to Enhance Humor

1. Develop a database of jokes, stories, sayings, etc. Every time you go to hear or see something funny, add the stories to your database. Be diligent about this activity and categorize information for easy use.

2. Search the Internet and read books on humor.

3. Always look for connections with your material. Do not just cut out a cartoon or funny joke. Write a short note on the back where it may fit with your material or activities.

4. As you complete a lesson plan or activity, be sure to plan out the jokes, stories, humorous overheads, etc. Look spontaneous and be prepared. Humor can be learned and planned; it does not have to be extemporaneous. I actually outline my lectures and write in the jokes in the proper places where they should work the best.

5. Collect overheads and videos (scanned onto your computer), label and categorize them. Share jokes and cartoons with your colleagues. A picture is worth a thousand words.

6. Keep track of the reactions you get with various jokes and activities. This will take some work, but any improvement takes time. Of course, go ahead and reuse the things that work and do not be afraid to eliminate the ones that don't. Remember, if the horse is dead, dismount.

7. Look at reality for some of the funniest things to discuss. Individuals will be able to make more connections between humor, knowledge, and real-life situations.

8. Do not be afraid to encourage students, friends, and staff to develop a sense of humor. Humor can be very contagious—let it happen.

9. Just do it. Don't be afraid to make mistakes and look less than perfect. Individuals will respect you for the chances you take—maybe.

10. Be sure that you have job security before you try any of the suggestions in this article, or at least a second career to fall back on.

It is not a question of IF you should use humor, but HOW to use it.

REFERENCES

Avolio, B., Howell, J. M., & Soski, J. J. (1999). A funny thing happened on the way to the bottom line: Humour as a moderator of leadership style effects. *Academy of Management Journal, 42*(2), 219–227.

Begley, S. (2000, October 9). The science of laughs. *Science & Technology*, pp. 75–76.

Berger, A. A. (1993). *An anatomy of humor.* New Brunswick, NJ: Transaction Publishers.

Berk, R. A. (2000, Fall). Does humor in course tests reduce anxiety and improve performance? *College Teaching, 48*(4), 151–158. (ERIC Document Reproduction Service No. EJ 619 990)

Brooks, G. P. (1992). *Humor in leadership: State of the art in theory and practice.* (ERIC Document Reproduction Service No. ED 417 113)

Crawford, C. B. (1994, May). *Strategic humor in leadership: Practical suggestions for appropriate use.* Paper presented at the meeting of the Kansas Leadership Forum, Salina, KS. (ERIC Document Reproduction Service No. ED 369 107)

Dandridge, T. C., Mitroff, I., & Joyce, W. F. (1980). Organizational symbolism: A topic to expand organizational analysis. *Academy of Management Review, 5,* 77–82.

Dickmeyer, S. (1993, April). *Humor as an instructional practice: A longitudinal content analysis of humor use in the classroom.* (Eric Document Reproduction Service No. 359587)

Edwards, C. M., & Gibboney, E. R. (1992). *The power of humor in the college classroom.* (ERIC Document Reproduction Service No. ED 346 535)

Fiegelson, S. (1998). *Energize your meetings with laughter.* Alexandria, VA: Association for Supervision and Curriculum Development.

Fink, E. I., & Walker, B. A. (1977). Humorous responses to embarrassment. *Psychological Reports, 40,* 475–485.

Garner, R. L. (2006). Humor in pedagogy: How ha-ha can lead to aha! *College Teaching, 54*(1), 177–180.

Gruner, C. R. (1970). The effect of humor in dull and interesting informative speeches. *Central States Speech Journal, 21,* 160–166.

Gruner, C. R. (1985). Advice to the beginning speaker on using humor—what the research tells us. *Communication Education, 34,* 142–147.

Gunning, B. L. (2001). *The role that humor plays in shaping organizational culture*. Dissertation, University of Toledo, 62(12A).

Hudson, G. (1979). *The role of humor in John F. Kennedy's 1960 presidential campaign*. Dissertation, Southern Illinois University.

Humphreys, B. R. (1990, May). *A cheerful heart is good medicine: The emotional and physical benefits of humor*. (ERIC Document Reproduction Service No. ED 317 892)

Jennifer, L. W. (2001). *Funny you should ask, what is the effect of humor on memory and metamemory?* Dissertation, The American University.

Johnson, S., & Foley, D. (2003, April). Laughter. *Discover, 24*(4). Retrieved from www.discover.com/apr_03/featlaught.html, part of the Learning Series: The Brain and Emotions, part 2.

Priest R. F., & Swain, J. (2002). Humor and its implications for leadership effectiveness. *Humor,* 169–189.

Provine, R. (2000). *Laughter: A scientific investigation*. New York: Penguin Books.

Rareshide, S. W. (1993). *Implications for teachers' use of humor in the classroom*. (ERIC Document Reproduction Service No. ED 359 165)

Roberts, W. (1990). *Leadership secrets of Attila the Hun*. New York: Warner Books.

Scriven, J., & Hefferin, L. (1998, February). Humor: The "witting" edge in business. *Business Education Forum*, pp. 13–15.

Stephenson, S., & Thibault, P. (2006). *Laughing matters: Strategies for building a joyful learning community*. Bloomington, IN: Solution Tree.

Thompson, J. L. (2000). Funny you should ask, what is the effect of humor on memory and metamemory? (Doctoral Dissertation, American University). *Dissertation Abstracts International, 61(8-B)*, 4442. (UMI 9983671)

Weinstein, M. (Speaker). (1986). *Lighten up: The power of humor at work*. (Cassette Recording). Greenwich, CT: Listen USA.

Wooten, P. (1996). Humor: An antidote for stress. *Holistic Nursing Practice, 10*(2), 49–55. http://www.jesthealth.com/artantistress9.html

Ziegler, V., Boardman, G., & Thomas, M. D. (1985). Humor, leadership, and school climate. *Clearing House, 58*, 346–348.

Ziv, A. (1984). *Personality and sense of humor*. New York: Springer.

PETER M. JONAS has been an associate professor and Chair of the Doctoral Leadership Studies Department in the College of Education and Leadership at Cardinal Stritch University since 1997. He has been actively involved in consulting and speaking for the past 20 years in the areas of research, leadership, and humor, and has presented at a variety of national conferences, many of them dealing with the subject of humor in education. In addition, he has written numerous books, manuals, and book reviews, as well as published more than 30 articles in professional periodicals. Peter received his Ph.D. degree in American history from Marquette University.

Innocents Abroad in the New Millennium: How Well Does the American Leadership Model Travel?

By Mark Bagshaw

WHEN IT COMES TO ANALYZING LEADERSHIP IN AN INTERNATIONAL OR non-U.S. context, concepts that are closely associated with the American model of leadership—so much so that they often are thought of as leadership "universals"—do not always travel well. The principal reason for their lack of portability is that they derive from a political, economic, legal, cultural, and social context that is almost unique in the world's history. Leadership in America takes place in a societal context comprised of a particular type of *democratic political system*, a largely *market-driven economic system*, a *transparent legal system* which accords every citizen equal rights under the law, a system of *cultural values* that shape American values and attitudes toward leaders and leadership, and a *liberal social system* emphasizing the primacy of *individual freedom over individual responsibility* to serve the needs of society. All of these contextual factors condition leadership in America but are not uniformly present in other parts of the world, and where they are present, they appear to differing degrees and in different configurations. In this paper, I challenge the idea that certain core concepts in the study of American leadership that devolve from the American context are universally applicable around the world.

The reason that we in the field of leadership have not been more circumspect in applying the American model of leadership to other world contexts is an uncomplicated manifestation of scholarly ethnocentrism. Since the end of World War II, most of the scholarship focused on leadership has been conducted by Americans or foreign scholars living and working in North America. As a result, much of what we know about leadership *anywhere* in recent times is based on what American leadership scholars have discovered about leadership in America. Although leadership studies are now conducted in many countries—and often with regional, cross-country, and cross-cultural comparisons—there is still, as Den Hartog and Dickson observe, "a strong North American bias in the leadership theories, models, and measures that are used and published in mainstream social science literature" (2004, p. 253).

In general, scholars in the field of leadership have been careful about the more obvious dangers of overgeneralizing. At our most parsimonious, we in the field of leadership have said, "Well, so long as it involves leaders, followers, and shared goals, we'll call it leadership" (Wills, 1994, p. 13)—*wherever* it takes place; on the other hand, at our most ambitious, we have argued for the universal application of a more ideological and more discriminating definition that embraces both descriptive and prescriptive elements, such as the definition of leadership offered by Rost (1991, pp. 102–103), which asks us to judge whether it is indeed leadership by: (1) determining whether an influence process is taking place; (2) distinguishing intentions for real changes from intentions for nominal or everyday changes; (3) ascertaining whether the putative influence process is occurring among leaders and followers, and therefore is multidirectional; and (4) ensuring that the purposes of those engaged in said influence processes toward real changes are also mutual—neither exclusively the purposes of the leader nor exclusively those of the other group members the leader seeks to lead.

In Figure 1, there are listed seven conditions that typically are taken to be universally characteristic of leadership in all situations. The ordering of the items in this list is not random but a deliberate concatenation wherein each successive item devolves from the item that precedes it. Of these seven supposed leadership universals, it is my contention that at least six of them (Items 1 through 5 and Item 7 in the figure) require reassessment based on relevant disconfirming evidence found in cultures outside of the United States. The terminology of "agent" and "target" in Supposed Leadership Universal #5 comes from Gary Yukl's *Leadership in Organizations* (2002, p. 142) but can be found in a number of sources. This terminology is not in dispute; what is dubious about this item when applied to world locations beyond the U.S. is the contention that, in the context of leadership, agents' attempts to influence universally are intended to "affect the thinking and enlist the will" of their targets. Supposed Universal #6 is related to #5, and seems beyond dispute when framed by an appropriately broad definition of what constitutes a power resource. The idea that the ability to influence depends on power resources is well supported throughout the leadership and social sciences literature. If we define influence conventionally as "power enacted by an agent to affect the behavior of one or more targets," as Yukl does (2002, p. 142), then it is apparent that sources of power—power resources—are indispensable for influence to occur. With these qualifications in mind, in the six sections that follow, I challenge the universality of each of the six contested items in Figure 1.

Figure 1. Seven Supposed "Leadership Universals."

1. That leadership is a social or *group* phenomenon (<u>not</u> the possession by an individual of particular personal traits or behaviors).

2. That leadership is a *process* or dynamic (<u>not</u> a static condition or positional arrangement).

3. That this group process is *purposive* or goal-oriented (<u>not</u> based on preserving the status quo; or on clan membership, kinship, or relational commitments).

4. That seeking to accomplish group goals derives from *influence* (as distinguished from coercion).

5. That the use of influence involves at least one person (an "agent") attempting to *affect the thinking and enlist the will* of one or more others (a "target").

6. That the ability of an agent to influence a target depends on *controlling and dispensing power resources.*

7. That the primary power resource in enacting leadership in contemporary societies is *persuasion*—the ability to communicate persuasively.

Does Leadership Adhere in the Group or in the Leader?

Supposed Leadership Universal #1 suggests that leadership is a social or group phenomenon, and not the behavioral outcomes that result from an individual's traits. This is uncontested to the extent that leaders, whether charismatic or positional, do need followers for leadership to occur. As Wills observes in *Certain Trumpets* (1994, p. 13), "If you want to lead, the one thing you can't do without is followers"; consequently, merely possessing the personal traits of a leader, or performing certain behaviors associated with such traits doesn't constitute leadership in itself. Or does it? When GLOBE Project researchers (House et al., 2004) used more than 160 investigators to study the responses of 17 thousand managers in more than 950 organizations in 62 societies worldwide, in order to identify what constitutes effective leadership, their methodology led them to consolidate 21 "first-order" dimensions into the six "second-order" dimensions shown in Figure 2.

Figure 2. The GLOBE Project's Six Global Leadership Dimensions.

1. Charismatic/Value-Based Leadership (e.g., being visionary, inspirational, having integrity and decisive elements)

2. Team-oriented Leadership (e.g., acting collaborative, integrating, and diplomatic)

3. Participative Leadership (e.g., being non-autocratic and allowing participation in decision making)

4. Autonomous Leadership (e.g., being individualistic, independent, and unique)

5. Humane Leadership (e.g., modesty, tolerance, and sensitivity) ["paternalistic" in some cultures]

6. Self-Protective Leadership (e.g., being self-centered, status conscious, and a face-saver)

(House et al., 2004)

Although the GLOBE researchers refer to these six variously as global leadership "dimensions," "attributes," or "behaviors" (House et al., 2004, pp. 14, 41–42), it is clear from their accompanying descriptions that most of them are imputed traits of group leaders that manifest as effective leader behavior. GLOBE Project researchers found that some sets of leader traits were seen to lead to effective leadership in all cultures; in other words, they were universally effective. Some of the sets of traits were seen as universally ineffective in all cultures; and in some cases, particular sets of leader traits were seen as effective in some cultures and ineffective in others; in other words, these latter sets of leader traits were culture-dependent or context-specific (House et al., 2004, pp. 39–40).

In observing the characteristics of the six second-order sets, it is easy to see that they are defined principally in terms of leader traits and leader behaviors, and offer very little to suggest the importance of group dynamics involving follower traits or behaviors, or group goals. If we were to take the one set of the six that does seem to at least imply a group interaction—Item #3, Participative Leadership—we find Participative Leadership involves leaders who are non-autocratic and encouraging participation in decision making ("involving others in making and implementing decisions") (House et al., 2004, p. 14). GLOBE researchers found that this type of leadership was not enthusiastically endorsed by respondents in the Middle East, Eastern Europe, and East and South Asia—that is, four of the ten groups of "culture clusters" that comprise the universe of the GLOBE study (House et al., 2004, pp.

42–43, 683). In many societies studied by the GLOBE Project scholars, the type of leadership that looks most like a group phenomenon is less in evidence than one might expect. Indeed, leadership as defined by the behaviors of paternalistic leaders, autocratic leaders, and even self-protective leaders are very much in evidence in the GLOBE Project results, and very much define the form that leadership takes in many of the GLOBE Project culture clusters.

One of the chief arguments for seeing leadership as a social or group phenomenon under all circumstances is the idea that the activities of a group doing leadership is not just an extension of the will of the leader: group members are imagined as being required to commit their own individual wills to the activity. Burns (1978, pp. 18–21), Rost (1991, pp. 105–106), and Wills (1994, p. 18), as prominent examples, all rule out the use of coercion to carry out the plans or desires of the leader. If coercion, the act of compelling others to act in response to an aversive stimulus (force or the threat of force), is used, Burns, Rost, and Wills are unwilling to call that type of social interaction leadership. Yet, the strong, charismatic leader who sweeps followers off their feet by force of personality traits, or whose behavioral history suggests predictability along the dimensions of competence and ethical behaviors (Heifetz, 1994, p. 107), and whose trustworthy demeanor therefore engenders trust in the group, is clearly documented by research. Indeed, as any reputable newspaper with a foreign desk testifies, the autocratic and paternalistic model of leader is alive and well and directing human traffic in Caracas, Kolkata, Kinshasa, and Tashkent. The point is not that Burns, Rost, and Wills are wrong; it is, rather, that *we* are misguided to assume that a single model which adequately describes the phenomenon of leadership in North America can be used to analyze leadership in many other parts of the world. In examining Supposed Leadership Universal #4, we will return to the prohibited use of coercion as a prime example of what Storti has termed the "ethnocentric impulse" (2001, p. 66f.).

Is Leadership a Dynamic or a Condition?

Supposed Leadership Universal #2 states that leadership is a process or dynamic, not a static condition or positional arrangement. One implication of this supposed universal is that leaders can be followers, and followers can be leaders: simply having a superior position or formal title does not automatically make one the leader of group activities, nor does a subordinate status or job description rule out the possibility of leading. The idea of leadership as a dynamic that empowers all group members is grounded in such concepts as "roving leadership" (De Pree, 1989, p. 48), the Janus-like "leader-follower" described by Gardner (1990, p. 4), and the conception of leadership as a "mutually determinative" activity on the part of leaders and followers delineated by

Wills (1994, p. 14). But these ideas also ignore the important relationships between hereditary or hierarchical position and the ability to act as leader in more traditional societies such as those of the Middle East and Central, South, and East Asia, where organizational position or hereditary role are often the chief enablers for group leadership to occur.

Geert Hofstede (1997) points out that in societies with high power distance, that is, large and accepted differentials in power between superiors and subordinates, "there is a norm that less powerful people should be dependent on the more powerful, subordinates expect to be told what to do, and the ideal boss is a benevolent autocrat or good father" (p. 37). Hofstede's observation is germane and representative. In my research on managers in multinational corporations operating in China in the opening years of the 21st century, indigenous Chinese middle managers typically did not consult with their subordinates before issuing directives (partly from the desire not to be perceived as requiring advice or appearing to be uncertain), and subordinates did not expect to offer advice to their superiors unless specifically asked (partly from fear of causing the superior to lose face). Managers expected to make decisions autocratically and paternalistically for the good of all. Subordinates were often reluctant to disagree with their superiors for fear of reprisals and were reluctant to trust their opinions and ideas with each other. Leadership based on position or hierarchy was also a source of harmony and stability in these organizations. In China, generally, to have everyone in a group attempting to influence each other, and attempting to lead, would be to invite conflict and chaos (*luan*) (Bagshaw, 2002, 2004, 2005, 2006).

Is Leadership About Accomplishing Purposes or About Maintaining Relationships?

According to Supposed Leadership Universal #3, the group process articulated in Supposed Universal #2 is purposive, focused on goal accomplishment, and not focused on preserving the status quo. Nor is the group process invested in enforcing or reinforcing kinship or other relational commitments and configurations. If purposiveness in attaining goals is indeed the operative model for all cases of leadership, it seems fair to ask who gets to set the goals the group pursues? The American model says "the group sets the goals." John W. Gardner, one of the most insightful writers on the nuances of leadership, suggested that "shared values are the bedrock on which leaders build the edifice of group achievement" (1990, p. xvi). Although the American model allows the vision of one group member to frame the purposive activities of the whole group, the model also requires that other group members embrace that vision in a consensual manner—by sharing values—before effective leadership, and effective pursuit of the vision's implied goals, can occur. As Smircich and Morgan (1982) phrase it, "Leadership is defining a reality that can gain a consensual following" (p. 259). In the context of the American model, any attempt at leading requires accreting enough support and agreement from the group for a leader-candidate's vision to be pursued. If the group agrees with the reality that the would-be leader defines through his or her vision, then the leadership game is afoot; otherwise, more caucusing, more campaigning, and more attempts at defining the reality that the group inhabits are necessary. In other societies, less openly democratic approaches, some approaches closer to the notion that "silence gives consent," appear to be the rule, rather than the exception.

> **❝ IN THE CONTEXT OF THE AMERICAN MODEL, ANY ATTEMPT AT LEADING REQUIRES ACCRETING ENOUGH SUPPORT AND AGREEMENT FROM THE GROUP FOR A LEADER-CANDIDATE'S VISION TO BE PURSUED. ❞**

The idea that it is not leadership if it does not involve purposiveness—the pursuit of goals—is at the heart of the American leadership model. The American model says that leadership, in its essence, is all about change: First, we scan the environment looking for problems and opportunities, and when we perceive a match between our group, our organization, and some issue in our environment, we try to articulate the nature of the issue, how it will affect us, and what we should do about it—how we should change. If that change is a rather large, ambitious undertaking, we call what we should do about our situation "the vision." Then, we try to sell the vision to our fellow group members as a vision of change. In effect, we say,"For us to avail the opportunity or ward off the problem, we will have to change what we do, in the following ways, in order to arrive at the improved future state that I envision and will now go on to describe." That's how the American model sees leadership.

Elsewhere in the world, however, one encounters diverse examples of prominent persons who in other respects appear to be leaders, but whose vision is *not* about change but about preserving harmonious relations or preserving the status quo. In some group contexts around the world, change is viewed as an invitation to entropy, a falling off from goodness, the enemy of a group's stability and peace. (Consider, as an example, the views on the relative desirability of Westernization held by mullahs in Iran at the time the Shah was deposed.) In China, there is still strong support for the idea that the leader is not so much a dramatic doer as the embodiment of the stable center, the *zhongyang*. The father of modern China, Dr. Sun Yatsen, was known in China by the honorific title *Zhongshan*—"Central Mountain." *Zhongshan* captures the idea of a source of stability at the center of social action, around which a society that seeks to preserve harmony and stability can be ordered and developed. Much the same may be said about the tribal leadership that we see today in Anbar Province in Iraq. Brigadier General John Allen's idea of viewing tribal social structures as the tectonic plates of country culture, the underlying unit of social infrastructure in parts of the Middle East and Central Asia, has serious merit. "Tribal leaders in Anbar Province in Iraq take money from the U.S. military and use it to shore up and reinforce their leadership of their tribal groups, not so much to achieve the *status ante*—the way it was before the war—as to secure and perpetuate the tribal status quo" (Jaffe, 2007, p. 1).

Is Leadership Free of Coercion—or Not?
Supposed Leadership Universal #4 says that this purposive group process we call leadership involves influence, influence free from the taint of coercion. As noted earlier, the contemporary American model delimits influence to noncoercive means. According to Burns (1978, p. 18), those who hold power are of two types: power-wielders and leaders. Power-wielders are motivated to achieve their own goals by marshaling resources to influence the behaviors of persons who respond to their influence efforts; these influence efforts may include any means (including coercion) that causes these target persons to respond. Leaders, on the other hand, are motivated to realize goals held in concert with their followers, and leaders do this by mobilizing resources to arouse, engage, and satisfy the motives of followers—causing followers to commit their wills (not simply yielding their compliant behaviors) and thus precluding the use of coercion.

But is commitment of the follower's will necessary? Is compliance not enough? Burns's analysis makes sense when applied to American leadership (with its individualistic and empowered group members clamoring to participate in group decision making and to own their individual contributions to group achievement), but the analysis falls short of accounting for situations in other cultures (for example, in Russia or Turkmenistan) where characteristically strong autocratic leaders marshal resources to achieve *their own* goals (which may be intended, ultimately, to benefit followers), but where followers seem more like respondents to stimulus than followers being aroused, engaged, and motivated. Conversely (for example, in Japan), leaders often appear to be no more than respondents to the consensually derived desires of other group members (followers?) and appear to have no goals of their own, and little impetus to action, other than standing in front of the group and representing the group will.

Outside of the United States, the prescription of a coercion-free leadership "lacks legs" (Nye, 2008, p. 30). Even in America, as recently as the late 1950s, French and Raven's (1959) typology of the sources of social power lists coercion—the ability to punish—right alongside the ability to reward as one of five major sources of social power or potential influence over others. The *locus classicus* for including coercion as a form of influence is Machiavelli's sphinx-like riddle in *The Prince*, written around 1513 CE: If you wish to be a leader, is it better to be loved or feared? The best answer, according to Machiavelli, is *not* "to be feared" *or* "loved" but to be *both*: loved *and* feared. In other words, the best answer vaults the horns of a false (but categorically convenient) dichotomy.

When I teach Machiavelli in my leadership classes, this riddle typically precipitates a teachable moment, and I typically pause on Machiavelli's assertion to let realization sink in: "How can this be? Isn't it a paradox to be both loved AND feared? Are not love and fear opposites? Can someone give us an example of how a leader, or any person, could be both loved AND feared?" When I get a good answer to this question from the class, the example offered usually is an authority figure from the student's life (a father, a grandmother; occasionally, a coach or teacher). Usually, the authority figure is someone the student loves and respects but who also threatens their sense of continued well-being in a way that causes them to modify their behaviors in ways consistent with the authority figure's desires. Even in America, there seem to be some conditions that make it difficult to remove the use of coercion from the leader's toolkit of influence sources.

Enlightened Commitment or Stimulated Compliance?

Supposed Leadership Universal #5 states that when an agent influences a target, this action is an attempt to "affect the thinking and enlist" the target's will. Clearly, if shared goals are the result of "mutually determinative activity" as Wills argues (1994, p. 14), or if intended "real changes" are the reflection of "mutual purposes" as Rost argues (1991, pp. 118–123), then this idea of enlisting or engaging the wills of group members makes some sense. Nevertheless, although goals mutually shared by leaders and followers are critical in America, it is not so elsewhere. One manifestation of this lack of universal mutuality is that cultural differences frequently preclude mutuality by the way power is distributed and wielded in decision making. For example, Pye states:

> Harold Laswell's definition of power—"Participation in the making of significant decisions"—rings true in American culture . . . [but] in no traditional Asian culture would such a definition of power have been acceptable. . . . [In China,] leaders tend to see themselves as all-powerful, and the Chinese people continue to crave leaders who can solve all their problems. (1985, p. 21)

Thus, for instance, in the traditional model of Chinese decision making, there is minimal mutuality, and little need or effort to "affect the thinking" of followers, or to "enlist their wills." In Japan, conversely, decision making that involves a strong central leader is uncommon. To underscore the point that Japan does not favor strong leaders, Pye asks his readers how many names of Japanese prime ministers they can recall (1985, p. 183). The presumed paucity of relevant names that comes to mind reflects Pye's insight that the Japanese "have never had an ideal of leadership comparable to the American concept of chief executive" (Pye, 1985, p. 171). The contrasting Chinese model of a central powerful leader who serves the needs of the group for harmony and stability and whose authority obviates the need for much critical and analytical thinking by followers was rejected by the Japanese in favor of a model in which, when required, some person is pushed forward from the group to represent its consensus to others. In the Japanese situation there also is little mutuality, but now it is the leader who is the target of influence attempts that make minimal demands on the leader's thinking and have little need to enlist the leader's will.

The mechanisms by which the Japanese group conveys its consensus to its Japanese leaders are subtle. At one time, the *ringi seido* or *ringi sho*—in which a proposal for a particular decision outcome is circulated in document form by a person or persons at a lower level in an organization to various people at higher levels, in order to develop group consensus in favor of the particular decision outcome desired to be enacted at the highest executive level—was endemic in large business organizations and was characteristic of the diffused use of power by the group. *Ringi* is not only a group-consensus-seeking device, but it is also a method of communication. Many people who are directly or indirectly affected by the proposal learn about it informally before it is implemented. Although the contemporary Japanese bureaucracy has adopted more Western ideas of businesslike behavior, *ringi*-like group behaviors continue to be used to achieve consensus and avoid decisive, authoritarian-style decision making (Pye, 1985, p. 172).

Other characteristic Japanese decision-making processes include *sake* parties (after-work drinking sessions), *nemawashi* (informal opinion surfacing), and *jyomukai* (executive meetings) (Misumi, 1984). The protocol of *sake* parties after work hours allows subordinates, under the cover of drunken camaraderie, to say what they like in the presence of their superior without fear of reprisal. Drinking parties are a ritual that permits frustrations and criticisms to be brought to the attention of higher levels without loss of face. *Nemawashi* is an informal preliminary sounding out of opinions, which gives minority views an adequate hearing and prepares the ground for consensus before a formal vote. If the proposed course of action is formally voted down, this would involve loss of face, and that would be unseemly. *Nemawashi* allows everybody, including dissenters, to come out of the process without public humiliation or shame. *Nemawashi* works better with simple or routine matters and becomes less effective when opinions are sharply divided on important issues. In such cases, principally to reduce embarrassment, *jyomukai*, or executive meetings, tend to be used. *Jyomukai* held behind closed doors permits a face-saving resolution of any decision-making situation which falls between total rejection and total acceptance in a swift, subtle, and suitably harmonious manner. Note that in the case of both Chinese followers and Japanese leaders as targets, the purpose is not to convince them by rational argument that will enlist their wills but to apprise them of the direction that the Chinese leader and the Japanese followership, respectively, wish to proceed.

The Primacy of Verbal Communication or Other Forms of Suasion?

As noted earlier, the terminological aspects of Supposed Leadership Universal #5, and Universal #6—the mechanics of how influence works, and that an agent's ability to influence depends on power resources (broadly defined)—are concepts whose use is not in dispute, and whose application indeed does seem to be universal. This leaves us, then, with Supposed Leadership Universal #7: the idea that a primary source of the leader's ability to influence others lies in his or her ability to use verbal communications—written or oral—to persuade others to give their will to a proposed group purpose. Typical U.S.-derived descriptions of leadership, such as Smircich and Morgan's "defining a reality that can gain a consensual following" (1982, p. 259) and Wills' "mutually determinative activity" (1994, p. 14), lend support to the view that persuasion of group members is essential for leadership to take place, and that acts of persuasion implicitly involve convincing followers—either through one's compellingly articulated vision of reality or one's persuasive skills in argument—to join in defining and then pursuing a particular course of action. At the very least, we are hard pressed to imagine, with either of these definitions, a contemporary American leadership context that would not, as a practical matter, principally involve persuasion through verbal communication.

However, the importance attached to verbal communication in precipitating the event of leadership is not so great elsewhere. The anthropologist Edward T. Hall—first in *Beyond Culture* (1976), and later with Mildred D. Hall, in *Understanding Cultural Differences* (1990)—has noted that in low-context societies such as the U.S. and Germany, much information needs to be stated explicitly in situations with action implications for it to be understood; in high-context societies such as Japan, China, or Korea, and in much of the Middle East, verbal communication frequently is not required or used, nor is it necessary, for meanings to be understood and acted upon. Influence is more often brought to bear in these cultures by nonverbal means.

Hierarchical position, a sense of deference to the will of the leader or the will of the group, or a sense of reciprocal obligation—for example, the concept of *guanxi* in Chinese culture, and the concept of *giri* in Japanese culture—all may be potent, albeit mute, sources of influence.

> **❝ WE ARE HARD PRESSED TO IMAGINE A CONTEMPORARY AMERICAN LEADERSHIP CONTEXT THAT WOULD NOT, AS A PRACTICAL MATTER, PRINCIPALLY INVOLVE PERSUASION THROUGH VERBAL COMMUNICATION. ❞**

Nahavandi (2009) remarks suggestively that "in high-context cultures the ability to generate trust is more highly valued than written communication or legal contracts" (p. 37). If we look at countries outside the 30 member states of the Organization for Economic Cooperation and Development—those usually labeled "developing" countries—we find that in such countries organizational communication patterns are often indirect, nonassertive, nonconfrontational, and one-directional—invariably, from the top of the hierarchy downward (Den Hartog & Dickson, 2004, p. 266). Negative feedback is avoided or given indirectly to avoid seeming personally destructive and disruptive to group harmony, which would result in a loss of face for individuals and groups. Further, as observed in discussing China and Japan earlier, extensive communication can be seen as a sign of weakness or uncertainty on the part of the leader (as is the case of China) or lack of confidence or consensus in the group (as is the case of Japan).

Conclusion

In summary, much remains to be done to rationalize the use of the American model of leadership with the cultural expectations for leaders and followers in many places outside the U.S. As seen in the GLOBE Project results, leader traits often are more important as determinants of effective leadership in a culture than a more participatory group dynamic based on rational-legal exchanges among the relative equals composing the group. Similarly, creating change by purposeful action is in many non-U.S. world contexts less central than understanding and observing one's place in the proper order of things and preserving a desired but precarious *status quo*. It is also often the case elsewhere in the world that leadership is less about identifying and achieving goals than about enacting and affirming relationships. Further, it is not clear, even in America, that influence processes are free from coercion, and outside the American arena it decidedly *is* clear that a more complex *realpolitik* of power usage is routinely in play.

Finally, although persuasive communication through the spoken and written word is the central influence tool in the American model of leadership, in other cultures verbal communication frequently is supplanted by culturally embedded understandings of appropriate behavioral patterns that do not arise from seeking, as in the American model, to persuade others to create change or achieve goals. Indeed, in some cultures, persuasion efforts channeled primarily through verbal communication are perceived as so much "white noise."

REFERENCES

Bagshaw, M. (2002). Leading your way to competitive advantage in China: Some cultural impediments. In P. Thistlewaite (Ed.), *Emerging issues in business & technology 2002* (pp. 288–295). Macomb, IL: Western Illinois University.

Bagshaw, M. (2004). The art of mediation: Transferring a foreign company's cultural values to the Suzhou Industrial Park in the PRC. In R. Bauerley & S. Meixner (Eds.), *Emerging issues in business & technology 2004* (pp. 434–443). Macomb, IL: Western Illinois University.

Bagshaw, M. (2005). Chinese middle managers as leaders and followers in the lower Yangtze River delta. In R. Bauerley & S. Meixner (Eds.), *Emerging issues in business & technology 2005* (pp. 137–146). Macomb, IL: Western Illinois University.

Bagshaw, M. (2006). Managerial initiative and innovation in the lower Yangtze delta. In R. Wahlers (Ed.), *Proceedings of the Academy of Business Disciplines* (pp. 15–25). Ft. Myers Beach, FL: Academy of Business Disciplines.

Burns, J. M. (1978). *Leadership.* New York: Harper & Row.

Den Hartog, D., & Dickson, M. W. (2004). Leadership and culture. In J. Antonakis, A. T. Cianciolo, & R. J. Sternberg (Eds.), *The nature of leadership* (pp. 249–278). Thousand Oaks, CA: Sage.

De Pree, M. (1989). *Leadership is an art.* New York: Doubleday.

French, J. R. P., & Raven, B. (1959). The basis of social power. In D. Cartwright (Ed.), *Studies in social power* (pp. 150–167). Ann Arbor: Institute for Social Research, University of Michigan.

Gardner, J. W. (1990). *On leadership.* New York: The Free Press.

Hall, E. T. (1976). *Beyond culture.* Garden City, NY: Doubleday.

Hall, E. T., & Hall, M. D. (1990). *Understanding cultural differences.* Yarmouth, ME: Intercultural Press.

Heifetz, R. A. (1994). *Leadership without easy answers.* Cambridge, MA: Belknap Press.

Hofstede, G. (1997). *Cultures and organizations: Software of the mind.* New York: McGraw-Hill.

House, R. J., Hanges, P. J., Javidan, M., Dorfman, P. W., & Gupta, V. (Eds.). (2004). *Culture, leadership, and organizations: The GLOBE study of 62 societies.* Thousand Oaks, CA: Sage.

Jaffe, G. (2007, August 8). Tribal connections: How courting sheiks slowed violence in Iraq. *The Wall Street Journal*, p. A1.

Misumi, J. (1984). Decision-making in Japanese groups and organizations. In B. Wilpert & A. Sorge (Eds.), *International perspectives on organizational democracy* (pp. 525–539). New York: John Wiley.

Nahavandi, A. (2009). *The art and science of leadership* (5th ed.). Upper Saddle River, NJ: Prentice Hall.

Nye, J. S., Jr. (2008). *The powers to lead.* New York: Oxford University Press.

Pye, L. (1985). *Asian power and politics: The cultural dimensions of authority.* Cambridge, MA: Belknap Press.

Rost, J. C. (1991). *Leadership in the twenty-first century.* Westport, CT: Praeger Publications.

Smircich, L., & Morgan, G. (1982). Leadership: The management of meaning. *Journal of Applied Behavioral Sciences, 18,* 257–273.

Storti, C. (2001). *The art of crossing cultures* (2nd ed.). Yarmouth, ME: Intercultural Press.

Wills, G. (1994). *Certain trumpets: The nature of leadership.* New York: Simon & Schuster.

Yukl, G. (2002). *Leadership in organizations* (5th ed.). Upper Saddle River, NJ: Prentice Hall.

MARK BAGSHAW, PH.D., is tenured professor of leadership and management at Marietta College in southeastern Ohio. In recent years, his research and published work has focused on participants in international organizations in China. Professor Bagshaw teaches courses in strategic management, international business, and leadership.

Discovering the Power of the Intercultural Development Inventory as a Global Leadership Development Tool

By Karen Lokkesmoe

*How do you know where you are going if you don't know where you are? —*Terry Callahan

ALTHOUGH THE STATEMENT ABOVE WAS MADE IN A CORPORATE BUSI-ness context, it applies equally well to education, public, and nonprofit contexts. As the demand for effective global leaders increases dramatically (Adler, 2001; Black & Gregerson, 2000; Goldsmith, 2003; Jokinen, 2005; Osland, Mendenhall, & Osland, 2006; Rosen & Phillips, 2000; Rost, 1991), having effective, reliable, and valid assessment tools becomes increasingly important. Being able to measure global leadership capacity in both individuals and organizations would not only be useful (Osland, 2008), it is essential if we are to effectively design and deliver development training and assess capacity for those in, or who aspire to, global leadership roles.

Many organizations seek to build this kind of global leadership capacity through leadership development programs, but many of these programs are less effective than they could be. Even more troubling, organizations often don't have a clear understanding of what makes an effective development program. How often have we encountered development programs that miss the mark, either by expecting too much or too little of the audience, alternately threatening or offending the participants? Training or development programs that don't meet the participants where they are at are almost certainly doomed to fail. But how do we know what type of intervention, training, or development option is the right one?

Knowing where you are going, what it might look like when you get there, and from where you are starting the journey is an essential element of successful leadership, management, and personal development. Development goals that are grounded in a solid understanding of past and present influences, and that can clearly articulate a vision for the future, have a much better chance to succeed.

> ❝ BEING ABLE TO MEASURE GLOBAL LEADERSHIP CAPACITY . . . IS ESSENTIAL IF WE ARE TO EFFECTIVELY DESIGN AND DELIVER DEVELOPMENT TRAINING AND ASSESS CAPACITY FOR THOSE IN, OR WHO ASPIRE TO, GLOBAL LEADERSHIP ROLES. ❞

The Intercultural Development Inventory (IDI) developed by Hammer and Bennett (Hammer, 1999; Hammer, Bennett, & Wiseman, 2003) can be of invaluable assistance in this effort. The IDI was not designed to, nor does it pretend to, specifically measure global leadership capacities. It is, however, "the premier, cross-culturally valid and reliable measure of intercultural competence" (Hammer, in press, p. 248), which is highly related to global leadership competence (Beechler & Javidan, 2007; Bird & Osland, 2004; Goldsmith, 2003; House et al., 2004; Javidan et al., 2006). Over the past two decades intercultural competence has been recognized as indispensable to effective leadership in our global community (Adler, 2001; Black, Morrison, & Gregerson, 1999; Brake, 1997; Harris, Moran, & Moran, 2004; Javidan et al., 2006; Osland, 2008).

Harris, Moran, and Moran (2004) define global leadership as "being capable of operating effectively in a global environment while being respectful of cultural diversity" (p. 25). Bhawuk and Brislin (1992, p. 414) define intercultural sensitivity as a sensitivity to the importance of cultural differences and to the points of view of people in other cultures. Hammer defines intercultural development as "the movement from a monocultural mindset to an intercultural mindset that reflects increasingly more complex perceptions and experience of cultural differences" (Hammer, 2008, handouts, p. 5).

Although there are some who may still wish to argue that leadership is leadership, wherever you are, and that global leadership is little more than effective leadership done globally, I believe that question has been resoundingly answered by others (Adler, 2001; Bird, 2008; Chhokar, Brodbeck, & House, 2008; Crosby, 1999; Goldsmith, 2003; Osland, 2008) and will therefore proceed based on that assumption. Let me take a moment now to define this and other assumptions upon which this paper has been based as they do have a bearing on the arguments presented here. I will define these underlying assumptions only briefly here and refer to supporting research for those interested in a more complete discussion.

Underlying Assumptions and Definitions

The first assumption is that global leadership is not just leadership done globally, but that there is something distinctly different about global leadership and global leaders. The consensus from recent reviews of global leadership literature (Hollenbeck, 2001; Jokinen, 2005; Osland, 2008; Suutari, 2002) is that "global leadership [is] far more complex than domestic leadership" (Osland, 2008). Adler (2001) says:

> Global leaders, unlike domestic leaders, address people worldwide. Global leadership theory, unlike its domestic counterpart, is concerned with the inter-action of people and ideas among cultures, rather than with either the efficacy of particular leadership styles within the leader's home country or with the comparison of leadership approaches among leaders from various countries—each of whose domain is limited to issues and people within their own cultural environment. A fundamental distinction is that global leadership is neither domestic nor multidomestic. (p. 77)

The second assumption is that the demand for effective global leaders is increasing dramatically. Whether addressing issues such as climate change or energy resources at an international level, or working within their own school district with students and families who speak more than 90 languages, or managing a family tea farm in India, many more leaders today find themselves in highly global contexts. Stories abound of ways in which these leadership challenges have met with poor to disastrous results. And even when not of monumental proportions, it is easy to see that being able to function effectively and respectfully with people from many cultural backgrounds is required of far more people today than in the past (Black et al., 1999; House et al., 2004; Mendenhall et al., 2008). A study by the Spartacus Group regarding diversity-related incidents (DRIs) revealed that 61 percent of those surveyed had witnessed a diversity-related incident at the workplace (Clayton, 2004). The study goes on to elaborate the potential cost of such incidents due to lost work time, diminished commitment to the workplace, or even departure from the workplace. The need for global leadership skills can no longer be denied.

The third assumption is that global leadership skills can be learned. It is now well established that leadership skills can be learned (Bass & Stogdill, 1990; Bennis,

1989; Burns, 1978; Crosby & Bryson, 2005; Terry, 1993). This is also true for global leadership and intercultural competencies which are both developmental and based on experience. Gregerson, Morrison, and Black (1998) maintain that global leaders are born and then made. They posit that some characteristics of successful global leaders are part of a person's psyche, while many other aspects can be acquired. How a person interprets past and present experiences of difference and the degree to which he or she is open to developmental experiences as well as which experiences he or she seeks out changes over time. The consensus is that much of what a global leader needs to do to be successful is based on skills that can be enhanced through experience and training and that some methods for enhancing these skills are more effective than others.

The final assumption is that intercultural competence is a foundational and essential global leadership skill. Although intercultural competencies are not synonymous with global leadership competencies, they do represent a significant portion of the competencies listed in global leadership models. All six dimensions of global leadership outlined by Mendenhall and Osland (Osland, 2008, p. 55) contain elements that are either explicitly (e.g., global mind-set, cross-cultural communication, cultural sensitivity, thinking globally) or implicitly (e.g., open-mindedness, flexibility, ability to deal with ambiguity) related to intercultural competence. Additionally, it is not hard to imagine how highly developed intercultural skills would have a positive impact on those capacities that do not directly reference intercultural skills (e.g., conflict management, team building, change agentry). The work of global leaders is carried out in intercultural contexts and therefore the importance of highly developed intercultural skills is difficult to overestimate.

I readily acknowledge that there are other assessment tools available and in development. I have focused this work on the IDI for three reasons. First, because my own research has convinced me that intercultural competencies lie at the core of global leadership development (Adler, 2001; Bennett, 2001; Black et al., 1999; Brake, 1997; Osland, 2008; Peterson, 2004). Second, my own work has been highly focused on the development and management of intercultural competencies among very diverse groups, and it is a tool with which I have extensive personal knowledge. Third, because the IDI is the premier cross-culturally validated intercultural assessment available (Hammer, in press). It has been rigorously tested under development and has been proven to be effective through ten years of consistent use (Bennett, 1986, 1993; Hammer, 2007; Hammer, in press; Paige, 1999; Paige et al., 2003).

At this point, it would be useful to describe the theoretical framework of the IDI and begin to make some parallels to global leadership development.

What Is the IDI?

The IDI is a 50-question inventory that measures a person's primary orientation toward cultural difference. The original pen-and-paper format was developed in 1998 and since 2006 it is also available online. Through a person's own responses and interpreted through the background of their personal experiences, the IDI indicates the primary worldview from which an individual experiences and responds to cultural difference. The inventory (v.3) is based on the Intercultural Development Continuum (IDC) (Hammer, in press) which was adapted from Bennett's (1986, 1993) Developmental Model of Intercultural Sensitivity (DMIS).

The IDI posits a continuum of five core orientations toward cultural difference progressing from the less complex or monocultural mind-sets of *denial* and *polarization,* through the transitional mind-set of *minimization,* to the more intercultural or global mind-sets of *acceptance* and *adaptation.* In the first two orientations a person interprets and interacts with intercultural difference using his or her own cultural lens, "from his/her point of view." In the transitional orientation of *minimization,* a person begins to understand there are alternate cultural perspectives from which to interpret the world, but still primarily relies on his or her own cultural framework when searching for commonalities to bring people together. In the two final orientations a person begins to understand and integrate the perspective of the "other" as he or she encounters and reacts to cultural difference and to increasingly be able to adapt his or her behavior in appropriate cultural ways.

Figure 1: Intercultural Development Continuum.

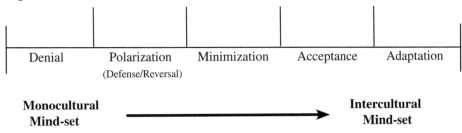

The first orientation is ***denial***. This orientation is often reflective of persons from a dominant culture group who have little experience with other cultural groups (Hammer, in press), or who feel little need to interact with others. At an organizational level, this may manifest itself as a seeming lack of awareness of a need to accommodate others, leaving it up to them to learn how to fit in. The developmental task for those with a denial orientation is to begin to see and recognize cultural difference.

Unfortunately, this increased recognition of and interaction with cultural difference frequently results in a more polarized orientation.

> ❝ THE INTERCULTURAL DEVELOPMENT INVENTORY IS A 50-QUESTION INVENTORY THAT MEASURES A PERSON'S PRIMARY ORIENTATION TOWARD CULTURAL DIFFERENCE. ❞

In the second orientation of *polarization* (consisting of *defense* and *reversal*) the individual recognizes that other cultures exist, but judges them as being better or worse than one another. In *defense*, one values one's own culture above the other and in *reversal* one values the other culture above one's own. In either case, there is an "us versus them" polarization which is often experienced as divisive and threatening (Bennett, 1993). This can be especially true when the increased level of interaction is not sought out, but imposed upon a person through demographic or policy changes beyond their control. At an organizational level, this can manifest itself through an insistence that others need to learn to fit in and that the role of diversity programs is to teach them how to adopt our ways (Hammer, in press).

The third orientation of *minimization* demonstrates a transitional state where one begins to move from a monocultural worldview to a multicultural worldview. In this orientation one tends to focus on either universal or humanistic concepts and minimize differences leading one to seek commonalities rather than acknowledge differences. As a response to the earlier orientation of *polarization*, this is a natural and necessary progression. In fact, for a long time this was seen as being the goal of intercultural understanding, especially among those from the dominant culture group. It is in this orientation that color blind and equity policies are pursued whereby organizations seek to enact procedures to eliminate inequity by ensuring equal treatment for all based on assumptions that the policies equally advantage everyone. The disadvantage of such policies is that there is a tendency to make assumptions that we are all alike, and that those making the decisions and setting the policies are still from the dominant group. Those from nondominant culture groups may not feel as included as was intended. Alternately, for members of the nondominant group, *minimization* may be "a more conscious strategy for getting things done within the dominant culture context" (Hammer, in press). The developmental task for those using a *minimization* orientation is to gain a deeper understanding of one's own culture as well as of other cultures. This cultural learning, in essence, encourages the individual to become a cultural learner in ways that allow him or her to appreciate difference rather than be threatened by it.

In *acceptance,* the fourth orientation toward cultural difference, the individual adopts a multicultural frame of reference regarding cultural difference. Here, one accepts and begins to appreciate a greater level of cultural complexity of other cultures as well as his or her own. There is a genuine curiosity and interest in cultural diversity and a willingness to adapt one's behavior to accommodate others. This does not mean that one abandons one's cultural identity, but rather that a person is able to "experience others both as different from oneself yet equally human" (Hammer, in press). At the organizational level this represents a genuine interest in learning and accommodating cultural differences. The challenge and the development task for both individuals and organizations is to learn how to adapt one's behavior to new cultural contexts and to simultaneously maintain a commitment to one's core values (Bennett, 2004).

The fifth orientation is *adaptation*, where one develops the capacity to adapt one's behavior and understanding of the world to that of other cultural perspectives. At this stage one can at least partially take the perspective of one or more cultures, bridge between cultures, and change behavior in culturally appropriate (Hammer, 2007) and authentic ways. This typically is developed through rather extensive interaction with other cultures. Organizations operating with an *adaptation* worldview would demonstrate willingness for all members to adapt behaviors in culturally appropriate ways (rather than just those from nondominant groups). In addition, cultural differences are seen as a resource for creativity and development rather than as a challenge to overcome.

A final element measured by the IDI, though not a part of the intercultural development continuum, is *cultural disengagement* (Hammer, 2007; Hammer, in press). *Cultural disengagement* is experienced as a sense of being disconnected from and not fully a part of one's own cultural group (Hammer, 2007). This can result from a person having significant experience with one or more cultural groups. For example, through the process of adapting to multiple cultural contexts, a person's cultural identity no longer feels tied to any one culture (Bennett, J. M., 1993; Bennett & Bennett, 2004).[1] Other possible reasons for cultural disengagement may include a person having had significant negative experiences with his or her own cultural group that results in a feeling of alienation (Hammer, in press).

The Development, Reliability, and Validity of the IDI

The IDI derives from Bennett's (1986, 1993) Developmental Model of Intercultural Sensitivity (DMIS). As Bennett originally conceived his model, it consisted of six developmental stages.[2] Hammer subsequently modified this model into the five-stage continuum that is now the basis of the IDI. A brief review of the development, reliability, and validity testing of the IDI follows. More extensive discussions are available in Hammer (2007), Hammer, Bennett, and Wiseman (2003), Paige (1999), Paige et al. (2003), and Bennett (1986, 1993). A full list of readings and research on the IDI and its uses can be found at http://www.intercultural.org/documents/IDIbiblio_Author.pdf.

The IDI was developed through a multistage process beginning with qualitative interviews with 40 people from 18 countries. The inventory questions were derived from the statements of this culturally diverse group. The statements were rated independently by four researchers and checked for interrater reliability. These research results verified that the IDI measured intercultural competence along the following five dimensional scales: DD = denial/defense; R = reversal; M = minimization; AA = acceptance/adaptation, and EM = encapsulated marginality, with *alpha* scores ranging from .80 to .85 (Hammer et al., 2003, p. 421). As noted, in IDI v.1 and IDI v.2, the scales for denial and defense and for acceptance and adaptation were combined. Subsequent research with 4,763 individuals from 11 distinct, cross-cultural groups by Hammer (in press) has further confirmed the fit of the data and has allowed for the expansion of the measurements of the model to the following seven scales: denial, defense, reversal, minimization, acceptance, adaptation, and cultural disengagement.

To date, the IDI has been translated through a rigorous back-translation process into 12 additional languages (Bahasa, Chinese, French, German, Indonesian/Malay, Italian, Japanese, Korean, Norwegian, Portuguese, Spanish, and Russian).

How Has the IDI Been Used?

The IDI has been used effectively with individuals and groups in education, business, public, and private settings. Over 1,200 people from more than 15 countries have been trained as certified IDI administrators (Hammer, 2007). Because the IDI has been in use only since 1998, much of the research regarding its use is available in unpublished manuscripts or from personal experience of working and talking to IDI-qualified administrators. For a full list of the research on the IDI see http://www. intercultural.org/documents/IDIbiblio_Author.pdf.

In the education sector the IDI has been used to assess current capacity; to design intercultural development training for school administrations, staff, and faculty; to aid in dealing more effectively with cultural differences in the classroom and the community; in training and development classes in higher education; to prepare and debrief international exchange participants; to evaluate programs; and to assess institutional capacity to deal with cultural difference (Greenholz, 2000; Lohmann, Howard, & Hoey, 2006; Machi, 2003; Roberson, Kulik, & Pepper, 2002; Shaheen, 2004; Paige, 2004; Paige & Emert, 2005).

In corporate environments, the IDI has been used for pre-departure training for executives and their families; for staff development and candidate selection for foreign assignments; for diversity efforts in hiring and retaining staff; with global teams; for executive coaching; to diagnose existing or potential areas of conflict in mergers or multinational operations; for research and marketing teams; and to evaluate program effectiveness (Bennett, 2004; Bennett & Bennett, 2004; Brooks, 2005; Burke, 2001; Osborn, 2001; Yamamoto, 1998).

The IDI has also been used in similar ways with public and nonprofit organizations such as hospitals, police departments, military units, and NGOs (Abu-Nimer, 2001; Altshuler, Sussman, & Kachur, 2003; Bartolini, 2001; Greenholz, 2005; Paige et al., 2003; Sheffield, 2007). Increasingly, public and private organizations are using the IDI to provide a more comprehensive understanding of intercultural development; to assess self-awareness and intercultural capacity; to design individual and group development goals, strategies, and training programs; to aid in personal coaching; and to evaluate program effectiveness.

How Can the IDI Be Used in Global Leadership Development?

Operating from the assumption that intercultural competence plays a significant role in the effectiveness of a global leader, the utility of a tool that assesses that capacity and can, through its use, increase a person's self-awareness and understanding of intercultural competence is significant. But it is worthwhile to go beyond the obvious and explore the utility of the IDI as an explicit part of global leadership development. How does it relate to global leadership development models and processes and what assessments are available?

The Global Competencies Inventory (GCI) (Kozai Group, 2002) measures 17 dimensions of effective intercultural behavior and global managerial skills that fall into three management categories:

- *Perception management*: nonjudgmentalness, inquisitiveness, tolerance of ambiguity, cosmopolitanism, and category inclusiveness;

- *Relationship management*: relationship interest, interpersonal engagement, emotional sensitivity, self-awareness, behavioral flexibility;

- *Self-management*: optimism, self-confidence, self-identity, emotional resilience, non-stress tendency, stress management, and interest flexibility.

With the possible exception of *category inclusiveness,* it is easy to see a connection between each of these competencies and intercultural competencies. Effective intercultural skills either encompass or enhance the dimensions listed. More research is needed to fully define how and to what extent these concepts are positively correlated.

The second assessment, reviewed by Bird (2008), is the Global Executive Leadership Inventory (GELI) developed by Manfred Kets de Vries and his associates

(2004). The GELI defines two broad roles of global leaders—one being primarily charismatic and one primarily architectural (Bird, 2008, p. 77) consisting of the following 12 dimensions: visioning, empowering, energizing, designing and aligning, rewarding and feedback, team building, outside orientation, global mind-set, tenacity, emotional intelligence, life balance, and resilience to stress. Here the connection to intercultural capacities is less obvious until you examine the definitions of how and with whom the global leader needs to carry out these tasks. All are defined within a global (or intercultural) context making it is easy to see how intercultural competence would significantly enhance a global leader's ability to carry out these tasks. As Bird (2008) points out, most of these "assessments focus on soft competencies—that is, characteristics of personality or worldview or attitude" (p. 79).

Global Leadership Development Processes

We have looked at models, skills, competencies, and dimensions of global leadership, but what about the process of developing global leaders? How does IDI-based development fit the global leadership development processes? There are two primary ways in which IDI assessments and IDI-based training would be of great benefit for the design and delivery of global leadership development programs. First is the IDI assessments themselves. This allows organizations and individuals to assess, based on their own responses, where they are in the journey toward intercultural competence and their current capacity to engage effectively with cultural differences.

The second benefit is using IDI-based training. Using the IDI and the developmental continuum to design developmental programming allows one to provide training activities to meet individuals and staff members where they are, rather than where you think they are (or should be). A major downfall of training programs in the past is that they have attempted to deliver the same content to everyone, sometimes with limited or poor results.

For example, a person who is just beginning to gain an understanding and appreciation for cultural diversity (i.e., at the beginning stage of minimization) and who may still feel challenged by the need to accommodate increasing levels of diversity may feel that they are being asked to give up their own cultural understandings before they are ready. They have not yet gained comfort and skill in balancing the unity that known systems and norms provide with the diversity of other perspectives. Asking them to adopt too many new communication or cultural norms could backfire causing them to revert to a more defensive stage. On the other hand, providing trainings focused on superficial differences between cultures and focusing only on commonalities may offend and alienate members who do not feel represented by those commonalities or who are ready to embrace more substantive concepts. For those who know and have already learned to appreciate the creativity of multiple perspectives, such trainings can seem simplistic and insulting.

What global leadership development models exist? Because global leadership development is such a nascent field, little research has been done in this area. Although more than these five models exist, I will mention here those for which empirical research is available. The first, although initially designed for local leader development, provides a useful framework for global leadership development programs as well. The model used by the Center for Creative Leadership (Van Velsor & McCauley, 2004) is based on a process of *assessment*, *challenge*, and *support*. Participants go through an initial self-assessment process and are then encouraged to challenge themselves or are provided with incremental challenges in areas identified for growth within a system that supports them throughout the process. Accommodations are required with the shift to the global arena. First, for greatest impact, the challenges need to be of an international/intercultural nature and those providing support need to have global experience. Second, care needs to be taken to ensure cultural sensitivity in the assessment process as comfort levels with personal and public assessments and reflective practice vary a great deal. In cultures that use indirect communication styles, public assessments such as 360-degree or in-class peer assessments could be highly stressful and not as well received; however, individual results can remain confidential whether or not group assessments are utilized. Osborn (2001) says, "the [IDI] instrument fits well in the context of an assessment-for-development program like the Leadership Development Program offered by the Center for Creative Leadership and its Network Associates" (p. 5).

Another process model for global leadership development is Black and Gregerson's (2000) "remapping" model. This model consists of three phases through which a global leader is encouraged to create new mental maps. According to Black and Gregerson, "high-impact global leadership training . . . makes participants aware of cultural contrasts . . . confronts [them] with those contrasts in ways that heavily engages their senses for a significant period of time . . . [and] provides conceptual frameworks that enable [them] to radically redraw their mental maps" (2000, p. 179). As stated, this model is based on redrawing mental maps based on cultural contrasts. This is just what intercultural competence training does—allows one to recognize and understand cultural difference, and to move toward acceptance and appropriate behavioral and cognitive adaptations.

In addition, Osland and Bird (2008) review three process models that have emerged since 2001[3]. All three models begin with a set of factors (*moderating variables*, *antecedents*, or *talent*), proceed through a process of (*experiences, encounters, decisions, and challenges; transformational process consisting of a multiplicity of experiences, decisions and challenges*; or *contextualized experience*) to arrive at a state of enhanced global leadership capacity (*new mental models, global leader expertise,* or *the right stuff.*) Intercultural competence plays a central role in all of these models.

Let's take a look at how leadership from the various IDI orientations might impact an organization and a leader's effectiveness. Attempting to lead an organization or team from a *denial* or *defense* perspective, as you can imagine, would encounter significant difficulties. Given enough power and position to call the shots, a certain level of initial success is possible, but serious impediments are sure to follow. A start-up venture or an expansion into a new market would almost certainly fail either through ignoring the skills and abilities of those with diverse perspectives, or by actively alienating them, thus creating conflict or diminishing the organization's capacity for creative, inclusive policies.

A leader who leads from a *minimization* mind-set is less likely to alienate or offend others, but may still not reach beyond superficial similarities to take advantage of the creativity and innovativeness of his or her team. In the long run, it may be difficult to recruit and retain employees from diverse backgrounds because though they would not feel hostility, they may not feel included either. An advantage of this orientation is that by focusing on commonalities, a leader is able to bring people together and begin to bridge differences and conflict. Still, being able to bridge differences through a more inclusive perspective will have more enduring results. When a leader can openly accept and appreciate differences, a greater range of options becomes available to him or her for understanding and solving conflicts as well as for seeing and meeting the needs of his or her clients. With *acceptance* and *adaptation* orientations, a leader can draw on a broader range of ideas and strategies to meet market demands and begins to be able to authentically adapt his or her behavior and company policy to be inclusive and welcoming of difference.

Let's consider a couple of examples that illustrate how intercultural orientations can impact outcomes. "When IKEA first entered the United States, the company tried to replicate the formula that helped it succeed in Sweden, including having a Swedish-style cafeteria and selling beds that conformed to Swedish sheet sizes. Initially, sales were disappointing" (Cohen, 2007, p. 179). However, IKEA stores throughout the U.S. and elsewhere are experiencing tremendous success today (Burt, Johansson, & Thelander, 2007; Jonsson, 2008; Jonsson & Elg, 2006), and Ouchi (2006) even attributes the success directly to cultural understanding.

Another recent example of adaptive behavior is the efforts made by the Chinese Olympic planning committee to provide good customer service to international visitors during the Olympics. Knowing that other cultures interpret smiling or not smiling differently than the Chinese, "smile training" was provided to the young women selected as medal presenters (Macartney, 2008).

Conclusion

One can no longer doubt that the need for more and effective global leaders is increasing. Current research and literature indicates that developing effective strategies for enhancing global leadership skills is a high priority for public, private, and educational institutions (Adler, 2001; Black & Gregerson, 2000; Oddou & Mendenhall, 2008; Yukl, 2006). A majority of global leadership development strategies focus on the development of a "global mind-set" as a core strategy in much the same way as intercultural competence training. They both stress the need to be curious about and open to differences around us and to be flexible enough to adapt cognitive and behavioral responses in appropriate ways. Clearly there are other skills required to be an effective leader, but what sets global leaders apart is a global mind-set (Black & Gregerson, 2000; Brake, 1997; Javidan et al., 2006). A growing body of research demonstrates that the IDI could beneficially be used for the development of cross-cultural leaders (Osborn, 2001).

As the opening quote indicates, being able to chart a course for where you want to go is a critical factor in facilitating success. World leaders are increasingly acknowledging the importance of eliminating barriers and encouraging collaboration across social and cultural boundaries. In a recent speech in Berlin, Barack Obama stated that "the walls between old allies on either side of the Atlantic cannot stand. The walls between the countries with the most and those with the least cannot stand. The walls between races and tribes; natives and immigrants; Christian and Muslim and Jew cannot stand. These now are the walls we must tear down" (CNN.com, July 24, 2008).

With respect to intercultural competence, the IDI assesses current capacity, increases intercultural awareness, and assists in effectively mapping development goals and charting a course for how to achieve them. And finally, because intercultural competence and a global mind-set are such an essential part of global leadership, the IDI can be a powerful tool for global leadership development.

NOTES

1. This concept of cultural marginality was originally developed by Janet Bennett (Bennett, J. M., 1993; Bennett & Bennett, 2004).

2. Bennett's sixth orientation is *integration* and describes the capacity of a person to move fluidly between cultural groups feeling at ease in each. This, however, is not measured by the IDI and refers to cultural identity rather than a worldview of cultural difference. For these reasons, it has not been included in the revised Intercultural Development Continuum (Hammer, in press).

3. Please see Osland and Bird's chapter "Process models of global leadership development" for a thorough review of the Chattanooga model of global leadership development, the Global Leader Expertise Development model, and McCall and Hollenbeck's model for developing global executives.

REFERENCES

Abu-Nimer, M. (2001). Conflict resolution, culture, and religion: Toward a training model of interreligious peacebuilding. *Journal of Peace Research, 38*(6), 685–704.

Adler, N. J. (2001). Global leadership: Women leaders. In W. Mendenhall, T. Kuhlmann, & G. Stahl (Eds.), *Developing global business leaders: Policies, processes and innovations* (pp. 73–97). Westport, CT: Quorum Books.

Altshuler, L., Sussman, N. M., & Kachur, E. (2003). Assessing changes in intercultural sensitivity among physician trainees using the Intercultural Development Inventory. In R. M. Paige (Guest Ed.), Special issue on Intercultural Development. *International Journal of Intercultural Relations, 27*(4), 387–401.

Bartolini, W. F. (2001, Winter). Using a communication perspective to manage diversity in the development office. *New Directions for Philanthropic Fundraising, 34,* 47–75.

Bass, B. M., & Stogdill, R. M. (1990). *Bass & Stogdill's handbook of leadership: Theory, research, and managerial applications* (3rd ed.). New York; London: Free Press; Collier Macmillan.

Beechler, S., & Javidan, M. (2007). Leading with a global mindset. In M. Javidan, R. M. Steers, & M. A. Hitt (Eds.), *Advances in International Management, 19,* 131–169.

Bennett, J. M. (1993). Cultural marginality: Identity issues in intercultural training. In R. M. Paige (Ed.), *Education for the intercultural experience* (pp. 109–135). Yarmouth, ME: Intercultural Press.

Bennett, J. M., & Bennett, M. J. (2004). Developing intercultural sensitivity: An integrative approach to global and domestic diversity. In D. Landis, J. M. Bennett, & M. J. Bennett (Eds.), *Handbook of intercultural training* (3rd ed., pp. 147–165). Thousand Oaks, CA: Sage.

Bennett, M. J. (1986). A developmental approach to training for intercultural sensitivity. *International Journal of Intercultural Relations, 10*(2), 179–196.

Bennett, M. J. (1993). Towards ethnorelativism: A developmental model of intercultural sensitivity. In R. M. Paige (Ed.), *Education for the intercultural experience* (pp. 21–71). Yarmouth, ME: Intercultural Press.

Bennett, M. J. (2001). Developing intercultural competence for global leadership. In R.-D. Reineke & C. Fussinger (Eds.), *Interkulturelles Management: Konzeption–Beratung–Training* (pp. 207–226). Wiesbaden, Germany: Gabler.

Bennett, M. J. (2004). Becoming interculturally competent. In J. Wurzel (Ed.), *Toward multiculturalism: A reader in multicultural education* (2nd ed., pp. 62–77). Newton, MA: Intercultural Resource Corporation.

Bennis, W. (1989). *On becoming a leader.* Reading, MA: Addison-Wesley.

Bhawuk, D. P. S., & Brislin, R. (1992). The measurement of intercultural sensitivity using the concepts of individualism and collectivism. *International Journal of Intercultural Relations, 16*(4), 413–436.

Bird, A. (2008). Assessing global leadership competencies. In M. Mendenhall, J. Osland, A. Bird, G. Oddou, & M. Maznevski (Eds.), *Global leadership: Research, practice and development.* New York: Routledge.

Bird, A., & Osland, J. (2004). Global competencies: An introduction. In H. Lane, M. Maznevski, M. Mendenhall, & J. McNett (Eds.), *Handbook of global management* (pp. 57–80). Oxford: Blackwell.

Black, J. S., & Gregerson, H. B. (2000). High impact training: Forging leaders for the global frontier. *Human Resource Management, 39*(2/3), 173–184.

Black, J. S., Morrison, A. J., & Gregersen, H. B. (1999). *Global explorers: The next generation of leaders*. New York: Routledge.

Brake, T. (1997). *The global leader: Critical factors for creating the world class organization*. Chicago: Irwin Professional Pub.

Brooks, D. C. (2005, May-August) Learning tolerance: The impact of comparative politics courses on levels of cultural sensitivity. *Journal of Political Science Education, 1*(2), 221–232.

Burke, M. (2001). *Befriending difference: Intercultural sensitivity training for ministers*. Unpublished doctoral dissertation, Catholic Theological Union, Chicago, IL.

Burns, J. M. (1978). *Leadership* (1st ed.). New York: Harper & Row.

Burt, S., Johansson, U., & Thelander, Å. (2007). Retail image as seen through consumers' eyes: Studying international retail image through consumer photographs of stores. *International Review of Retail, Distribution & Consumer Research, 17*(5), 447–467.

Callahan, T. CCE, President, Credit Research Foundation. Retrieved March 25, 2008, from http://www.crfonline.org/surveys/dso/PerformanceMeasures.pdf

Chhokar, J., Brodbeck, F., & House, R. (2008). *Culture and leadership across the world: The GLOBE book of in-depth studies of 25 societies*. Mahwah, NJ: Lawrence Erlbaum Associates.

Clayton, C. B. (2004). *Linking employee commitment & workplace incivility to corporate earnings*. The Center for Human Capital. Retrieved March 20, 2008, from http://www.thespartacusgroup.com/images/dEPS_White_Paper_Ver.12.2005.v17.pdf

CNN.com. (2008, July 24). Accessed August 18, 2008, http://edition.cnn.com/2008/POLITICS/07/24/obama.words/index.html

Cohen, E. (2007). *Leadership without borders: Successful strategies from world-class leaders*. Hoboken, NJ: Wiley & Sons.

Crosby, B. C. (1999). *Leadership for global citizenship: Building transnational community*. Thousand Oaks, CA: Sage.

Crosby, B. C., & Bryson, J. M. (2005). *Leadership for the common good: Tackling public problems in a shared-power world* (2nd ed.). San Francisco: Jossey-Bass.

Goldsmith, M. (2003). *Global leadership: The next generation*. Upper Saddle River, NJ: FT/Prentice Hall.

Greenholz, J. (2000). Assessing cross-cultural competence in transnational education: The Intercultural Development Inventory. *Higher Education in Europe, 25*(3), 411–416.

Greenholz, J. (2005). Does intercultural sensitivity cross cultures? Validity issues in porting instruments across languages and cultures. *International Journal of Intercultural Relations, 29*(1), 73–89.

Gregerson, H. B., Morrison, A., & Black, J. S. (1998). Developing leaders for the global frontier. *Sloan Management Review, 40*, 21–32.

Hammer, M. R. (1999). A measure of intercultural sensitivity: The Intercultural Development Inventory. In S. M. Fowler & M. G. Fowler (Eds.), *The intercultural sourcebook* (Vol. 2, pp. 61–72). Yarmouth, ME: Intercultural Press. (IDI v.1.)

Hammer, M. R. (2007). *Intercultural Developmental Inventory Manual* (v.3). Ocean Pines, MD: IDI, LLC.

Hammer, M. R. (2008). *Intercultural Developmental Inventory Manual*. Training seminar handouts, June 23-25, p. 5. Ocean Pines, MD: IDI, LLC.

Hammer, M. R. (in press). The Intercultural Development Inventory (IDI): An approach for assessing and building intercultural competence. In M. A. Moodian (Ed.), *Contemporary leadership and intercultural competence: Exploring the cross-cultural dynamics within organizations*. Thousand Oaks, CA: Sage.

Hammer, M. R., & Bennett, M. J. (1998, 2001). *Intercultural Developmental Inventory Manual* (v.1, v.2). Portland, OR: Intercultural Institute.

Hammer, M. R., Bennett, M. J., & Wiseman, R. (2003). Measuring intercultural sensitivity: The Intercultural Development Inventory. In R. M. Paige (Guest Ed.), Special issue on Intercultural Development. *International Journal of Intercultural Relations, 27*(4), 421–443.

Harris, P. R., Moran, R. T., & Moran, S. V. (2004). *Managing cultural differences—global leadership strategies for the 21st century* (6th ed.). Oxford: Butterworth-Heinemann/Elsevier.

Hollenbeck, G. P. (2001). A serendipitous sojourn through the global leadership literature. In W. Mobley & M. W. McCall (Eds.), *Advances in global leadership* (vol. 2). Stamford, CT: JAI Press.

House, R. J., Hanges, P. J., Javidan, M., Dorfman, P., & Gupta, V. (Eds.). (2004). *Culture, leadership, and organizations: The GLOBE study of 62 societies.* Thousand Oaks, CA: Sage.

Javidan, M., Dorfman, P., Sully de Luque, M., & House, R. (2006, February). In the eye of the beholder: Cross cultural lessons in leadership from Project GLOBE. *Academy of Management Perspectives*, pp. 67–90.

Jokinen, T. (2005) Global leadership competencies: A review and discussion. *Journal of European Industrial Training, 29*(2/3), 199–216.

Jonsson, A. (2008). A transnational perspective on knowledge sharing: Lessons learned from IKEA's entry into Russia, China and Japan. *International Review of Retail, Distribution & Consumer Research, 18*(1), 17–44.

Jonsson, A., & Elg, U. (2006). Knowledge and knowledge sharing in retail internationalization: IKEA's entry into Russia. *International Review of Retail, Distribution & Consumer Research, 16*(2), 239–256.

Kets de Vries, M. F. R., Vrignaud, P., & Florent-Treacy, E. (2004). The Global Executive Leadership Inventory: Development and psychomentric properties of a 360-degree feedback instrument. *International Journal of Human Resource Management, 15*(3), 475–492.

Kozai Group, Inc. (2002). *The Global Competencies Inventory.* St. Louis, MO: Kozai.

Lohmann, J. R., Howard, A. R., & Hoey, J. J., IV (2006, March). Defining, developing and assessing global competence in engineers. *European Journal of Engineering Education, 31*(1), 119–131.

Macartney, J. (2008, January 10). Lessons in how to smile for China's Olympic hostesses. *The Times OnLine.* Retrieved August 18, 2008, from http://www.timesonline.co.uk/tol/news/world/asia/article3162656.ece

Machi, E. (2003, June 28). *Applying the developmental model of intercultural sensitivity to teaching intercultural communication.* Paper presented at the SIETAR Japan 2003 Conference, Tokyo, Japan. (Available through the Intercultural Communication Institute in Japanese.)

Mendenhall, M., Osland, J., Bird, A., Oddou, G., & Maznevski, M. (Eds.) (2008). *Global leadership: Research, practice and development.* New York: Routledge.

Oddou, G., & Mendenhall, M. (2008). Global leadership development. In M. Mendenhall, J. Osland, A. Bird, G. Oddou, & M. Maznevski (Eds.), *Global leadership: Research, practice and development.* New York: Routledge.

Osborn, N. (2001). *Diagnosing and developing cross-cultural expertise in global leaders.* Retrieved December 6, 2004, from www.team-inc.net/Docs/Crossculturalexpertise.doc

Osland, J. (2008). An overview of the global leadership literature. In M. Mendenhall, J. Osland, A. Bird, G. Oddou, & M. Maznevski (Eds.), *Global leadership: Research, practice and development.* New York: Routledge.

Osland, J., & Bird, A. (2008). Process models of global leadership development. In M. Mendenhall, J. Osland, A. Bird, G. Oddou, & M. Maznevski (Eds.), *Global leadership: Research, practice and development.* New York: Routledge.

Osland, J., Bird, A., Mendenhall, M., & Osland, A. (2006). Developing global leadership capabilities and global mindset. In G. K. Stahl & I. Bjorkman (Eds.), *Handbook of research in international human resource management* (pp. 197–222). Cheltenham, UK: Edward Elgar.

Ouchi, M. (2006, October 17). Culture key to assembling success at IKEA in Renton. *The Se-attle Times*. Accessed August 5, 2008, http://community.seattletimes.nwsource.com/archive/ ?date=20061017&slug=ikea17

Paige, R. M. (1999). *Culture as the core: Integrating culture into the language curriculum: Selected conference proceedings*. Minneapolis: Center for Advanced Research on Language Acquisition, University of Minnesota.

Paige, R. M. (2004). Instrumentation in intercultural training. In D. Landis, J. M. Bennett, & M. J. Bennett (Eds.), *Handbook of intercultural training* (3rd ed., pp. 85–128). Thousand Oaks, CA: Sage.

Paige, R. M., & Emert, H. (2005, May 4-7). *Bridging conflict through language and culture learning strategies and use in study abroad.* Paper presented at the 2005 Conference of the International Academy for Intercultural Research, Kent, OH. (Available through the Intercultural Communication Institute.)

Paige, R. M., Jacobs-Cassuto, M., Yershova, Y. A., & DeJaeghere, J. (2003). Assessing intercultural sensitivity: An empirical analysis of the Intercultural Development Inventory. In R. M. Paige (Guest Ed.), Special issue on Intercultural Development. *International Journal of Intercultural Relations, 27*(4), 467–486.

Peterson, B. (2004). *Cultural intelligence: A guide to working with people from other cultures*. Yarmouth, ME: Intercultural Press.

Roberson, L., Kulik, C. T., & Pepper, M. B. (2002, February). Assessing instructor cultural competence in the classroom: An instrument and a development process. *Journal of Management Education, 26*(1), 40–55.

Rosen, R. T., & Phillips. C. (2000). *Global literacies: Lessons on business leadership and national cultures: A landmark study of CEOs from 28 countries*. New York: Simon & Schuster.

Rost, J. C. (1991). *Leadership for the twenty-first century*. New York: Praeger.

Shaheen, S. (2004). *The effect of pre-departure preparation on student intercultural development during study abroad programs.* Unpublished doctoral dissertation, Ohio State University, Columbus.

Sheffield, D. (2007, January). Assessing intercultural sensitivity in mission candidates and personnel. *Evangelical Missions Quarterly, 43*(1). Retrieved March 10, 2008, from http://sheffield.typepad. com/Articles/AssessingInterculturalSensitivityinMission CandidatesandPersonnel.pdf

Suutari, V. (2002). Global leadership development: An emerging research agenda. *Career Development International, 7*(4), 218–233.

Terry, R. W. (1993). *Authentic leadership: Courage in action* (1st ed.). San Francisco: Jossey-Bass.

Van Velsor, E., & McCauley, C. (2004). Our view of leadership development. In C. D. McCauley, E. Van Velsor, & Center for Creative Leadership (Eds.), *The Center for Creative Leadership handbook of leadership development* (2nd ed., pp. 1–22). San Francisco: Jossey-Bass.

Yamamoto, S. (1998). Applying the developmental model of intercultural sensitivity in the Japanese context. *Journal of Intercultural Communication: SIETAR Japan, 2.*

Yukl, G. (2006). *Leadership in organizations* (6th ed.). Upper Saddle River, NJ: Pearson Prentice Hall.

KAREN LOKKESMOE is a doctoral candidate at the University of Minnesota in the Department of Education and Public Administration. Her dissertation, teaching, and consulting have focused on global leadership development, public and nonprofit management, and intercultural training. Karen is a certified IDI consultant and has consulted with area schools and organizations in IDI-guided development. She coordinated the Humphrey Fellowship program for four years, and has consulted with UNICEF, Hennepin County in Minnesota, and served on the boards of several nonprofit organizations.

"Worldly" Leadership for a Global World

By Sharon Turnbull

THIS PAPER DISCUSSES THE ADVANCES AND POTENTIAL LIMITATIONS of current global leadership theory, and goes on to examine the implications for global leadership development. It proposes that thinking about one of the manifestations of this phenomenon as "worldly" leadership enables a new and important conceptualisation to emerge. The paper builds on Mintzberg's (2004) worldly mind-set, and in turn advances our thinking about leadership development within this frame.

The paper analyzes the perspectives and experiences of 26 global managers from 14 nationalities and five continents. These managers formed one cohort of the International Masters Program in Practicing Management (IMPM), one of the first global management programmes for senior leaders launched over a decade ago. The data was collected from the privileged viewpoint of the role of Cycle Director (with overall responsibility for the participants' learning as they traversed the globe, attending five modules at six business schools).

A managerial exchange involving four solid days of observation of another participant engaged in their own work in another country and sector adds to the process, and accelerates the emotions of disorientation and disbelief to enable the deep sensitivity, empathy, and worldliness that can ultimately lead to Mintzberg's "worldly manager."

As Mintzberg (2004) has noted, worldliness contrasts with the rapidly growing globalisation discourse which "sees the world from a distance that encourages homogenization of behaviour . . . . A closer look, however, reveals something quite different: This globe is made up of all kinds of worlds" (Mintzberg, 2004, p. 304). The worldly mind-set, therefore, is not globalisation repackaged, but something quite different that results in the emergence of a different conception of the leadership process.

This paper draws on the accounts and writing of these leaders. It also engages with a range of recent studies, books, and articles on global leadership to uncover how this growing phenomenon is currently constructed and understood by scholars in this field. The discourses embedded in this so-called global leadership theory and current thinking about the development of so-called global leaders is then compared with the experiences and concepts which make up the idea of worldly leadership and the IMPM pedagogy that has been developed to support its development.

Global Leadership

Global leadership is a label that has been attached to numerous differing concepts for as long as economic globalisation has been on the world agenda. It is a contested term. Not only is *leadership* a word with countless definitions and interpretations, but *globalisation* has a multitude of meanings as well. Mendenhall (2008) traces global leadership back to the emergence of international business as a separate field of study in the 1950s and 1960s. The 1970s then saw an increase in studies of expatriate managers working in cultures different from their own. He suggests it was not until the 1990s, however, that the term globalisation came to mean more than this, and to focus on the increased complexity, difference, interdependence, and ambiguity that managers were starting to face as a result of these shifts on the world economic stage.

A plethora of books and articles have been published on the subject, seeking to identify what this means for both research and practice, along with a range of offerings for how to develop these individual and organisational competencies. Indeed, as recently as March 2008, an Internet discussion on the Network of Leadership Scholars discussion site took up the question, "Is there such a thing as global leadership?" This prompted animated debate over a period of a few days, demonstrating the lack of clarity and diversity of views that this term engenders. Some of the respondents felt that global leadership is about universally endorsed leader attributes. For others, global leadership represents a subfield of leadership differing from traditional leadership due to the demands of globalisation.

Nevertheless, the vast majority of research studies conducted in the field of global leadership have been seeking to define a set of global leadership competencies, and there are many such studies. Jokinen (2005) set out to draw together these studies to establish a more integrative framework, suggesting that "increasing understanding of different aspects of globalization and interrelationships of various factors and their changes will help organisations to meet the new challenges brought about by globalization, whether their primary operation environment is domestic, international or global" (pp. 199–200). However, she concludes that there is little agreement amongst researchers on what constitutes these global competencies, nor about what competencies are vital for global leadership, because the definition of global leadership is so unclear. She also points out that much of the early research was focused solely on expatriates, a much narrower perspective than the one adopted by many researchers today.

The quest for an understanding of the term often seems circular in nature, with Moran and Riesenberger (1994), for example, suggesting that for globalisation, one of the competencies that managers should have is "a global mindset," which sounds something of a tautology! Indeed, many of the competencies identified for global leaders do not sound dissimilar to the competencies required by domestic leaders. For example, "global literacies" are defined by Rosen, Digh, Singer, and Philips (2000) as "personal, social, business and cultural literacy." Another study (Bueno & Tubbs, 2004) has proposed (1) communication, (2) motivation to learn, (3) flexibility, (4) open-mindedness, (5) respect for others, and (6) sensitivity as the key global leadership competencies. Kets de Vries and Florent-Treacy (2002) take the perspective that the global leadership competencies are indeed the same as domestic leadership competencies, but suggest that global leaders are ones who "retain these capabilities even in completely unfamiliar situations" (p. 305), labelling this ability "emotional global intelligence." Many of the studies conducted to date, however, are limited by being primarily based on a narrow conception of global leader as expatriate leader, or are based on a homogenous sample of data from one country.

Osland's (2008) comprehensive survey of the global leadership literature identified 56 global leadership competencies (a list too long to be useful, as she herself notes). She has distilled these into six core categories of (1) cross-cultural relationship skills, (2) traits, (3) global business expertise, (4) global organising expertise, (5) cognitive orientation, and (6) visioning. She recognises that few leaders live up to these ideals, however, and points to the need for further research, specifically into how these competencies are best developed in leaders.

Clearly the term global leader is highly contested, and the competencies required are either too diverse or too broad to assist in shaping a curriculum for global leadership development. Given this confusion, this paper seeks to go beyond the competency debate to uncover alternative ways to conceptualise global leadership, and then to reflect on the implications for leadership development. Moving away from the psychological and behavioural perspectives, and adopting alternative lenses from organisational theory, the idea of worldly leadership is explored as an alternative way of thinking about this phenomenon.

Limitations of the Competency-based Perspective

A number of limitations of adopting a purely competency-based approach to researching and understanding so-called global leadership have been identified by scholars in the field and are discussed in this section.

1. *Global leadership is often a shorthand for exporting Western managers over-seas, and the skills identified often differ very little from those required at the home base.*

As Adler (1997) and others have pointed out, there is an Anglo-American and mas-culine bias in much of the work conducted in this field. As a result, she concludes that "most leadership theories are domestic theories masquerading as universal theories" (p. 174).

Ayman, Kreicker, and Masztal (1994) extend this point, also challenging this Western-centric perspective, suggesting instead that global "represents a sense of unity across multiple borders." The corporate global leader, Ayman et al. posit, "would not impose a model of management that represents only one particular culture's perspective. . . . A global leader understands different viewpoints and has the ability to synthesize them into a vision which respects all cultures" (p. 64).

Ghoshal (2005) also alludes to the limitations of the Western perspective of leadership for understanding global leadership when he contended that "a series of worn out mindsets" dominate management and managerial thinking, at least in North America and the United Kingdom.

2. *Defining a universal set of global leadership traits may be an impossible pursuit.*

The idea of defining a universal set of global leadership traits has been challenged by a number of culture specialists. Both Hofstede's (2003) work as well as the findings of the GLOBE Project (Chhokar et al., 2007; House et al., 2004; Javidan et al., 2006) indicate that there is no such thing as a universal economic, psycho-logical, or cultural rationality, making the defining of a universal set of global competencies problematic.

3. *Leadership is inextricably linked to context.*

Leadership has often been studied as though it were context free. More recently, however, there has been a growing interest in context as a strong influencing factor in leadership study. Bird, for example (Network of Leadership Scholars commu-nication, 21 March 2008), sees global leadership as a combination of outcomes, process, and context, and suggests that in understanding global leadership, more than ever "context matters." Hannum (cited in a Network of Leadership Scholars communication by Martineau, 20 March 2008) also points out the importance of the contextual frame. She argues: "In the past 'global leadership' often meant being able to lead in other cultures, now it is increasingly about 'working with multiple cultures at the same time and often at a distance' . . . . The ability to create and adapt mental models based on contextual information is part of the skill set for the global leader."

❝ LEADERSHIP HAS OFTEN BEEN STUDIED AS THOUGH IT WERE CONTEXT FREE. ❞

4. Global leadership may be seen as a dynamic social process and as a constantly shifting network of networks instead of as individualised skills and competencies.

For Behrens (Network of Leadership Scholars communication, 24 March 2008) the idea of *the* global leader is limiting: "Rather than elusive 'global leaders' we should be looking for a global network of local leaders" he suggests, thus re-conceptualising the debate and moving it away from the identification of individual capabilities to the idea of building *networked capability*. Related to this point is the domination of the leadership debate by the leader-follower relationship. The pervading emphasis on this dyadic relationship, which narrows scholarly focus to the behaviours of either leader or follower (or both), is starting to be challenged by organisational scholars working from post-structural or process perspectives, as well as by those who argue that leadership is not only about *top* leaders but can more usefully be seen as a "dispersed," "distributed," or shared *process* within and across organisations (Adler, 1997). These newer research paradigms tend to de-emphasise the person-centred approach in favour of understanding the processual dynamic of leadership, and may therefore help to deepen our understanding of global leadership and leadership development.

Adler's work is one such example. Focusing on women leaders across the globe, she reaches the conclusion that "Global leadership theory is concerned with the interaction of people and ideas among cultures" (1997, p. 175). Her research points to the nonhierarchical model of broadly dispersed leadership, which she notes is often favoured by women leaders who tend to seek to empower many leaders within society rather than focufsing on themselves as a single leader. Adler also concludes that women leaders tend to be driven by vision, not status, and to use broadly based popular support to achieve their outcomes. Adler is very clear that global leadership is not just an extension of domestic or multi-domestic leadership, but is a different phenomenon altogether which can be understood as a process by which people across the world work together synergistically toward common objectives that enhance quality of life.

Also focusing on women leaders in a globalised world, Werhane (2007) builds on Adler's worldview to propose a move away from the leader-follower paradigm to a more distributed understanding of the global leadership process:

> ... in a global multicultural economy where interaction is between managers from various cultures and perspectives, this leader-follower model may be outdated ... leadership is an interactive, dynamic, and mutually inter-relational process between leaders and managers, where each participant contributes to the vision and progress toward change in the company. (p. 427)

Mendenhall's (2008) authoritative book on the subject helpfully seeks to combine the person-centred approach with the processual understanding of global leadership as follows:

> Global leaders are individuals who effect significant positive change in orga-nizations by building communities through the development of trust and the arrangement of organizational structures and processes in a context involving multiple cross-boundary stakeholders, multiple sources of external cross-bound-ary authority, and multiple cultures under conditions of temporal, geographical and cultural complexity. (p. 17)

The Emergence of "Worldly Leadership"

The idea of worldliness contrasts with the globalisation discourse which "sees the world from a distance that encourages homogenization of behaviour" (Mintzberg, 2004, p. 304) by engaging at close proximity in the many different worlds within worlds that make up our globe and enrich our experience of it. But worldly leadership is not simply about observation. It is also about the way that we engage with, and act within and across these world(s). The worldly mind-set, then, is not globalisation repackaged, but something quite different that results in the emergence of a different type of leadership construct altogether. This leadership process comes much closer to the view conceptualised by Adler and by Werhane, and extends our thinking about the global leadership agenda into new spheres.

For Werhane (2007), one of the key omissions from the literature so far on global leadership is ethics: "Ideally the best global leaders are not merely values driven but are what we have called 'ethical leaders' who embody their values in all that they do and promote" (p. 433). For her this is more than a competency; instead it is a whole way of being.

Morrison (2001) goes further to propose that "integrity forms the bedrock of character and is essential in sustainable global leadership" (p. 65). For these voices, global leadership is much more than managing in other cultures: "Global leaders are those who successfully impact the actions and beliefs of others on a worldwide basis" (p. 65) and "creating and maintaining a moral environment for a global organisation is a never-ending job" (p. 76).

This increasing call for a worldly focus on integrity, ethics, and shared leadership toward global prosperity and sustainability is also echoed by Petrick et al. (1999) who focus on leading sustainability through stewardship:

> Excellent global leaders demonstrate their leadership substance by acting as responsible stewards of human and natural resources who promote concurrent economic, social, biological, and ecological development. (p. 61)

This, they suggest, will head to "reputational capital," thus solidifying credibility, reliability, responsibility, trustworthiness, and accountability.

Although their starting points may be different, these scholars share a common vision of leading across the world to ensure prosperity and sustainability for future generations.

> Reliance on stewardship sustainable development for global leadership substance has created social capital that is as important as financial capital in creating conditions for global prosperity. (Petrick et al., p. 62)

Crosby and Bryson's (2005) emphasis on "leadership for the common good" focuses primarily on public policy and political leadership for social change, and can be seen as relevant to our understanding of worldly leadership. Their work focuses, for example, on the dynamics of a shared-power world; the main settings in which leaders and constituents foster policy change in a shared-power world; and effective navigation of the policy change cycle.

Leadership for sustainability is also a topic of growing interest to the worldly leadership agenda. Ferdig (2007), for example, outlines this agenda as: a catalyst for change; whole systems thinking; dealing with complexity; meaning-making through conversation and interaction with others; and meaningful connection with other human beings and the earth. Sustainability leadership (an important element of worldly leadership) recognizes that the experience of change, and the dissonance it creates, becomes the fuel for new discoveries and innovations that can sustain the health of the organisation, the community, and ultimately, the planet.

From Global to Worldly? The Leadership Perspectives of the IMPM Participants

Twenty-six of the IMPM global leaders were asked during the first module of the programme (and prior to any discussion on leadership) to write down what the word *leadership* means to them, and then their rules of thumb for being a "good leader." No further guidance or explanation was given, and they were asked to e-mail their thoughts to us independently. Their definitions were then analysed thematically. Not surprisingly, many of the responses given were framed as competencies, thus echoing the dominant literature, although, as in this literature there was little consensus on the core competencies required. At the same time, however, an alternative and worldly focus was found in their descriptions, indicating that their understanding of leadership in many cases went beyond the identification of competencies. These worldly definitions are the focus of the following discussion, and in turn have informed our thinking on the development of worldly leadership.

Vision and Inspiration

The leaders demonstrated a focus on building deep engagement amongst their followers, and on generating a shared and common understanding of a dynamic and evolving vision for the future. Many wrote of looking beyond the organisation's immediate environment into the world to help people to imagine the future, and then developing a climate in which ideas are shared and co-created. They wrote of using all available antennae and tapping into all available networks to continually create new knowledge inside the organisation. This knowledge includes understanding trends and shifts in society, technology, markets and people, looking for tipping points and spotting them early, assessing the speed and destination of these changes, and then interpreting these to determine how they will affect the organisation and its purpose over time:

> *Making others have a vision, a dream, and all of them having similar visions. Inspiring them. Making people feel like themselves and proud of what they have done, and making people feel more than the sum of their parts.*

> *By vision I mean the ability to develop and build a consensus about what direction to pursue without dictating or "hard-selling" one's own ideas.*

> *The ability to show the directions with clear visions or values, respect/trust others, take initiatives, take risks, stick to the values, to be consistent, to be persistent, execute with conviction, challenge the hardship and never give up, have widely webbed network.*

Integrity, Humility, and Wisdom

Three of the most common words that the participants associated with good leadership were integrity, humility, and wisdom. These qualities were summarised by one leader as:

> *Integrity: People trust me because I am truthful, keep my commitments and have the courage to stand up and be open. Humility: People respect me because I respect them, I listen to them with no bias and I am not selfish/heroic. Wisdom: People are influenced by my thoughts because I share my knowledge and experience which is enriched by learning and synthesis.*

We found that these values recurred frequently in their descriptions of good leadership:

> *Ground your values in truth, commitment and courage*
> *Stay true to your values*
> *Do the 'right' thing*
> *Don't do anything just for money*
> *Live by example*
> *Display the highest levels of honesty*
> *Do not impose yourself or intimidate others*
> *Be constantly present alongside others*

For one leader the essential measure of success is that

> *. . . others can trust absolutely that you will not "lead them astray"; that in all aspects you will endeavour to look after their best interests; yet that you will not sacrifice yourself to the point you are left an "empty' shell."*

For another,

> *Leadership is a continuous process that involves living by example, displaying highest levels of honesty, humble presentation without imposing oneself or intimidating others and being constantly present to go along with the others.*

Authenticity and Courage

Authenticity and authentic leadership are relatively new to the mainstream study of leadership but were important to the IMPM participants. In the words of one of the leaders:

Authentic leadership implies that you do not "pretend," that you are not an "actor," that you recognize your limitations and that you "strive for excellence."

For another, his desired state is:

. . . to be open, speak and act with conviction rooted in values, build relationships based on trust . . . reason with an open mind, balancing inquiry and advocacy, asking the right questions, encouraging others to share their views openly without being defensive.

Balance and Responsibility

One manager from Korea used the aquatic metaphor of a stream to define leadership as a collective process:

People and organization should be well-balanced by natural leadership like as a stream. Act less artificial, more natural. A good leader is defined as acting like the nature of water. The reasons are as follows:

1. *Water gets joined together and becomes one.*
2. *Water flows from up to down, interconnected together.*
3. *Water purifies everything, even if any muddiness.*

Or put more conventionally by an Irish manager:

Leadership and responsibility go hand and as do understanding motivation and consequences of actions. A good leader cares about people and recognises that people and consensus are central to achieving results.

Worldly Leadership—A Definition

For the purposes of this research, and for the leadership development research agenda that follows, I define *worldly leadership* by combining some of the key themes identified within the alternative literature reflecting Mintzberg's idea of the worldly mind-set, with the definitions given by the leaders in the International Masters Programme in Practicing Management. Starting from Mintzberg's definition that "worldly" is about seeing "all kinds of different worlds" (and often worlds within worlds) from close up and taking action, worldly leadership can be seen as aiming for unity and collaboration (as opposed to homogeneity) across borders through a shared humanity. Above all, it can be seen as being about shared power, dispersed and flexible networks, stewardship, integrity, responsibility for the common good, and an emphasis on a sustainable world.

The qualities and ways of living required for this go beyond competency frameworks as they are about ways of being, to include: vision and inspiration; integrity, humility, and wisdom; authenticity and courage; and balance and responsibility.

> **66 ABOVE ALL, WORLDLY LEADERSHIP CAN BE SEEN AS BEING ABOUT SHARED POWER, DISPERSED AND FLEXIBLE NETWORKS, STEWARDSHIP, INTEGRITY, RESPONSIBILITY FOR THE COMMON GOOD, AND AN EMPHASIS ON A SUSTAINABLE WORLD. 99**

Conclusion

It has been argued that worldly leadership goes further than most definitions of global leadership. It goes beyond individual competencies to include leadership as a networked process of interconnectedness and boundary-spanning. It goes beyond the emphasis on top leaders to include shared leadership and a focus on giving a voice to the disenfranchised or marginalized. Furthermore, worldly leadership has been shown to encompass stewardship, leadership for the common good, as well as for sustainability. It is a way of seeing the world and living in the world. It requires the qualities of vision and inspiration; integrity, humility, and wisdom; authenticity and courage; and balance and responsibility.

Developing worldly leadership has been shown to be a challenge for individuals and organisations. It has been argued that this is achieved most quickly and sustainably by deep immersion and encounters at close proximity in new and alien settings, and with leaders who themselves exemplify and embody these qualities. These experiences, followed by a shared reflective sense-making process, ideally within a culturally rich and diverse group, followed by the collaborative and joined up translation of the ideas into action within the real worlds of the leaders and their practice, combine to produce sustainable transformational learning at many levels, and a form of leadership that is needed in the world today.

REFERENCES

Adler, N. J. (1997). Global leadership: Women leaders. *Management International Review, 1,* 171–196.

Adler, N. J., Brody, L. W., & Osland, J. S. (2000). The Women's Global Leadership Forum: Enhancing one company's global leadership capability. *Human Resource Management, 39*(2/3), 209–225.

Ayman, R., Kreicker, N. A., & Masztal, J. J. (1994). Defining global leadership in business environments. *Consulting Psychology Journal, 46*(1), 64–77.

Bueno, C. M., & Tubbs, S. L. (2004). Identifying global leadership competencies: An exploratory study. *Journal of American Academy of Business, 5*(1/2), 80–87.

Chhokar, J. S., Brodbeck, F. C., & House, R. J. (Eds.). (2007). Culture and leadership across the world: The GLOBE book of in-depth studies of 25 societies. Mahwah, NJ: Lawrence Erlbaum Associates.

Crosby, B., & Bryson, J. (2005). *Leadership for the common good: Tackling public problems in a shared power world*. London: Jossey-Bass.

Ferdig, M. A. (2007). Sustainability leadership: Co-creating a sustainable future. *Journal of Change Management, 7*(1), 25–35.

Ghoshal, S. (2005). Bad management theories are destroying good management practice. *Academy of Management Learning and Education*, pp. 75–91.

Hofstede, G. (2003). *Culture's consequences: Comparing values, behaviors, institutions and organizations across nations*. London: Sage.

House, R. J., Hanges, P. J., Javidan, M., Dorfman, P. W., & Gupta, V. (Eds.). (2004). *Culture, leadership, and organisations: The GLOBE study of 62 societies*. Thousand Oaks/London: Sage.

Javidan, M., Dorfman, P. W., Sully de Luque, M., & House, R. J. (2006). In the eye of the beholder: Cross cultural lessons in leadership from Project GLOBE. *The Academy of Management Perspectives, 20*(1), 67–90.

Javidan, M., & House, R. J. (2001). Cultural acumen for the global manager: Lessons from Project GLOBE. *Organizational Dynamics, 29*(4), 289–235.

Jokinen, T. (2005). Global leadership competencies: A review and discussion. *Journal of European Industrial Training, 29*(2/3), 199–261.

Kets de Vries, M. F. R., & Florent-Treacy, E. (2002). Global leadership from A to Z: Creating high commitment organizations. *Organizational Dynamics, 30*(4), 295–309.

Martineau, J. (2008, March 20). [Network of Leadership Scholars, LDRNET-L] "Is there such a thing as "global leadership"?

Mendenhall, M. E. (2008). The elusive, yet critical challenge of developing global leaders. *European Management Journal, 24*(6), 422–429.

Mendenhall, M. E., Osland, J. S., Bird, A., Oddou, G. R., & Maznevski, M. L. (Eds.). (2008). *Global leadership: Research, practice and development*. Abingdon, Oxon: Routledge.

Mintzberg, H. (2004). *Managers not MBAs: A hard look at the soft practice of managing and management development*. San Francisco: Berrett-Koehler.

Moran, R. T., & Riesenberger, J. R. (1994). *The global challenge, building the new worldwide enterprise*. London: McGraw-Hill.

Morrison, A. (2001). Integrity of global leadership. *Journal of Business Ethics, 31,* 65–76.

Osland, J. S. (2008). The multidisciplinary roots of global leadership. In M. Mendenhall, J. Osland, A. Bird, G. Oddou, & M. Maznevski (Eds.), *Global leadership: Research, practice and development* (pp. 18–33). Abingdon, Oxon: Routledge.

Petrick, J. A., Scherer, R. F., Brodzinski, J. D., Quinn, J. F., & Ainina, M. F. (1999, February). Global leadership skills and reputational capital: Intangible resources for sustainable advantage. *The Academy of Management Executive.*

Rosen, R., Digh, P., Singer, M., & Philips, C. (2000). *Global literacies: Lessons on business leadership and national cultures*. New York: Crown.

Werhane, P. H. (2007). Women leaders in a globalized world. *Journal of Business Ethics, 74,* 425–435.

SHARON TURNBULL is Director of the Centre for Applied Leadership Research at The Leadership Trust Foundation in Ross-on-Wye, Herefordshire, UK. Her research interests are leadership, leadership development, organizational culture, and change. She taught for many years at Lancaster University prior to joining The Leadership Trust. She is a Visiting Professor at both the University of Gloucestershire and the University of Worcester, Senior Research Fellow at Lancaster University Management School, and Chartered Fellow of the Chartered Institute of Personnel and Development. She currently directs the International Master's Program in Practicing Management, a program taught at six business schools across the globe.

Mutiny—Some Failures of Military Leadership, 1943 to 1972

By Kevin Baker and James Warn

THE MOST SERIOUS FAILURE OF LEADERSHIP OCCURS WHEN THERE is an outright rejection of leadership—refusal to follow directions or instruction. Nowhere is such failure more serious than in the armed forces, where rejection of leadership by a group of subordinates—failure to obey a command—is the crime of mutiny. There have been few instances of mutiny in the English-speaking armed forces in the twentieth century where all the blame can be placed on the mutineers (even if they usually wore the penalty of their action). In some cases, it is difficult not to sympathise with the mutineers, especially if their complaint was commanding officers who spent their time drinking and womanizing (as was a complaint after the Indian Navy mutiny). One perceptive comment on mutiny (and pertinent to leadership generally) is attributed to Admiral Collingwood—Admiral Nelson's second in command at Trafalgar. Collingwood stated that if men mutinied, the fault was not with them but with their leaders. In the following case studies, the mutinies came about more because of what the leaders failed to do rather than because of what they did. In some of these cases the commanders had a passive role—ignoring the needs of their men or failing to respond effectively, rather than exhibiting extreme behaviours.

This paper considers six mutinies over the period 1943 to 1972, in the Canadian and Indian navies, the British Army, and the New Zealand, Australian, and United States navies. In most of the mutinies, an ever-present theme is that the challenge to leadership occurred after the leader or leaders had been perceived to have neglected the interests of followers. In New Zealand in 1947, in a situation of dissatisfaction with conditions, senior naval leaders threatened sailors with disciplinary action, made no attempt to address grievances, and a mass walkout ensued. In contrast to this response, in 1970 Australian naval authorities reacted to a serious situation with good sense and a preparedness to consider the grievances of sailors, and a crisis was averted.

In other cases personnel mutinied in response to a failure to attend to their needs for respite and rest. The mutiny of the British Army soldiers of the 13 Parachute Battalion occurred after they had been accommodated in a camp that was "crowded, unsanitary and in a poor state of repair." These soldiers were mainly veterans who had been fighting continuously since D-Day and had been engaged in major battles such as the Ardennes and the Rhine crossing. In the example of mutiny in the Royal Canadian Navy, sailors mutinied in response to being refused shore leave in their home base, where they would be reunited with family and loved ones. This crew had experienced an arduous spell of convoy duty where they had faced the constant threat of death in cramped and confined quarters.

In the other two cases, in the Indian and United States navies, the trigger events are more complex to unravel. In the case of the mutiny in the USS *Constellation*, there was evidence of overcrowding, but this seemed only to exacerbate racial tensions on board. This situation no doubt reflected wider tensions in U.S. society at the time, but in the context of leadership onboard a ship, it pointed to a rift in the bond between officer and sailor. In this case the breakdown was in the mutual exchange of respect between individuals and in the social setting, and race was the fault line. In the case of the Indian Navy mutiny, grievances over poor food and unfair pay and conditions were keenly felt. Again the leaders failed to build a bond based on respect with followers and again the division was along racial lines.

66 MUTINY . . . IS THE ULTIMATE FAILURE OF LEADERSHIP. 99

Canadian Navy Mutiny

On 19 July 1943, around 190 men on the Tribal-class destroyer *Iroquois* shut themselves in the fore mess decks of their ship in what was the largest mutiny to affect the Royal Canadian Navy.[1] The men had chafed under the tight discipline enforced by their captain, Commander "Scarface" Holmes, and the night before the message had gone around the mess decks—the ratings of the *Iroquois* would not answer the pipe to fall in for work at 8:00 A.M. the next day, preparatory to taking the ship to sea. Moreover, they would close and lock the mess deck doors to deny access to the ship's officers.

To the extent that any mutiny is justified, the men of *Iroquois* had cause for complaint. Their ship had been hard-pressed during long service in the North Atlantic during the hardest times of the war at sea. As an indicator of the widespread discontent, almost all the seamen of the ship joined the action—the normal complement of a Tribal-class destroyer, including officers and petty officers, was just 240, and nearly 80 percent of the complement were involved in the mutiny.

What had brought matters to a head was the Captain's decision to restrict leave after an arduous spell of convoy duty, during which they had seen ships sunk and rescued survivors. Just six weeks before, the *Iroquois* men had taken on board no fewer than 628 survivors of a sunken merchant ship. They had been looking forward to their "run ashore" as a break from the tension and danger of the war against submarines and aircraft, but it was denied them. Captain Holmes announced that because of a relatively minor breach of discipline, the crew would be refused shore leave in Halifax, their home base. This was clearly an unreasonable decision, but because of the limited grievance channels, the only response that the crew could make in the face of this bad leadership was to take the ultimate step of mutiny. They chose an imaginative tactic that both spared them punishment and made it difficult for the Captain to respond aggressively to the challenge thrown down to his leadership. The mutineers closed and locked the mess deck doors.

The tactic of closing and locking the mess deck doors was a very effective one for mutineers, because it prevented officers identifying ringleaders or spokesmen and it also provided grounds for a legal defence that the men involved could not hear orders directly addressed to them. Their demands were listed on a piece of paper affixed to the doors. The demands included the removal of both the Captain and the Executive Officer.

The matter was clearly at an impasse, for the ship's authorities could not break into the mess decks without causing substantial damage to the ship. It went quickly to the Vice Chief of Naval Staff. It was crucial that the matter be resolved quickly, for the *Iroquois* was urgently needed for convoy escort duty and the timetables of dozens of ships could not be held up. Although it set a precedent for the exercise of naval discipline (and would haunt the Canadian Navy for years after the war), the Admiral did not hold a formal investigation (for which he was criticised)[2] but immediately removed Commander Holmes and the Executive Officer from the *Iroquois*. Under new senior officers who showed better leadership, the destroyer quickly returned to normal and proceeded to sea.

A second mutiny took place soon after the war which involved many ships, not just one, but once again the basic cause seems to have been the poor leadership by middle-ranking officers, and initially an aggressive response that made matters worse.

Indian Navy Mutiny

On 18 February 1946, Indian naval ratings at the signals station at Mumbai refused to obey their officers and took control of their barracks. Their example was quickly followed by Indian seamen in warships in Mumbai harbour. Their actions were motivated by growing tensions between British officers and Indian ratings and had far-reaching ramifications. It was a ". . . momentous event . . . which threatened that ultimate mainstay of British rule, the military."[3] The mutiny undermined British military leadership and confidence in that leadership, for the British were forced to recognise the "questionable loyalty of the Indian services by the Royal Indian Navy mutiny."[4]

> ❝ ON 18 FEBRUARY 1946, INDIAN NAVAL RATINGS
> AT THE SIGNALS STATION AT MUMBAI REFUSED TO
> OBEY THEIR OFFICERS AND TOOK CONTROL OF
> THEIR BARRACKS. ❞

A Board of Enquiry of the Admiralty examined all aspects of the affair. Evidence given at the enquiry in May 1946 pointed to specific reasons for the mutiny, and these reasons revolved around the quality of leadership. An Indian officer named Lieutenant Surendra Kohli criticised the attitude of the British officers toward the sailors they led.[5] A seaman of the frigate HMIS *Jumna* told the enquiry that he had experienced three commanding officers who "spent their time in drinking and with girls."[6] In its report, the Board of Enquiry was scathing in its comments about the competence and quality of leadership of British officers and added that there was evidence of "harsh and even inhuman treatment by quite a number of officers . . . essentially because of the 'colour bar' and feelings of racial superiority."[7]

The catalyst for the walkout involved a telegraphist at the signals station named Dutta. The commander of the station was one of the officers subsequently accused of frequent use of racial epithets, which, given the circumstances of the time, was an appalling example of leadership. The strikers initially complained about poor food and instead demanded "the best type of Indian food."[8] The next day the mutiny spread to ships in Mumbai harbour until another three thousand men were involved. The British Ensign was hauled down and replaced by the flags of Congress and the Muslim League. British and Indian officers were forced off their ships, and the guns of a frigate were trained on two symbols of British rule—the Taj Mahal Hotel and the Royal Yacht Club. Initially, the mutiny was not violent, but on 19 February large numbers of men went ashore from the ships and more men gathered on the naval base. They crammed into the base gymnasium, and there were more than two hours of oratory from various quarters that resulted in the crowd becoming inflamed. Then the mutineers rampaged through the base, armed with a range of weapons from steel hammers and crowbars to hockey sticks. British officers were attacked and beaten, although no one was killed. The sailors also resented the American presence, and the U.S. Information Services Library was surrounded, its windows smashed and the American flag ripped from its flagpole.

On 20 February, the mutiny spread to other shore stations and warships, and it was clear that the situation had become one of open mutiny. Besides the mutinous state of the fleet's main base at Mumbai, another 1,500 men mutinied in the shore bases in other parts of India at Madras and Calcutta and Vizagapatam. In HMIS *Hindustan* the crew mutinied because they felt that the Captain had insulted them. At HMIS *Adyar* at Madras, when officers attempted to address the crew, they were stoned by their men. There were mutinies in more than 50 warships and shore bases and the Board of Enquiry later estimated that ten thousand men took part in mutinous actions.

The Viceroy's Council met in urgent session and instead of negotiating, and investigating whether the mutineers might have just demands, the Council vowed to react to the situation with a firm hand, and they agreed that the mutiny would have to be put down, that there would be "no question of parley," and that they would seek unconditional surrender by the mutineers.[9] The fleet commander, Vice Admiral Godfrey, vowed to bring the mutinous sailors under control, "even if it means the destruction of the Navy of which they have been so proud."[10] Once again, when naval leadership was put under challenge, it rejected the option of negotiation, even though their uncompromising reaction only made the situation worse.

Because the Admiral had no naval resources to back up the Council's hard line, he had to call on his army colleagues for assistance. They resolved to follow a policy of using "overwhelming force on hand"[11] to return the mutinous sailors to obedience. Four British regiments were brought to the Mumbai harbour area to enforce the ultimatum. On 21 February, English and Scottish soldiers began moving into the base, arresting any sailors who did not immediately disperse.[12] When news of the mutiny reached the civilian population, riots broke out in the city, fuelled by nationalism and intercommunal hatreds and sparked by the example of insurrection. Two hundred seventeen people were killed and over a thousand injured in the civil rioting over the next five days before calm returned. The respected Indian Nationalist leader J. Nehru called for the sailors to surrender unconditionally.[13] Neither Congress nor the Muslim League wanted the Raj to collapse in violence. In the naval base, a small group of sailors wanted to resist Nehru's call to lay down their arms, but most ratings responded and they resolved to return to discipline. On 22 February 1946, the mutiny in Mumbai was over. In the course of the rioting and the entry of the troops, one RIN officer had been killed. A British officer and seven British soldiers were injured, and a number of ratings of the RIN were also injured. Armed soldiers were sent on board the warships, and would maintain on guard until 5 March, when the base and the ships were considered to be under control and quiet again. It is significant that the mutiny was, in the end, not resolved by force but by the exercise of a better quality of leadership—that of Nehru, whose moral authority was respected by the mutineers. Many of the mutineers were charged and jailed for short periods until Indian independence, when they were all released as heroes.

British Army Mutiny

Shortly after the Indian mutiny, there was a military mutiny that involved almost an entire battalion of paratroopers—254 men in all were convicted of mutiny by a Field General Court Martial and punished by jail sentences ranging from three to five years. In this case, although the mutiny was sparked by complaints about living conditions, the military leadership concerned were not overtly bad leaders—they were simply bound by military disciplinary practices and their own prejudices and allowed themselves to be put in a situation where a clash was inevitable.[14] In May 1946, 13 Para Battalion of the British Army based in Malaya moved into a pre-war camp that was overcrowded, and was also in a poor state of repair after being used for other purposes during the Japanese occupation. At 7:00 A.M. on 14 May, a number of paratroopers gathered near the canteen and let the orderly officer know that they had prepared a list of grievances and would not go on parade until they could present the list to their commanding officer, Lieutenant Colonel Leyland. The orderly officer refused to hear their grievances and ordered them to fall in, but the men refused to move. Lieutenant Colonel Leyland came out to meet the men near the canteen and he also told them that he would not accept their list of grievances, that they would have to forward them through official grievance channels, and then he also ordered them to fall in on parade. Once again the soldiers refused the order; both sides had been put at an impasse, largely through the officers' refusal to bend an army regulation. The situation escalated. The men stayed gathered in groups until after lunch, when the commander of the Second Division, Major General Arkwright, arrived to confront them. The General repeated the mistake of the Lieutenant Colonel and bluntly told the paratroopers that he could not consider their grievances unless they were submitted through formal channels. He then made the further mistake of making the affair even more serious by invoking his authority and telling the men that they were committing mutiny. He demanded that they immediately fall in on the company markers, or else he would have them arrested for their mutiny. Far from meekly obeying the ultimatum, the men responded with whistles and murmuring, but no one fell in on parade.

Having painted himself into a corner and having to save face, the General ordered all the men to be arrested. At the courts martial (which must have presented logistical problems), some men offered the defence that they had not been at the gathering, but instead were asleep in their tents. This defence was not accepted. Others argued that they had misunderstood the purpose of the gathering, which they had been told was an official one to consider their grievances. They also were found guilty. A third group tried the novel defence that they should have been called out by their NCOs to fall in on the company markers, not by officers, and hence they were not technically disobeying an order. This defence too was rejected. The upshot was that the War Office in London was informed of the lengthy jail sentences imposed on 254 men of 13 Para Battalion, and formal confirmation of the proceedings and the sentences was requested.

One would have liked to have been a fly on the wall of the office where the file landed on the desk of a senior officer and the implications were raised. It was unimaginable to hold such a large number of soldiers, and men of an elite unit at that, in post-war Malaya, where imperial prestige had already been badly damaged by the debacle of the fall of Singapore in 1942. The alternative was to ship the men back to Britain, and their numbers were such that hundreds of guards would be required to supervise them—an entire ship would be required, and imagine the publicity when a whole shipload of mutineers arrived in the country. Then more than 250 well-trained soldiers, many of them battle-hardened and experienced paratroopers, would be dropped into Britain's penal system. A message was sent from the War Office to the GOC-in-C Malaya Command: the charges were quashed. The men of 13 Para Battalion went back to being soldiers instead of convicted mutineers. They were shortly needed to combat a Communist insurgency that was about to break out.

The following year there was another naval mutiny, and in this case the obduracy of leadership was at the very highest political levels. The naval leaders on the spot attempted to react responsibly and sensibly, but they were overruled from above with disastrous consequences for the navy involved, the Royal New Zealand Navy.

New Zealand Navy Mutiny
The Royal New Zealand Navy in 1947 consisted of just a handful of ships, and the two main units were Dido-class cruisers—*Black Prince* and *Bellona*. There was discontent among the seamen regarding pay and conditions, and they hoped that a new Labour government would improve their situation. In March 1947, *Black Prince* was at the Auckland naval base with HMNZS *Philomel*, along with the corvette *Arbutus*.

On the morning of Monday, 31 March, the sailors learned that new pay rates and conditions changes left them generally worse off, and there were other broken promises regarding conditions. Incensed, the sailors of the base resolved to protest next morning, 1 April, when the commanding officer was informed that the men would not accept duty as a protest against the failure of the government to keep its promises. This group of seamen, numbering about 100, then left the parade area and word was spread that there would be a meeting of all seamen of the ships in the base canteen at twelve o'clock. The base commander was the well-respected Commander Phipps, and he passed on to the naval authorities in Wellington the no-doubt surprising news that they had a mutiny on their hands. However, he held off taking action until he saw how events would unfold.

The noon meeting was inconclusive. Older seamen emphasised that the action was against the government and not the service itself. It was noted that the seamen who walked off the *Black Prince* were punctilious in saluting the Ensign as they left. Observers commented that the seamen were very calm and controlled at all times. One man who had had a glass of rum was prevented from taking part in the mutiny by his comrades, in order to make sure that no one could accuse the mutineers of being affected by alcohol.

When the bosun's pipe sounded the signal for the return to work at one o'clock, the *Philomel* men, now joined by ratings from the crew of the *Black Prince,* instead resolved that they would "go on strike as a protest against the government's failure to carry out a formal promise. . . ."[15] The mood was very tense. Discipline on the base was in the hands of the Master-at-arms and his boat's crew, but they were outnumbered by the mutineers.

The crew of the corvette *Arbutus* decided for the mutiny and went ashore, leaving only the officers and petty officers on the ship. The group of mutinous seamen, now numbering well over 200, waited in the canteen area for a reply from the Naval Board to their petition. By 4:00 P.M., the Naval Board replied to the men's petition, but the response was couched in vague and uncertain terms, insisting that the men had to return to duty before their complaints would be considered.

The men walked off the base. A group of leading seamen drafted a message to the press, reiterating that the protest was "solely a protest against the government in its failure to live up to the stated promise of the Prime Minister."[16] The only seamen still on the base were 18 Imperial ratings and the sick berth staff in the naval hospital. There was a Cabinet meeting in Wellington, and that night the Prime Minister announced that the pay rates would be made retrospective to 1 April 1946, but the men would have to take the consequences of their mutiny.

The seamen met again on the Devonport Reserve at 8:00 A.M. next day. The Prime Minister's announcement was considered. The meeting lasted barely ten minutes. It ended in a unanimous resolution that contained two demands—there should be no "victimisation" of the mutineers, and lower-deck welfare committees should be established to consider a range of shipboard issues. The men then marched to the dockyard gates to present these demands to Commander Phipps who came to the gates to meet them. Many seamen wore the good conduct badges representing eight years continuous service, and a majority wore one or two rows of war service ribbons—they were hardly the malcontents of the services.

Commander Phipps (who went on to a distinguished career) was constrained by the government's attitude and he could do little more than try and persuade the men to return to duty and to accept punishment for mutiny. The seamen heard the commander out in silence, and when he had concluded they dispersed.

Overnight consideration did not incline the government toward concession or sympathy. Their hard-line approach was to damage the New Zealand Navy for years. When the mutinous seamen, some 200 strong, returned to the dockyard gates at 10:00 A.M. on Thursday, Commander Phipps had been instructed to offer them a blunt alternative—return to duty immediately or face immediate discharge. The Naval Board had lain down that the men had to accept naval discipline or be discharged. It was the same unbending line used in response to earlier mutinies—there could be no consideration of the rights and wrongs of a situation that drove men to refuse orders.

A leading seaman spoke to the group, hundreds strong, and finished with the question, "Do you want to be civvies?" The reply was "… a thunderous 'Yes!'"[17] There then took place one of those spontaneous actions which, even many years afterwards, loses none of its poignancy.

Long-serving seamen who the day before had emphasised their loyalty to their country, a loyalty that was already well-proven, but who had had that loyalty thrown back in their faces, now stripped off their badges of rank, good conduct awards and medal ribbons, and walked away from the navy.

If the authorities believed that the mutiny was over, they were rudely disabused. In Lytellton, the minesweeper HMNZS *Hautapu* docked. Notwithstanding the harsh example of the dismissal of the Auckland men, the *Hautapu* ratings refused duty. Once again, there was a strong reaction. The seamen were warned of the consequences of their action—there seems to have been little attempt to negotiate genuine grievances. The seamen, stokers, able seamen, and leading hands left the ship.

The police were called in and warrants for the arrest of the seamen were issued. The charges were "wilfully disobeying orders and improperly leaving their ship."[18]

More than 200 of New Zealand's naval ratings were thus dismissed in the course of three days. The navy suffered. *Black Prince* could not be manned. Most of the crew of the corvette *Arbutus* were discharged, and that ship could only be adequately manned by seconded seamen from a number of other sources. A week after the event, a reporter stated that Devonport base "retains its deserted appearance."[19]

66 LONG-SERVING SEAMEN . . . STRIPPED OFF THEIR BADGES OF RANK, GOOD CONDUCT AWARDS AND MEDAL RIBBONS, AND WALKED AWAY FROM THE NAVY. 99

Australian Navy Mutiny

In the Royal Australian Navy, there was unrest over pay in early 1970, and it came to a head in August of that year. Their grievance was very similar to that of the New Zealanders in 1947, in that a pay rise had been granted to merchant seamen and the government had promised that the increase would flow on naval personnel, but they were slow in approving the move. Discontent grew during the year, and by August it reached a high point. On 17 August, informal communication channels carried a message that there would be a "stop-work" after lunch that day. No one determined where the message started or who started it, but it must have been one of the engine personnel, for they were the men who responded. Around 200 engine room personnel of the aircraft transport HMAS *Sydney,* and the destroyers and frigates *Brisbane, Yarra, Anzac,* and *Swan,* left their duties and gathered in the courtyard of the Garden Island dockyard, still within the precincts of the base, where they waited fairly quietly but determinedly. News of their action was quickly carried to the Flag Officer Commanding the Australian Fleet, Rear Admiral H. D. Stevenson.

Against all the protocols, Stevenson himself went to where the men were gathered and stood on a box so they could all see him. Then he asked them to state their reasons for their actions. Several did so (despite the risk of being identified as ringleaders of what was technically a mutiny). When they had finished, Stevenson spoke and, although he would not commit to any specific response, he promised he would pass on their concerns to the government in Canberra. His promise immediately defused the situation. When Stevenson then "asked" the men to return to duty, there was only a brief hesitation before the personnel returned to their respective ships. Their "stop-work" had lasted one and a quarter hours. It had no tangible affect on operations. The pay rises were soon approved by a somewhat-startled government.

However, the affair had been reported in the media, and Navy Headquarters had to announce that no disciplinary action would be taken against the men who had participated in what media sources were calling the "Navy walk-off." The authorities, recognizing that the situation could have had severe consequences but for Stevenson's prompt and unusual action, said that in future the men would be expected to comply with the formal Navy procedures for handling complaints.

The official reaction was a sensible one for the times. In the years of civil protest over Australia's involvement in the Vietnam conflict, any strong action against the incipient mutineers would probably have drawn substantial support for them. This was in contrast with earlier mutinies when public opinion was very strongly against seamen who resisted naval authority. Another difference in 1970 was the fact that dissatisfied seamen could more easily resign, and hence a heavy-handed disciplinarian approach could have seen large numbers of skilled men leave the navy at a time when their skills were in demand.

United States Navy Mutiny

The sixth case study of mutiny presented here relates to the United States Navy, and in this instance an observer would conclude that the ship's officers handled the disturbance well, and that the causes of the mutiny were beyond their control. This underscores a point that whereas poor leadership can make a bad situation worse, sometimes not even good leadership can salvage a bad situation.

In November 1972, the aircraft carrier USS *Constellation* was at the large United States naval base at San Diego in California, undergoing training preparatory to sailing for "Yankee Station" in Vietnam. Racial tension was also evident on this aircraft carrier, with certain recreational areas of the ship becoming exclusive territory either for blacks or whites. The tension was made worse by overcrowding in the ship, which, in addition to its 4,500 man crew, had an additional 250 personnel for its aircraft squadrons embarked.

To relieve the overcrowding, the Captain of the *Constellation* sought permission to discharge some crew members who were near the end of their service, and this permission was given.[20] He chose to include among the discharges 15 sailors who had been reported as adding to the racial tensions on board by supporting meetings of black seamen and spreading information of what had happened on another carrier, the USS *Kitty Hawk*, the month before.

Rumours spread among the 400 black crewmen of the *Constellation* that their "brothers" were being victimised. Tension increased and on the morning of 3 November, the Captain was informed that around 60 black sailors were involved in a sit-down protest in the forward mess. The ship's Master-at-arms was sent to disperse them, which he did, seemingly without trouble, but within the hour the group, now numbering a hundred, reassembled in the aft mess.

The ship's officers planned an open forum to allow all crewmen the opportunity to raise and discuss grievances. When the forum was convened late in the afternoon, it degenerated into a noisy argument with a number of radical sailors at the core of the protest. The situation was at an impasse. The Captain decided that the only way to resolve it was to send ashore the dissidents. On the morning of 4 November, he sent a black lieutenant to supervise a "beach detachment" of seamen who preferred to leave the ship. To his surprise, a total of 144 men, including a small number of white crewmen, walked off the ship and were taken to a naval air station, where they continued their discussions for another five days. They were officially considered to be on shore leave.

As there was a pressing need for the *Constellation* to undertake operations on "Yankee Station," the negotiations were terminated, gangways were raised, and the carrier sailed for Vietnam. More than 120 seamen remained. They were charged with being absent without leave and received minimal punishments such as extra work duties before being transferred to other ships and postings.

The incident resulted in a number of enquiries in Washington, one by the Senate Armed Services Committee, which reviewed issues of what constituted a mutiny.

Lessons of Leadership That Can Be Learned from These Case Studies of Mutiny

The bond between follower and leader has been described either as functioning around agreed-upon transactions in its poorly developed state,[21] or relationship-based in its more mature form.[22] These two approaches to explaining the leader-follower bond are presented as alternatives in the research literature or at least as separate states with the transactional stage preceding the development of the relationship. The above narratives of mutinies suggest that such a clear division may be more arbitrary than actual.

Transactionally founded leadership occurs when the leader relies on hierarchical status within the organizational setting, contractual sanctions, and control of economic rewards to influence and direct the subordinate.[23] In response, the subordinate provides a limited form of followership that meets the required expectations in order to gain rewards. The motive of the subordinate in this case is self-interest rather than consideration of more collective needs. In contrast, more mature leader-follower bonds, such as described by transformational leadership theory, occur when the leader is able to elevate followers' concerns from self-interest by raising their awareness and providing a cause that is merged with the needs of the wider group.[24] The military induction process moves the new recruit along a well-tried and tested training pathway that emphasises loyalty, obedience to rank, and teamwork. In the mutinies described above, the military personnel were experienced, well socialised in the values and culture of the military organisation, and their loyalty and performance had been tested under combat or operational pressures. These are indications that the leader-follower bond was functioning at a relationship level, where there was a strong emotional bond, respect for rank, and a clear sense of obligation to the wider group. Yet the breakdown occurred when the leaders defaulted at the transactional level.

The research on the psychological contract can also provide some useful insight into how the tipping point of rejection of authority might have been reached. The psychological contract is a mental model of what the employer and employee expect of each other, and it serves to guide the actions of both.[25] At its most basic a psychological contract might be expressed as a "fair day's pay for a fair day's work." It refers to an "exchange relationship between employer and employee."[26] The failure of one party to fulfill anticipated outcomes can have a strong negative impact on the other party, since the violation is perceived as having resulted in a loss of some kind. A strong emotionally based reaction can be expected where the contract revolves around a longer term relationship rather than an explicit transactional exchange—and especially when the relationship is admixed with strong feelings of patriotism and loyalty to the service. Offsetting the severity of the reaction is the increased likelihood of followers perceiving a relational-based contract to seek remedies that will maintain the relationship with the leader.[27] In the above cases, the mutineers only severed the relationship when expelled by their leaders.

The leadership theory and the research on the psychological contract assume a dyadic bond and make little mention of the wider social context. In the case of the Indian mutiny in particular and the other mutinies a full understanding of the failure of the leader-follower bond can only be understood in the wider social circumstances. Although the psychological contract may explain expectations between a single follower and leader, it is hard to assume that any group of mutineers shared exactly the same mental model. Recourse to social and cultural level belief need to be incorporated into how the mutineers espoused their concerns (e.g., wage equity with civilian counterparts in the cases of the New Zealand and Australian mutinies).

A number of observations can be made and lessons learned for military and naval leaders. One, the leader-follower bond is dynamic and sensitive to situation. Distinctions between transactional and relational are conceptually neat but can be arbitrary for an actual leader since the nature of the relationship is more mixed in reality. Leaders ignore transactional commitments at their peril even if they are transformative and have formed strong relationships with dedicated, loyal followers.

Positing that violations at the relational level can trigger an emotionally strong response does provide an explanation of why previously loyal and dedicated troops and sailors would mutiny. Also, these events need to be understood in a wider social context. Psychological explanations address well the bond between an individual leader and follower but do not shed much understanding on why a group might mutiny. Finally, incorporating this social context is important where the grievances can be elevated in consciousness about wider causes or agendas (e.g., civil rights, nationalism), especially where there exists a clear fault line between race and authority.

Conclusion

On balance, there are indeed cases of mutiny attributed to reprehensible failure of leadership, but there are also examples of mutinies that came about despite the leadership abilities of commanders—Admiral Collingwood's comment that if men mutiny it is the fault of their leaders is insightful, but not always irrefutable fact.

NOTES

1. The source for this incident is Whitby, M. (1965), "Matelots, Martinets, and Mutineers: The Mutiny in HMCS Iroquois, 19 July 1943," *Journal of Military History* 65/1: 77-104.

2. Audette, L., "The Lower Deck and Mainguy Report of 1949," in Boutilier, J. (1982), *The RCN in Retrospect 1910–1968,* University of British Columbia Press, Vancouver, p. 238.

3. Omvedt, G., "Gandhi and the Pacification of the Indian National Revolution," in Jeffrey, R., et al., Eds. (1990), *India, Rebellion to Republic Selected Writings 1857–1990*, Sterling Publishers Private Limited, New Delhi, p. 73.

4. Ghosh, K. K. (1969), *The Indian National Army*, Meenakshi Prakashan, Meerut, p. 209.

5. Report of the Commission of Enquiry into the Royal Indian Navy Mutiny, February 1946, *Extraordinary Gazette of India*, 21 January 1947, National Archives of India, New Delhi, p. 128.

6. Ibid.

7. Ibid.

8. *The Times of India*, 18 Febuary 1946.

9. Moon, P., Ed. (1973), *Wavell: The Viceroy's Journal*, Oxford University Press, London, p. 215.

10. *The Times of India*, 21 February 1946.

11. *The Times of India*, 24 February 1946.

12. Ibid.

13. *The Times of India*, 26 February 1946.

14. The following account is drawn from War Office file WO 71/1011.

15. *The New Zealand Herald*, 2 April 1947.

16. Ibid.

17. *The New Zealand Herald*, 3 April 1947.

18. *The New Zealand Herald*, 8 April 1947.

19. *The New Zealand Herald*, 11 April 1947.

20. The main source for the following description of events is drawn from *The New York Times,* 26 November 1972, quoted in Guttridge, L. (1992), *Mutiny, A History of Naval Insurrection,* Ian Allan Publishing, Maryland.

21. Bass, B. (1995), Theory of transformational Leadership Redux, *Leadership Quarterly,* 6(4), 463–478.

22. Graen, G. B., & Uhl-Bien, M. (1995), Relationship-based approach to leadership: development of leader-member exchange (LMX) theory over 25 years: Applying a multi-level, multi-domain perspective, *Leadership Quarterly,* 6, 219–247.

23. Ibid.

24. Bass, op. cit.

25. Ibid.

26. Anderson, N., & Schalk, R. (1998), The psychological contract in retrospect and prospect, *Journal of Organizational Behavior,* 19, 637–647 (638).

27. Rousseau, D. M. (2004), Psychological contracts in the workplace: Understanding the ties that motivate, *Academy of Management Executive,* 18, 120–127.

KEVIN BAKER completed a bachelor's degree followed by a master's degree from the University of Sydney while working in the health and welfare sector. From 1992 to 1993, he completed a doctorate in economics in 18 months while managing a sheltered workshop. His interest in history came to the fore with the publication of six works of history from 1997 to 2006, ranging from church history to military history, including a book on naval mutiny coauthored with Dr. Tom Frame. His most recent books include a history of sedition in Australia and New Zealand, a biography of General Paul Cullen, and a history of the Orthodox Church in China, Japan, and Korea. He is currently a Visiting Fellow at the Australian Defence Force Academy, University of New South Wales.

JAMES WARN initiated the introduction of the academic leadership courses at the Australian Defence Force Academy and has been instrumental in developing enhanced academic programs contributing to the professional development of career military officers. He has a Ph.D. degree in psychology, has worked as a practising psychologist, and currently is investigating leadership culture and capability in an international collaborative research project.

Research and Service Learning Study Abroad Experience

A Context for Developing a Global Ethic of Care

By Liz Barber, Charles E. Wilson, Vanessa Duren-Winfield, Jacqueline Greenlee, and Tom Smith

WHAT KEY CULTURAL AND MORAL CONTEXTS PROVIDE THE SEEDING ground for envisioning better futures (for more than just the few) in a globally intertwined world? This paper examines the development of a global ethic of care within the context of an ongoing university-based leadership and service learning research study abroad in Malawi, Sub-Saharan Africa.

In 2006 the Interdisciplinary Leadership Studies Program at North Carolina Agricultural and Technical State University, under the directorship of Alexander Erwin, partnered with Virginia Polytechnic Institute and State University, Radford University, and three primary (Standards/Grades 1-8) schools located in Domasi Province in the Southern Region of Malawi, to provide opportunities for transnational mutual aid and self-help. Liz Barber, a professor in the Leadership Studies Program, initiated North Carolina A&T's involvement with the partnership and continues to serve as an advocate for international study abroad. One aim of this collaborative effort is to promote a more robust and rounded understanding of globally distant others through joining hands to accomplish much-needed work.

The inclusion of North Carolina A&T, an historic black college/university, cuts across the grain of the "white fathers" approach to service in Africa. In terms of student experience, summer 2007 traveler Jackie Greenlee describes best the sense of identification individuals of color feel in encountering "a sea of humanity where faces like mine are the majority." Working side-by-side with Malawian change agents, we gain a window into more than just leadership strategies for working successfully across cultural difference, or a sense of how the notion of leading is construed in a different culture. We come to know and care about friends in a far distant place.

Malawian educators, children, and others serve as informants, collaborators, and coauthors for the projects of university faculty and students. University coursework provides insight into Malawian culture, history and politics, and challenges the country faces in the areas of education, medicine, agriculture, and economic development. Summer 2007 students purchased a laptop for the one Domasi school that has electricity, to facilitate an ongoing exchange of ideas across distance and difference.

66 THE INCLUSION OF NORTH CAROLINA A&T ... CUTS ACROSS THE GRAIN OF THE 'WHITE FATHERS' APPROACH TO SERVICE IN AFRICA. 99

Grounding a Global Ethic of Care

To ground our work, we weave together several disparate lines of inquiry. Situated cognition (Lave & Wenger, 1991) locates development within specific communities of practice and serves as a bridge between cognitive (i.e., Mintzberg & Gosling, 2002) and life experience (i.e., Brugman, 2003; Callery, 1990; Gorman, Duffy, & Heffernan, 1994; Rogers, 2002) models of ethical development. Nell Noddings (2003) situates ethical development within the reciprocal relationship that exists between a caregiver and the one-cared-for. The caregiver gains gratification from observing the effects of his or her caring upon the one-cared-for. With experience, the caregiver's ethic of care grows to encompass unknown others with whom he or she is able to empathize, based upon previous reciprocal caregiving relationships.

The self-help or mutual aid approach we employ in Malawi engages students and faculty members from both sides of the globe in a participatory process of sharing common experiences, situations, or problems. In such an exchange, knowledge and experience are brokered in getting help, giving help, and learning to help oneself (Borkman, 1999, 2004). Such initiatives are voluntary in nature, with the primary focus on emotional support, practical support, and information exchange.

A service learning approach to difference provides a pathway for diverse others to unite in the achievement of common goals (Etzioni, 2004). In this approach individuals regard those who differ from themselves in a thoughtful effort to understand the fruitful ideas these others bring to the table. Empirical research has verified the impact of international service experiences on moral reasoning, cultural intelligence, and leader adaptability (Wilson, 2008). Liberation theorist Paulo Freire (2006) argued that awareness of one's humanity as nested among the humanity of others requires a reading of both "the word" and "the world." We argue that leader ability to envision better futures for the many requires the development of a global ethic of care that is fostered best when the classroom becomes the world.

> **❝ EMPIRICAL RESEARCH HAS VERIFIED THE IMPACT OF INTERNATIONAL SERVICE EXPERIENCES ON MORAL REASONING, CULTURAL INTELLIGENCE, AND LEADER ADAPTABILITY. ❞**

Learning to Care in Malawi

In Malawi three-quarters of the population live on less than $2 a day. A relatively new nation, Malawi gained its independence in 1964, launched its first universal public education initiative in 1994, and currently exists as one of the poorest countries in the world. Life expectancy is 37, slightly less for women; one-fifth of the adult population and more than 10 percent of children birth to age 14 test positive for HIV/AIDS. The only correlate of remaining free from HIV is staying in school. Remaining in school, however, is no easy accomplishment. Classes of 125 or more children are taught by a single teacher with an eighth-grade education and only a few weeks of training. Few children possess schoolbooks, paper, or pens for completing classroom work. Children whose families allow them to attend school (instead of working at home or in the markets) come speaking a number of indigenous languages, while instruction takes place in only one of these languages, the politically favored ChiChewa. English is taught as a second language through Standard 4, after which time it becomes the language of instruction. High stakes testing, a remnant of British domination, is conducted in English from Standard 5 on, greatly reducing the pool of students eligible for secondary education.

In recent years, however, the election of a more democratic-minded president, Bingwa Mutharika, has led to positive changes. Despite setbacks from insufficient or untimely rains that can decimate the population through famine, and a cloying poverty that makes development of any kind extremely difficult, the country is now in a season of hope as change agent leaders emerge in such fields as agriculture and education. Thus Malawi exists as fertile ground for mutual aid and self-help projects, which currently focus on education initiatives. Domasi Demonstration Primary, a laboratory school, provides a promising site for change, as efforts can be displayed there for educators across the country to observe and emulate. Teachers at this school are better educated, with all holding a Malawi Certificate of school completion, and some have completed college courses.

The recent addition of Malemia Village School to the partnership is significant for a number of reasons. Malemia provides a more accurate feel for how education is carried out in the rural areas that dominate in Malawi. During initial visits to Malemia we observed the signs of severe malnutrition: children with stunted growth, hair loss, legs bowed by rickets, and swollen bellies. So moved were the students that upon their return to the U.S. they raised the funds needed to reinstitute a lapsed donor aid feeding program at Malemia. As of summer 2008, close to a thousand children who once received donor-funded porridge two days a week, and then none, now get porridge enriched with peanut flour, milk, and sugar on every school day.

Based on input and co-planning with Malawian educators, service research projects have included a number of literacy-related projects including building and stocking libraries of children's picture books in English, and model teaching demonstrations employing giant poster-size "big books" (commonly used in the U.S. for early literacy instruction and equally useful in Malawian classrooms of 100+ children) for bilingual math, science, and social studies lessons. Another project built upon Malawian teachers' growing familiarity with big-book instruction by scaffolding their use of the photovoice participatory action research method (Wang & Burris, 1994) to create their own big books for teaching about HIV/AIDS prevention. Photovoice places cameras in the hands of those most affected by a social problem in order for them to document these realities. Reflections upon the photos prompt dialogue, text, and in this case, the authoring of culturally comprehensible HIV/AIDS teaching materials.

Other projects have included examining and supporting the efforts of effective change agent leaders; documenting the daily lives of Malawians; and networking a pen pal project that links at-risk sixth graders from a high-needs middle school in Greensboro, North Carolina, as English-language mentors for Malawian youth who need opportunities to use their English, and who, in return, will serve as cultural mentors. The study abroad program, which includes 18–20 students each summer, is now poised to involve participants from university schools of nursing, agriculture, social work, and business.

No Bananas: Learning About Zero in a Third World Country

In the summer of 2007, four North Carolina A&T students spent three and one half weeks in Malawi. They brought away differing impressions from their sojourn, but all spoke to a developing understanding of self among others, of a common humanity that allows individuals to envision and care not only for specific Malawian friends, but for many unknown others. Each traveler speaks in her own voice below.

Vanessa: Roofless Learning

Among the many things I learned during my service research, I learned how culture shapes how we think about what constitutes good leadership. Definitions of effective leadership vary from one culture to another. Leadership behavior that works well in one culture could be completely ineffective in others. For example, in Malawian classrooms, young "citizen leaders" emerged from just about everywhere. Secor and Tyasto (2005) identified citizen leaders as people who take on leadership responsibilities without any formalized position that accords them the authority and privilege of leadership. For example, whether Malawian teachers were present or not, older children functioned as leaders for younger ones. I recall how individual older youth stepped into roles of citizen leaders in their schools by serving as surrogates for the teacher or head teacher (principal) in their absence, to make sure their peers maintained civility and good order.

The leadership behaviors of the older Malawian children were those of protector and guardian. Attributes such as commitment, sensitivity, and responsiveness to others describe these surrogates well. The younger children would receive a strong switching with a hand-tied, straw-like broom when they behaved in a manner the older children considered inappropriate, such as chasing after our bus upon arrival or departure, or lingering on the outskirts of the classrooms after instruction began. Asserting protective leadership authority over peers would not happen as easily in America, where young school-aged children no longer feel the need for nor desire the guidance and protection of older children.

Family leadership in Malawi provides another example. In some families the notion of father as leader is viewed very differently from how we understand this in our culture. As past culture has allowed, some Malawian fathers have many wives. Such a man expects the wife to be faithful, wash, cook and clean, and take care of the home while he continues to procreate additional children with new wives. While most Malawians frown on such behavior, in some families the practice continues to this day.

Globalization has already impacted Malawi. Those who possess the ability to accept and administer change are ready for this new shift, and will become the future leaders. Annie Fletcher, a Malawian friend, is a female catalyst for globalization and social justice. As entrepreneur, founder, and CEO of Annie's Lodges, she brought tourism to Malawi and provided better jobs for many. Above-average wages are paid to her employees and she provides them with the only health care plan in Malawi among all lodge enterprises. Annie Fletcher is recognized as a change agent leader in Zomba and across her country, for her significant contributions to economic development in the cities where Annie's Lodges have been established, and for her continuous support for feeding programs for children in orphanages. As a former member of the Malawian Parliament she looked after the welfare of her country.

For change agent leaders like Annie there is much work to do. Political corruption still exists, and I saw this firsthand in the unfinished school houses at Malemia. To get a school in their village, villagers first make the bricks and fire them in pits in the ground. Next, they build the schoolhouse walls. Finally, they petition the government to come put a tin roof on each classroom. The government says that all the schoolhouses at Malemia have roofs on them, but there was Mr. Mwanja and his Standard 7 students—70 or more—having school in the rain with no roof on their classroom. Yet the children still come. They come to learn and they sit in the rain and inclement weather seeking knowledge.

In Malawi, happiness and joy are not measured in terms of what you have. The children did not have much in terms of finances, fancy clothes, or even shoes, but they had lots of joy, and shared it with us daily.

66 IN THE SUMMER OF 2007, FOUR NORTH CAROLINA A&T STUDENTS SPENT THREE AND ONE HALF WEEKS IN MALAWI. 99

Tonya: Humility

I learned much by interacting with Malawians, and humility ranked at the top of the list. It was easy to assume that I would have more to offer Malawians than they could offer me. Living in a country that is known for its progress and advances in many areas made me high-minded when it came to thinking about or interacting with those living in a developing country. I can imagine the feeling being similar to how I envision some privileged people reacting, interacting, and thinking about underprivileged people in the United States. As I entered the country I realized that it was not much different from some of the rural areas in North Carolina. Interacting with the people made it evident that not only did I not have any special knowledge or wisdom to offer, but in fact I could learn much from them. I was a stranger in their land, was viewed by them as wealthy and knowledgeable, but I was treated with the same love and respect that Malawians give to their own family, friends, and neighbors. I no longer felt like the leader/teacher from a privileged country, but a student learning from wise and experienced people.

I once heard Cornell West say, "In order to lead people you have to love the people, and in order to save the people you have to serve the people." As a leader, whether it's locally or globally, in order to connect with people, one must be humble.

How can one lead effectively without loving those being led? There has to be a connection and the connection is made through the humility of the leader.

Liz: The Long Way to Lilongwe

The notion of zero is not a concept in Malawi, where everything is something that can be used in some way. Children make toys from telephone wire, soccer balls from grocery bags. This idea dawned on me as we attempted, at a teacher's request, to teach multiplication to a Standard 4 class. We thought the children would benefit from knowing the identity property of multiplication by one, as well as what happens when you multiply by zero. However the children—about 100 in the classroom that day—continued to tell us that 4 x 0 should surely be at least 4 or so.

In exasperation, all of us—Tonya, Jackie, Vanessa, and I—lined up in front of the children, who possessed little English but knew well the word "banana." We each, in turn, mimed that we had "no bananas." Then the children helped us count: 1, 2, 3, 4 ladies, each with how many bananas? No bananas! So how many bananas do four ladies—with no bananas each—have? Whether the children caught on or not, from that day until our last, at whatever time of day, hordes of children could be heard mimicking our chant of "no bananas." Our struggle to teach zero should have told us something about how Malawians view their world, but the greater insight was yet to come.

On the final day before departing from Malawi we were traveling in the van that had served us from the day our plane landed in the country's capital city, Lilongwe. As we bumped our way across an infamous stretch of byway that was paved in a few spots, washed out by the rains in many, and never paved in others, we learned the meaning of the Malawian saying, "rough as the road to Mangochi." Once on a better road everyone breathed a sigh of relief until our driver signaled that something was amiss, stopped the van, and we got off, more than 50 kilometers from the nearest town, Salima. A bearing had frozen up and gotten so hot that it melted onto the van's axle. Nothing would do but for our driver to catch the next mini-bus to Salima to find a repairman and bring him back to fix the van. That was at noon. At 5:00 P.M. the Malawian winter sun was sinking as the driver returned with a young man carrying a hammer and a screwdriver. All flashlights were recruited to light the repairman's labors, which lasted long into the night.

To our dismay the village children who'd swarmed us all afternoon for pens, bits of candy and fruit, or American coins disappeared into the darkness. In the silence that remained we confronted our vulnerability. We were stranded by the side of the road in the African bush, many miles from our destination. There was no light and the coolness of the African winter night had begun to descend, along with our spirits.

Every household possessed a machete, and most of us had read about the uses of these as weapons in less hospitable African countries.

Then in the distance we spotted a procession of children moving in the darkness toward us, led by one bearing a coal to light a bonfire. Within moments American students and Malawian children were trading games, dances, and life stories around the light of a fire that warmed both hands and hearts. At one point the older boys retreated, then returned to lead the younger children in a rousing chorus of the Malawian national anthem. In the light of the fire with the Milky Way over our heads, we Americans rendered our best version of our own anthem, followed by a bicultural songfest of epic proportions. As I watched on the periphery, a man from the village gently touched my elbow and said, "Do not lose mind." Those words aimed at recognition and comfort linger in my memory to this very day.

> **66 WITHIN MOMENTS AMERICAN STUDENTS AND MALAWIAN CHILDREN WERE TRADING GAMES, DANCES, AND LIFE STORIES AROUND THE LIGHT OF A FIRE THAT WARMED BOTH HANDS AND HEARTS. 99**

At the flash-lit work station a loaves-and-fishes miracle was taking place in response to the young mechanic's paucity of tools. As he labored away with his small hammer, out of the bush came an anonymous helper with a bigger one. When a hacksaw was needed, one came, and when its blade broke, a larger hacksaw was proffered by yet another villager. Near midnight, when all songs had been sung, the old bearing was removed, a new one in place, and we loaded onto the van to arrive at our hotel in Lilongwe at 2:00 A.M. We climbed into bed in our clothes, and were awakened by hotel personnel telling us that one of our students' passports had been found that morning by the village fireside of the previous night's adventure. Our flight out of the country was that morning; no time was left to send a car all the way back to the scene of our roadside van repair. With no hope of recovering the missing passport, we stumbled through breakfast and prepared to leave for the airport. Yet an enterprising young man from the village miraculously caught a mini-bus and met our van, the passport in hand, at the last minute as we were leaving our hotel for the airport. All he asked in return was that we use his cell phone to call his boss and explain his absence from work that morning.

In our country we rate and rank everything from eggs to children. Zeroes abound in the American landscape, but Malawians see value in everything. Everyone is a dancer, musician, or artisan; everyone has a gift to give.

Jackie: Through the Lens and Looking Inside

Journaling offered me time for introspection and reflection. This was particularly beneficial when I could complete it in a timely manner that was relatively recent to the learning moment. Being able to review video clips of the previous day also provided a way for me to reconnect such that I was both observer and participant. Being able to literally re-play teachable moments gave me the opportunity to process the day's events and examine my own feelings about what had transpired and the lessons I had learned from those events. I found that both still photography and videography helped to isolate specific memorable moments, and these visualizations had the power to transport me to a time and place that I had forgotten about on my return to the U.S. The music and the children's voices, in particular, have the ability to remind me of the importance of service learning.

Leadership is not defined by one's station or position in life. It is defined by one's ability and willingness to openly share her knowledge base and value system with those who lack that knowledge. Different does not mean deficient. Real knowledge sometimes comes from unlearning what one has known for years. Change agent leadership has no boundaries.

Notes Toward a Global Ethic of Care

Since their return to the U.S., despite completing dissertations, articles, and research proposals while at the same time functioning as full-time leaders in their prospective fields, the 2007 Malawi travelers have continued their journeys of the heart. Their first act was to establish a scholarship that funds a Malawian student for four years of university education. This student began his classes to become a math teacher educator at Domasi College of Education in January 2008. Next they formed the Leadership Studies Program's first service organization, the Zikomo Leadership Society, to raise awareness of the needs of Malawians, and to fund-raise to continue their support of the Malemia child feeding program, future scholars at Domasi College of Education, and other similar projects.

Leaders shape visions of better futures that hold the power to move others to action. Yet those visions must come from somewhere—is it difficult to envision that which one has yet to see or experience. At no time has there been a greater need for leaders able to envision sustainable change for the many, instead of just the few. Such change integrates profitability with organizational integrity through:

Leadership for organizational longevity
Transparency that allows decisions to be scrutinized
Commitment to communities
Honesty in representation and transactions

Fair treatment and inclusion of workers in organizational decision making

Thoughtful approaches to the environment

Justice in all relationships

Respect for human rights across diverse global settings (Batstone, 2003, as cited in Hargreaves & Fink, 2006, p. 6).

Such leaders shape visions of better futures that hold the power to move others to action. Those visions emerge from a global ethic of care, a caring that begins in face-to-face relationships and extends to unknown others with whom they can now empathize. Leadership for the future must be able to imagine many unknown others, identify with them, and take their humanity into account. The Malawi study abroad experience provided a time and place for these leaders to find themselves among others. Preparation of leaders for the future must include similar opportunities for the development of a global ethic of care.

REFERENCES

Batstone, D. (2003). *Saving the corporate soul and (who knows?) maybe your own.* San Francisco: Jossey-Bass.

Borkman, T. (1999). *Understanding self-help/mutual aid: Experimental learning in the Commons.* Piscataway, NJ: Rutgers University Press.

Borkman, T. (2004). Self-help groups. In D. F. Burlingame (Ed.), *Philanthropy in America: A comprehensive historical encyclopedia, 2* (pp. 428–432). Santa Barbara, CA: ABC-Clio.

Brugman, D. (2003). The teaching and measurement of moral judgment development. *Journal of Moral Education, 32*, 195–203.

Callery, P. (1990). Moral learning in nursing education: A discussion of the usefulness of cognitive-developmental and social learning theories. *Journal of Advanced Nursing, 15*, 324–328.

Etzioni, A. (2004). *From empire to community: A new approach to international relations.* New York: Palgrave Macmillan.

Freire, P. (2006). *Pedagogy of the oppressed.* New York: Continuum.

Gorman, M., Duffy, J., & Heffernan, M. (1994). Service experience and the moral development of college students. *Religious Education, 89*(3), 422–431.

Hargreaves, A., & Fink, D. (2006). *Sustainable leadership.* San Francisco: Jossey-Bass.

Lave, J., & Wenger, E. (1991). *Situated cognition.* Cambridge: Cambridge University Press.

Mintzberg, H., & Gosling, J. (2002). Educating managers beyond borders. *Academy of Management Learning and Education, 1*(1), 64–76.

Noddings, N. (2003). *Caring: A feminine approach to ethics and moral education* (2nd ed.). Berkeley: University of California Press.

Rogers, G. (2002). Rethinking moral growth in college and beyond. *Journal of Moral Education, 31*(3), 325–338.

Secor, J., & Tyasto, M. (2005). Leadership for social change: Cross-cultural development of citizen leaders. In N. S. Huber & T. J. Wren (Eds.), *Building leadership bridges* (pp. 123–135). College Park, MD: International Leadership Association.

Wang, C., & Burris, M. A. (1994). Empowerment through photovoice: Portraits of participation. *Health Education Quarterly, 21*(2), 171–186.

Wilson, C. E. (2008). *The impact of international service experiences on adult development in moral reasoning and cultural intelligence.* Unpublished dissertation manuscript. North Carolina Agricultural and Technical State University.

LIZ BARBER is an experienced ethnographer whose literacy studies research extends across the pre- and postsecondary span, and into third world sites. She reviews articles for journals such as *Education Researcher* and the *International Journal of Qualitative Studies in Education*. A National Writing Project Fellow, Barber mentors the writing of doctoral students and teaches courses in globalization, and human development and relations, in the Interdisciplinary Leadership Studies Doctoral Program at North Carolina Agricultural and Technical State University.

CHARLES E. WILSON, M.Div., Ph.D., is a recent graduate (Spring 2008) of the Interdisciplinary Leadership Studies Program of North Carolina A&T State University. His area of academic interest is leader development, with specific attention to the developmental impact of international service experiences on moral development and cultural intelligence. He has presented at the International Leadership Association, the Academy of Management, the Asia Pacific Academy of Management and Business, and has most recently published an article on his research in the current issue (Fall 2008) of *Culture and Religion*.

VANESSA DUREN-WINFIELD, M.S., is a research coordinator and core faculty member of the B.S. in Health Care Management Program at Winston-Salem State University with 16 years of research experience. Her primary research interests include health literacy, CVD, diabetes, and HIV/AIDS, with special emphasis on the disparities in quality of care for minority populations. She has published both nationally and internationally, and has extensive experience in applying community-based research methods while working with diverse populations and multidisciplinary teams. She is a Ph.D. candidate (Fall 2008) at North Carolina A&T State University.

JACQUELINE GREENLEE is Director of Organizational Development for Guilford Technical Community College (Jamestown, NC). She earned her Ph.D. from the Interdisciplinary Leadership Studies Program at North Carolina A&T State University. The focus of her dissertation was "Lessons of Experience for Community College Leaders." Through her research Jackie identified the significant events by which community college administrators learn to lead and develop others. In her current role she is responsible for the development and implementation of her institution's comprehensive professional development program and strategic succession planning.

TOM SMITH is a professor of educational foundations at North Carolina A&T State University, has 13 years of experience as a public school teacher and 14 years as a professor at A&T. He is coauthor of the recent publication, *Chaos in the Classroom*, a text about dynamics, cognition, and classroom teaching. He currently teaches courses on service learning and social foundations. Smith actively searches for more enriching experiences for pre-service teachers. He also has an interest in student writing and the development of teacher beliefs.

Vision for Change: Partnering with Public Health Leaders Globally

By Nicola De Paul, Nancy M. Campbell, Anita Verna Crofts, Aaron Katz, and Elisabeth Mitchell

FOR SEVEN YEARS (SEPTEMBER 2000–2007), THE POPULATION LEADER-ship Program (PLP) at the University of Washington (UW) brought together outstanding professionals from selected developing countries who specialized in the areas of population, family planning, and reproductive health for a nine-month residential leadership development and management training in Seattle, Washington. Each year, a cohort of 10–12 such leaders worked together in a three-phase program to enhance their abilities, knowledge, and skills that would assist them in developing a vision and strategies for improving health services and policies in their respective countries. As a result, the PLP has a network of 78 Fellows in 24 countries, most of whom are making positive systemic change at the local, national, and international levels. Partnerships now exist between institutions in the Fellows' home countries as well as with the UW that are a direct result of the professional relationships developed during the PLP. The PLP experience[1] has provided an opportunity to learn about what program structure and strategies best support Fellows' growth as effective change agents in their unique cultural, political, and economic contexts. In this paper, the authors highlight and summarize the lessons learned from seven years of delivering the university-based, year-long residential leadership development and management training.

The PLP gained many valuable insights regarding what type of program design would best support participants in cross-cultural leadership development and management training, and also improve the transfer of knowledge and skills learned in the program to participants' home country environment. Based on these insights, the PLP is currently exploring variations of the U.S. university-based residential model of leadership development and management training that is described in this paper.

Program Overview

Consistent with the perspective that training is a process and not an outcome[2], the PLP included three distinct phases: Phase I, Readiness; Phase II, In-Residence; and Phase III, In-Country Implementation. Each phase included efforts to support Fellows' awareness of their leadership and management strengths and gaps, as well as their particular cultural orientation and how it supports or hinders their personal and professional vision for change. Each phase of the training was designed to integrate with and build on the activities and learning from the prior phase.

Phase I: Readiness. Effectiveness in all program phases began with Fellow selection. It was essential to identify participants who were well suited for the challenges of a nine-month (three academic quarters), in-residence program in a foreign country. The Fellows' level of motivation, ability to benefit from training, and ability to influence systems change are a few of the variables that were considered in the selection process. Due to the length of the In-Residence Phase, Fellows faced significant demands. Immersion in a new culture is stressful and requires a willingness and capacity to learn from unfamiliar circumstances. Fellows must have a desire to develop and grow at personal and professional levels. The resiliency essential to this type of program requires a "psychological hardiness," and adequate family, community, and organizational support.

For each year's cohort, program faculty and staff deliberately chose Fellows from both the public and nonprofit sectors with a commitment to gender balance and regional diversity. This mix of Fellows assured a variety of cultural perspectives and supported a focus on the whole person, not just the "academic self."

During the Readiness Phase, the staff and faculty modeled the type of communication Fellows could expect in all program phases, creating an environment conducive to knowledge transfer. Deliberate and thoughtful communication by staff and faculty that demonstrated responsiveness and cultural competence and emphasized the value of each Fellow to the overall Fellowship experience helped establish reasonable participant expectations. Well-planned communication also helped to build the critical trust that led to the collaborative relationships required for success in the subsequent In-Residence and In-Country Phases. What Fellows could expect from the program and what the program expected of Fellows was clearly presented. Cultural diversity within the cohort and differences in the U.S. such as pace of life, heavy use of e-mail communication, and graduate student lifestyles were discussed to better prepare Fellows for success in a new environment. This preparation laid the foundation for the development of strong relations among Fellows and with faculty and staff, which in turn promoted the development of a learning community and strengthened the likelihood of knowledge transfer.

Activities and assignments required during Phase I were designed to help the Fellows prepare for adjustment to issues ranging from a different climate, to the rigors of graduate school, to the challenge of a program that required continuous self-reflection. All incoming Fellows were encouraged to connect with their program mentor, "Friendship Connection," and alumni Fellows, and were required to complete a 360-degree leadership assessment during this phase. The assessment, which arguably reflects an American bias toward leadership, was used as one venue to discuss the impact of culture on leadership ideals and beliefs in Phase II. This helped the Fellows begin to think about their leadership and management capacities prior to their arrival for the In-Residence Phase, and making connections with people affiliated with the program helped prepare the Fellows for their cultural transition.

> 66 CULTURAL DIVERSITY WITHIN THE COHORT AND
> DIFFERENCES IN THE U.S. SUCH AS PACE OF LIFE,
> HEAVY USE OF E-MAIL COMMUNICATION, AND
> GRADUATE STUDENT LIFESTYLES WERE DISCUSSED
> TO BETTER PREPARE FELLOWS FOR SUCCESS IN A
> NEW ENVIRONMENT. 99

Phase II: In-Residence. The underlying premise of Phase I: Leadership opportunities present themselves daily in every environment. This phase was designed to help Fellows recognize these opportunities and translate classroom training and experience into personal, political, organizational, and systems thinking. Phase II, the In-Residence Phase, intentionally created networking, mentoring, and professional opportunities that carried over into Phase III.

This holistic approach to leadership development did not go unnoticed by the Fellows. One Fellow described the PLP's impact in an annual evaluation this way:

> ... what the PLP has to offer is far more developed and multi-layered compared to other leadership programs. Its strength lies in the complexity of exposures and experiences that the Fellow faces in the one-year residence in another (alien) culture ... the PLP eventually delivers a Leader who is more empowered, with a wider world vision and a deeper understanding of [the world], because she has been where few have ventured ever before.

A key strategy for Fellows to enhance their leadership skills and abilities was the deliberate creation of a multicultural and cross-sector cohort. Sharing the experience of being in a foreign culture, Fellows tended to learn, work, and play together, which resulted in lifelong friendships, strong professional ties, and collaborative cross-national initiatives. Examples of the nature and impact of these friendships, ties, and projects will be provided throughout the paper. This intensive peer interaction enhanced the learning that occurred in and outside the classroom. Although not visible to the Fellows at first, many of the issues they faced transcended cultures and political boundaries. The multicultural context shrank the world, removed countries from the abstract, and linked them inextricably with human faces, inspiring Fellows to think of their leadership path as interconnected with global leadership development and worldwide support. Often it was only following the fellowship year, when Fellows returned to their home countries, that they recognized the significance of the multicultural interaction facilitated by the PLP. For example, in sharing her experience one Fellow stated that

> *The new cultures in which the Fellows find themselves are never aggressively pushed onto them to accept or understand, but are revealed and unfolded through simple occasions like house parties, home get-togethers, etc., where opportunity to exchange intercultural ideas and lifestyles develops new dimensions of understanding. Learning is not just inside the campus but outside too . . . each Fellow challenges the views of others . . . biases and prejudice are shed to be replaced not just by tolerance but with some real understanding and empathy.*

In order to strengthen their skills, Fellows engaged in a variety of activities during Phase II. They took part in the Leadership and Reproductive Health seminars, two required weekly three-hour sessions, as well as additional classes of their own choosing. Fellows were also assigned individual mentors, provided opportunities for professional affiliations, and connected to the local community through social networks and host families.

The Population Leadership Seminar was designed to provide Fellows with opportunities to think about, apply, and learn about their own leadership skills and abilities. It provided a time for reflection about personal, academic, community, and professional experiences in a cross-cultural setting. The class design allowed for exploration of the social, psychological, spiritual, and physical dimensions that leaders must nurture within themselves. Although the seminar explored what leaders do within the context of teams and organizations, it focused primarily on an individual's efforts to demonstrate effective leadership.

In the seminar, program faculty provided the Fellows time to explore the meaning and role of leadership and how leaders adapt to different contexts by observing other leaders, undertaking a variety of assessments (including the Phase I 360-degree assessment), engaging with other leaders in discussion and developmental activities, public speaking, professional networking events, and ceremonial and award events that recognize and honor leaders. Practice and application of leadership skills and tools both inside and outside the seminar were used as opportunities for reflecting about the Fellows' leadership abilities. Each Fellow created a leadership development plan in the second quarter of the academic year to identify concrete strategies for skill development during the remainder of Phase II and Phase III of the program. The leadership development plan also included a component focused on strengthening various skills, including communication, public speaking, networking, collaboration, and leading through change.

66 ALTHOUGH NOT VISIBLE TO THE FELLOWS AT FIRST, MANY OF THE ISSUES THEY FACED TRANSCENDED CULTURES AND POLITICAL BOUNDARIES. 99

In the Reproductive Health (RH) Seminar, faculty helped Fellows examine the conceptual foundations of family planning and reproductive health policy and the social context in which health policies and services operate. Faculty addressed essential management skills such as planning, implementation, negotiation, ethics, financial and personnel management, public/private partnerships, policy analysis, advocacy, management of political environments, communication, and evaluation. The RH Seminar offered Fellows an opportunity to explore how the leadership knowledge and skills they gained in the Leadership Seminar could be applied to needed changes at the international, national, and local levels.

As their final project for the Leadership and Reproductive Health seminars, Fellows developed their own Home Plan, which equipped them for reentry, both in their professional and personal lives, and provided them with a concrete five-year roadmap for implementing their vision for change. As one Fellow said,

> Writing a Home Plan helped me to articulate what my ideal long-term goals and objectives are. When I got home it helped in strengthening my resolve to stay in the development sector even in the face of difficulties in securing jobs of choice. As stated in the plan, I know that my life work is improving the lives of people in whichever way I can and that is what I focus on.

A critical component of the fellowship year was to connect each Fellow with a mentor (UW faculty and professional staff and community leaders) who provided academic, professional, and career guidance. Fellows and mentors were carefully paired, generally based on common professional or geographic areas of work. In addition to quarterly meetings with mentors and Fellows and two social gatherings designed for mentors and Fellows only, the PLP provided minimal guidelines about the role of mentors and frequency of meetings and suggested discussion topics. As considerable flexibility was built into this component, mentor-Fellow relationships and frequency of contact varied depending on the individuals.

Mentors and program staff often worked in tandem, which resulted in the PLP being more responsive to Fellows' needs and to the development of deeper relationships during Phase II and Phase III. Many Fellows continued to collaborate with mentors once back in their home countries. For example, the executive director of a Seattle women's health clinic served as a mentor to a Mexican PLP Fellow who worked in Mexico City on issues of women's reproductive health rights. Professional and personal connections between this mentor and Fellow have continued to thrive as they share challenges, strategies, and successes. In another case, a Fellow and his mentor collaborated on developing and leading policy advocacy workshops organized by other PLP Fellows in Nigeria and Uganda. Still another mentor and Fellow were invited to present together at a conference in a second Fellow's country.

Fellows were also paired with "Friendship Connection" families from the Seattle community. These pairings provided Fellows with further opportunities to develop cross-cultural competence as they learned about the host culture and about themselves as they interacted with that culture. These relationships provided opportunities for Fellows to get to know their Friendship Connections well and, for some, to establish deep relationships that continue to support and enrich Fellows' personal and professional lives. Fellows often mention their experiences with their Friendship Connection families—going boating, attending a basketball game or child's birthday party, or having Thanksgiving dinner in the family's home—as unforgettable exposure to U.S. culture. With these shared experiences during the residential year and ever-increasing access to good communication technology, Fellows and Friendship Connection families are able to sustain their relationships.

Phase III: In-Country Implementation. The premise underlying Phase III of the PLP is that ongoing support and collaboration on in-country projects enhances knowledge transfer, retention of learned skills, and the effectiveness of initiatives undertaken by Fellows. The PLP recognized that the organizational culture Fellows return to may impede their ability to behave differently, use their new skills, or implement their visions for change. Knowledge transfer between cultures and countries is identified as a challenge throughout the program. Fellows were supported in Phase II to begin thinking about the nature of their home organization and community and how they may help or impede their knowledge transfer. Fellows received program support in Phase III through a variety of strategies that included: check-in regarding Fellows' Home Plans, connection to a virtual global community of leaders, annual Fellows conferences, small and large grants, professional development support, support for UW graduate student summer interns to work in returned Fellows' home organizations, and continued access to UW libraries and databases.

A key strategy for supporting the Fellows' transition to their home country was the Home Plan, which identified specific professional goals and challenges that would have to be overcome for knowledge transfer to be sustained. Fellows were encouraged to explore the various Phase III support mechanisms and to identify those that might be useful in implementing their Home Plans and affecting systemic change. Support for attending conferences, ongoing professional training, and Master-level education (for a limited number of Fellows), along with ongoing interaction with PLP staff and faculty, significantly contributed to Fellows' success as leaders. Follow-up regarding Home Plan implementation by PLP staff also supported knowledge transfer by providing a strong sense of encouragement and accountability for plan implementation.

A virtual community through a sophisticated program website design has created an avenue for Fellows to retain some of the social support and sense of connection developed during Phase II. The PLP website has a comprehensive resource section that houses presentations, documents, and other material that was originally introduced in the seminar, and is now accessible to Fellows and their organizations. In addition, Fellows submit papers of their work in-country, which are then housed on the website for wide distribution.

> **❝ A VIRTUAL COMMUNITY THROUGH A SOPHISTICATED PROGRAM WEBSITE DESIGN HAS CREATED AN AVENUE FOR FELLOWS TO RETAIN SOME OF THE SOCIAL SUPPORT AND SENSE OF CONNECTION DEVELOPED DURING PHASE II. ❞**

Fellows have also created in-country working groups to address shared issues. For example, five Fellows from Pakistan, the Philippines, and India formed an advocacy working group, and a series of advocacy training workshops were held by a group of six Fellows working collaboratively in Nigeria, Pakistan, the Philippines, and Uganda. Some of these collaborations have been funded, in part, by larger PLP grants, which Fellows leveraged to obtain additional support from other organizations.

Lessons Learned

Each year of the program lessons were learned about what makes an effective university-based, residential model of cross-cultural leadership development and management training. Lessons sprung from daily interactions with Fellows during the residential year and also from continued communication with Fellows who had returned to their home countries. The following seven lessons are highlighted as crucial to the development and maintenance of a successful program.

> **“ LESSONS WERE LEARNED ABOUT WHAT MAKES AN EFFECTIVE UNIVERSITY-BASED, RESIDENTIAL MODEL OF CROSS-CULTURAL LEADERSHIP DEVELOPMENT AND MANAGEMENT TRAINING. ”**

1. Use a formal evaluation process to assess the effectiveness of knowledge transfer.

One of the strengths of the PLP design was the inclusion of an ongoing, internal program evaluation. The PLP evaluation began when the first cohort of Fellows arrived in September 2000 and has continued throughout the life of the program. The evaluation included extensive interviews and questionnaires with Fellows at the beginning and end of their year in Seattle and written evaluations of specific program activities. In addition, follow-up interviews were conducted at PLP annual conferences, and e-mail surveys were conducted with Fellows who had returned home. Input was also solicited from PLP staff and mentors and representatives of organizations where Fellows held professional affiliations. A final, comprehensive, seven-year evaluation report provided rich data on the Fellows, the program, and trends over time.

The evaluation allowed program faculty to continuously assess the effectiveness of the program, and since the Fellows were highly skilled senior executives, they were invited to partner with faculty to enhance the program's strategy and design. The input regarding both Phase II and Phase III helped the faculty to understand how to improve program structure and strategies to increase the Fellows' ability to implement progressive change in their countries.

2. Support for knowledge transfer must begin as early as recruitment.

Choosing candidates who have the greatest likelihood of learning and growing is the first step in ensuring knowledge transfer and vision implementation. Careful screening and a thoughtful selection process identified Fellows with experience and goals consistent with the program mission. The alignment of Fellows' goals with the program mission contributed to improve Fellow satisfaction during Phase II, the In-Residence Phase, and increased success in vision implementation in Phase III, the

In-Country Phase. A thorough communication plan in the Readiness Phase allowed Fellows to learn more from the In-Residence Phase.

3. Focus on leadership and management skills and abilities.

A dedicated Leadership Seminar (originally, the PLP had a single seminar that included leadership, management, and policy topics) that focuses directly on the interpersonal leadership skills needed to effectively implement program, policy, and advocacy skills is essential to knowledge transfer. This program element should focus on the individual and how his or her personal mission and strengths and weaknesses will support or impede his or her implementation efforts.

4. The Phase II program must be long enough to build trusting relationships that can develop into professional partnerships among Fellows, their organizations, and institutions in developed countries.

Trust takes time. Trusting relationships are the foundation that has resulted in several successful Phase III initiatives. The trust developed during the lengthy Phase II resulted in Fellows reaching out to Fellows in other countries to achieve mutual goals. An example of this was an initiative among Fellows from Sudan, Ethiopia, and Uganda in which they conducted joint research on peer-to-peer public health education programs in internally displaced-person camps in greater Khartoum.

Another example of the importance of trust was the start-up of a "mapping project" funded by the Bill and Melinda Gates Foundation. A UW team identified 24 countries in Asia and Africa in which researchers would map the political environments in the health sector to understand the organizations and networks that were active and influential. The PLP program was asked to partner on the project because of the strength of the PLP Fellows network. For each target country, the project required an in-country coordinator who was experienced and well respected in that country's health sector so as to facilitate access to key organizations, and who could conduct interviews, circulate questionnaires, synthesize data from across the country (and in some cases, from multiple researchers), and prepare a comprehensive country report. In 15 countries, PLP Fellows served as country coordinators, readily accepting the invitation to participate despite modest compensation and (initially) a vague scope of work. In the nine target countries without PLP Fellows, the start-up time was at least double and the costs in staff time considerably more. The duration of the PLP meant that Fellows not only develop trusting relationships that facilitate such collaboration, but feel a kinship to work that involves the university they attended.

5. Use multiple approaches to create the social support needed for knowledge transfer.

Ongoing social support is necessary to nurture new skills, especially in the situation of an organizational environment that might not accept change. Creating methods for social support to maintain the desired behaviors is needed in all three program phases. Forms of social support can range from sharing accurate and timely information, to the assignment of mentors and Friendship Connections, to providing access to social and professional events, listservs and websites, and institutional partnerships.

6. Keep the program focused on change in the home environment.

Over the program's history, staff and faculty learned that Fellows would benefit from more active support when they returned home. Strategies that kept Fellows connected with each other and with their UW colleagues, including active e-mail listservs, a dynamic program website, and opportunities for networking at conferences, help to enhance the sense of a leadership community and, thus, to sustain knowledge transfer. In addition, small financial grants were provided specifically to support the initiatives that Fellows sought to carry out soon after returning to their home countries. For example, a Fellow in Sierra Leone used her small grant to expand the efforts of her work reintegrating young women (who were victims of sexual violence during the civil war) back into their communities with income-generation skills.

Many of the program changes made over time related directly to enhancing Fellows' ability to develop a clear personal and professional vision and to translate their vision into a mission that could be implemented in their organizations, networks, and countries. Faculty made changes that included enhancing Phase I communication, adding a seminar focused largely on interpersonal leadership skills, changing curricula of the two seminars, making additions to professional development opportunities during Phase II, and providing stronger support for and nurturing of the mentor relationships.

7. Understanding the organizational context of the Fellows is essential for success in Phase III.

Ultimately, Fellows return to a particular organizational context. One of the challenges of knowledge transfer in leadership development is lack of support in the home environment for the returning program participant. It is difficult for a Fellow to implement a vision for change if their newfound knowledge and skills are not valued or if no support exists for their strategy or goal in their organization. Phase III support must be designed to meet the needs of the organizational context of the Fellow. One strategy to support knowledge transfer is the formation of a network of Fellows within a country, which can bolster confidence and provide the support needed to assist Fellows in retaining the skills and abilities which may be rejected by their home organization. For example, a Filipina Fellow returned to her work in a national health program and encountered challenges in obtaining a promised promotion. Through careful counsel and support from both the Fellows in the Philippines and her PLP cohort worldwide, she was able to design strategies, receive support, and ultimately succeed at obtaining the promotion without creating disharmony in the workplace.

Another form of partnership is that between the training institution (the University of Washington) and the PLP Fellows' home institutions. An example of such a partnership is the Sudan Leadership and Management training program. Following his PLP fellowship year in Seattle, a Sudanese Fellow became the Deputy Director of the Sudanese National AIDS Program in the Ministry of Health (MOH). He invited the PLP to collaborate with the MOH on a multilayered effort to build the leadership and management capacity of Sudan's health system, one of his main goals upon returning home. The initiative began with a three-part pilot training for MOH program managers in one state, Blue Nile State.[3] The partnership is now in the process of scaling up the pilot into a national training program involving health system managers from ten states and will help build the federal MOH's capacity to conduct similar training programs in the future.

The PLP experience has provided an opportunity to participate in additional partnerships. Over time it has become clear that successful partnerships have several common elements, including: (1) Invitation: based on the interests and articulated needs of in-country partners; (2) True partnership: the PLP and in-country partners must commit staff, time, and money to the project, making it truly collaborative and ensuring a strong sense of shared ownership and purpose; (3) Mutual accountability: shared ownership naturally leads to mutual accountability; (4) Foster new connections: carefully selected training partners will connect previously disconnected sectors and organizations; (5) Promote knowledge transfer and sustainability; and (6) Build capacity through linking PLP network (Fellows) with various strategic organizations within the host country, to enhance policy development and implementation.

Long-term success, the ability of Fellows to use their training to successfully make progressive, systemic change, is greatly enhanced to the extent that the training institution has similar ongoing partnerships with home organizations. These partnerships provide an additional vehicle for Fellows to overcome resistance from their home organizations to their vision for change.

Summary

The PLP had a planning year and seven cohorts of Fellows from which to learn about knowledge transfer in a global health leadership and management development program. By using a rigorous evaluation system, the faculty and staff of the PLP have been able to continuously assess what strategies are most effective in supporting global leaders to improve health services and policies in their respective countries. The PLP experience supports the tenets of training transfer models[4] that suggest an individual's learning in training, performance after training, and ability to make organizational change are influenced by the trainee's capacity, the training program design, and the climate of the organization to which the trainee returns. The most effective PLP program design was one that had progressive stages of learning where each phase built upon the one that preceded it. Each phase was designed to support the ultimate program goal, which was enhancing the ability of the Fellows to implement change in their home country health system.

Selecting Fellows who aligned with the program mission was not enough to ensure learning in Phase II and therefore success in Phase III. Fellow selection was not based solely on professional status, education, and ability, but included a consideration of the Fellow's motivation and capacity to learn in a program that required not only full immersion in the American culture but the ability to work with and learn from Fellows from many very different cultures. Finding Fellows who were both highly motivated and also open to learning about themselves through a cross-cultural experience was a key predictor of how much the Fellow would learn in Phase II of the program. The program also moved away from selecting individuals from numerous countries and concentrated on building cohorts in eight countries[5]. This created a cohort of Fellows within a country who could better support and assist each other in all Phases, but particularly in Phase III of the program.

Next to Fellow selection, the clear communication of expectations and pre-Fellowship preparatory exercises were critical elements of Fellow success in Phase II. Clearly communicating expectations and creating venues for virtual introductions and communication between Fellows, faculty, and staff assisted in the entry to Phase II.

For effective knowledge transfer, Phase II must focus not only on management, policy, and advocacy skills. Extensive time must be devoted to enhancing the interpersonal skills of the training participants. It is a misnomer to call the PLP a training program. It is a leadership development program and, as such, concentrates on the conceptual, technical, and interpersonal skills of the participants. The added value of a cross-cultural cohort is the ability to hold up the mirror of culture so participants can understand their own strengths and weaknesses as leaders within the unique dynamics of their home culture.

Enhancing the development of interpersonal leadership skills and the transfer of those skills to the home culture of the participants requires sufficient time to establish trust. Trusting relationships between Fellows and with faculty and staff were the bridge to partnerships that enhanced knowledge transfer in Phase III and enabled work toward systemic change. Similarly ample social support was needed for all program phases. Each phase created transitions that resulted in challenges, moments of anxiety, and frustration. The difficulty of such moments was reduced when a social support network was available to help ease transitions. Whether dealing with the inability to negotiate a foreign culture or the rejection of new learning by the home organization, social support helps Fellows to continue with their efforts to use their new skills to innovate and improve health care systems.

Recognizing that the context that each Fellow returns to is very different, the PLP faculty and staff used a variety of strategies to support Fellows in Phase III. Knowledge transfer is easiest where the home organization or system respects the expertise and experience of the Fellows and welcomes their new ideas; unfortunately, this is not always the case. Fellows often returned to environments that did not embrace change and rejected the new approaches and strategies of the Fellows. Social support, while very helpful, is not always enough to support knowledge transfer. Program faculty discovered that creating partnerships with Fellows' home organizations or systems helps to create the opportunity and space for Fellows to use their new skills and thus to make system changes. These partnerships can come in the form of a small project grant from the PLP to a Fellow, collaborations between Fellows of different countries or within a country, or partnerships between global "north" organizations and those in the Fellows' home countries.

Creating a global health leadership program design that can facilitate knowledge transfer and system change requires time, commitment, and resources. It requires a willingness on behalf of the leadership development agency to partner with its participants to build the trust and relationships necessary for learning. As learning partners, participants, faculty, and staff can join together to create sustainable relationships and partnerships that can transform the health care delivery systems of the world.

NOTES

1. The PLP no longer provides an in-residence leadership development program but focuses on in-country training.

2. For a review of some of the literature on strategies used before, during, and after training, see M. Anthony Machin in K. Kraiger (Ed.), *Creating, implementing, and managing effective training and development* (pp. 263–301), San Francisco: Jossey-Bass.

3. This is another example of how personal relationships matter; the minister of health in BNS strongly supported the UW PLP partnership and advocated for the pilot to take place in his state, in part because he spent 18 months at UW conducting research in a postgraduate program.

4. See models such as Holton (1996).

5. Eight countries have a minimum of four Fellows. There are two additional countries that have three Fellows.

REFERENCES

Holton, E. E. (1996). The Flawed Four-Level Evaluation Model. *Human Resource Development Quarterly*, 7(1), 5–22.

Kraiger, K. (2002). *Creating, implementing, and managing effective training and development: State-of-the-art lessons for practice.* The professional practice series. San Francisco: Jossey-Bass.

NICOLA DE PAUL is Program Coordinator for the Population Leadership Program at the University of Washington. Since 2005 she has managed the logistical components of the program, coordinating the on-campus experience for the Fellows in-residence and acting as liaison to the international organizations with which the Population Leadership Program has partnered to conduct public health leadership trainings in Ethiopia, Sudan, and Pakistan. Nicola holds a B.A. degree in theology with a specialization in curriculum development from Seattle Pacific University.

NANCY M. CAMPBELL has 20 years of experience as an executive with both public and nonprofit agencies. As a senior lecturer for the Evans School of Public Affairs at the University of Washington, Nancy provides leadership development for mid-career professionals. As a consultant to government and nonprofit organizations, she uses training, coaching, and assessment to help individuals and groups increase self-awareness and self-management, lead high-impact change, align organizational practice with mission, and plan for succession and transition.

ANITA VERNA CROFTS is Director of Communication and Outreach for the Population Leadership Program at the University of Washington. In this capacity, she oversees both the documentation and promotion of continuing partnerships with 78 international PLP Fellows in more than 20 countries worldwide. She holds a B.A. degree from Haverford College in anthropology and East Asian studies, and a Master of Public Administration degree from the University of Washington.

AARON KATZ is a senior lecturer in the Department of Health Services, University of Washington School of Public Health and Community Medicine, and is director of the Packard-Gates Population Leadership Program. Aaron received the Award for Excellence from the American Public Health Association in 2006 and the UW School of Public Health's Outstanding Teaching Award in 2004. He received a B.S. degree from the University of Wisconsin–Madison in 1974 and a certificate [master] of public health degree from the University of Toronto in 1975.

ELISABETH MITCHELL is Director of Leadership Initiatives for the Population Leadership Program at the University of Washington. She served as a Peace Corps volunteer in the Sultanate of Oman from 1979 to 1982 and has recently relocated there. She is the recipient of the 2007 UW Distinguished Woman Award, the 2004 Evans School Award for Outstanding Staff, the 2003 Foundation for Understanding Through Students International Citizen Award, and is a nominee for UW Distinguished Staff for 2008. She holds a B.A. in political science and philosophy from Lewis and Clark College and a master's in Teaching English as a Second Language from the University of Washington.

Transitioning from Employee Portraits from the Past

Leadership and Employee Commitment in Modern Lithuania

By Dail Fields, Evaldas Andzius, and Ruta Krisciunaite

DURING THE PERIOD OF COMMUNIST RULE, THE LEADERSHIP AP-proaches used by Lithuanian managers were largely determined by the imposed social and political order. This roughly translated to domination of politics over economy, production targets over efficiency, and centralization over decentralization (Diskiene, 1997). The transition from a command economy to a market economy, in process since Lithuania's independence in 1991, has required not only major policy changes aimed at correcting macro-economic imbalances and micro-economic inefficiencies of the past, but also fundamental changes in the management culture and behavior (Diskiene, 1997; United Nations Development Program, 1995). Traditions of sound economic management existed in the pre–Second World War era, but the Soviet-imposed command economy eradicated most of these traditions in Lithuania (Diskiene, 1997). As a result, basic managerial and entrepreneurial skills have been neglected during the last decades, and considerable time and effort may be required to reintroduce them into the new generation of Lithuanian enterprises and business managers. The creation of a market economy in Lithuania and subsequent entry into the European Union in 2004 required a radical transformation of the values entrenched under the socialist economy, including a sense of security, conformity, obedience, self-effacement, and deference to the decisions of higher-level authorities. Managerial behaviors that grew into bureaucratic norms discouraged qualities of great importance in the transformed market economy including innovativeness, entrepreneurship, and strategic thinking about the future of the organization (Diskiene, 1997). These managerial norms included an implicit model of subordinate employees needing to be micro-managed in order to properly perform their jobs. For example, a survey of manufacturing companies in Lithuania conducted in the 1990s found that many managers within these organizations believed that employees needed close supervision and direction. Indeed, these managers expressed a prevailing view that highly authoritarian management practices that were frequently used in Soviet organizations are not only effective today but are actually preferred by employees within current Lithuanian companies (Diskiene, 1997).

❝ THE CREATION OF A MARKET ECONOMY IN LITHUANIA AND SUBSEQUENT ENTRY INTO THE EUROPEAN UNION IN 2004 REQUIRED A RADICAL TRANSFORMATION OF THE VALUES ENTRENCHED UNDER THE SOCIALIST ECONOMY. ❞

In this chapter, we present information from two recent studies of employees in Lithuanian organizations that were conducted by the three authors. The results of these studies led us to the conclusion that the traditional managerial view of Lithuanian employee needs and preferences is obsolete. The data from these studies show that the organizational commitment and loyalty of employees in modern Lithuania may depend on the use of leadership approaches that assure employees of just treatment and active concern for employee welfare and development, rather than authoritarian rule. Taking steps to implement management and leadership practices that increase the likelihood that employees are loyal and committed to Lithuanian companies is an increasingly urgent need, as immigration to other EU countries has been likened to a "brain drain" currently in Lithuania (Bagdanavicius & Jodkoniene, 2008; Miskinis, 2008). The results presented here suggest that contrary to prevailing views grounded in past practices, Lithuanian employees appreciate fair and concerned treatment from their leaders. Indeed, the willingness of these employees to be committed and loyal to an organization may depend on the degree to which leaders and managers provide such supportive and just behaviors (Cotton & Tuttle, 1986). Not surprisingly, Lithuanian employees, like those in the USA and other parts of Europe, choose to remain with their organizations longer when they perceive that leaders care about employee work outcomes like fair treatment and support for development (Hale & Fields, 2007; McFarlin & Sweeney, 1992).

In the following sections, we review two studies that we conducted in which the relationship between leadership practices and employee commitment was examined. We pay particular attention to those aspects of management and leadership behaviors that seem to be most strongly related to increased employee commitment and reduced interest in changing jobs. In these studies were two separate but related questions. In the first study, we examined the extent to which the commitment of Lithuanian employees to an organization is affected by the employees' perceptions of justice and support within the organization. In the second study, we examined the extent to which organizational commitment of Lithuanian employees is affected significantly by the extent to which the leaders in the organization show interest in the employees, exhibit humility, and involve the employees in creating the goals of the company. These investigations cover employees within both private- and public-sector employers. After reviewing the results of each of these studies, we will discuss the leadership implications for employing organizations and employers in modern Lithuania.

Empirical Studies

Study 1: Justice, Support, and Employee Commitment

The focus of this study was on the extent to which beliefs that employees are treated justly by an employer (referred to as organizational justice) are antecedents of organizational commitment among Lithuanian workers. The authors also consider the extent to which perceptions of organizational support for an employee are related to commitment to the organization.

First, some background on organizational commitment. The concept of organizational commitment is a way of characterizing the strength of an employee's identification with and involvement in an organization. It includes a strong belief in and acceptance of the organization's goals and values, a willingness to show considerable effort, and a strong desire to remain with the organization (Mowday, Porter, & Steers, 1982). Organizational commitment has been consistently related with positive organizational outcomes, such as reduced turnover and absenteeism and higher motivation and productivity (Meyer & Allen, 1997).

Organizational commitment is defined in terms of three components (Allen & Meyer, 1997). The first is *affective commitment*, defined as employees' emotional attachment and identification with the organization. Affective commitment is an employee's emotional attachment to the organization where an employee "wants to" rather than "has to" work in that organization (Allen & Meyer, 1990). Affective commitment is often related to an employee's job satisfaction, satisfaction with his or her supervisor, job autonomy, and the perceptions of organizational fairness. It reflects an employee's identification with the organization and can be characterized as a positive interaction between an individual and his or her employing organization. Affective commitment may also represent the employee's belief that he or she shares similar values with an organization (Abbott, White, & Charles, 2005). Commitment has been described as a measure of the strength of an individual's identification with and involvement in a particular organization (Allen & Meyer, 1991).

The second form of commitment is termed *normative*, defined as a feeling of obligation to be loyal to the organization, a need to fulfill a sense of duty. Normative commitment is a feeling of obligation to remain in the organization because of socialization experiences and a moral attitude of commitment. Normative commitment is seen as "the totality of internalized normative pressures to act in a way which meets organizational goals and interests," or the "moral thing to do" (Allen & Meyer, 1991, p. 66). The third type is *continuance commitment*, which is defined as an employee's commitment to the organization in light of assessment of the costs and benefit of leaving the organization for alternative employment. Continuance commitment is a behavior of remaining in the organization resulting from the possible costs of leaving the organization. One of the reasons why employees continue working in organizations is accumulation of "side-bets," which is individual investment and benefits within the organization such as pension, seniority, specific training or skills (Allen & Meyer, 1991).

❝ THE DATA FROM THESE STUDIES SHOW THAT THE ORGANIZATIONAL COMMITMENT AND LOYALTY OF EMPLOYEES IN MODERN LITHUANIA MAY DEPEND ON THE USE OF LEADERSHIP APPROACHES THAT ASSURE EMPLOYEES OF JUST TREATMENT AND ACTIVE CONCERN FOR EMPLOYEE WELFARE AND DEVELOPMENT, RATHER THAN AUTHORITARIAN RULE. ❞

The most widely studied consequences of organizational commitment are turnover and on-the-job performance (Allan & Meyer, 1991). Turnover of employees has been linked to organizational commitment because employees who are not "emotionally attached," have low "perceived costs" of quitting, or do not feel "obligated" to work for a particular organization will tend to quit that job (Allan & Meyer, 1991). Employees with strong affective commitment will have lower absenteeism behavior, higher individual effectiveness, and citizenship behavior because emotional attachment leads to higher motivation to perform well on the job (Mathieu & Zajac, 1990). Employees with strong normative commitment will also have a high job performance, work attendance, and organizational citizenship behavior because of the sense of obligation and duty. However, normative commitment generally has a modest relationship with on-the-job performance measures because "feelings of obligation are unlikely to involve the same enthusiasm and involvement associated with affective commitment."

Continuance commitment is generally not related to on-the-job performance because under normal circumstances, employees whose tenure in the organization is based primarily on need may see little reason to do more than is required to maintain their membership in the organization (Allen & Meyer, 1991). Some previous studies have found that employee perceptions of organizational justice and organizational support may be positively related to levels of affective and normative commitment (Allen & Meyer, 1991; Sweeney & McFarlin, 1997).

Organizational justice is defined in terms of two dimensions (Folger & Konovsky, 1989; Sweeney & McFarlin, 1997):

- procedural justice, which is an employee's perception about the fairness of the organization's procedures and standards for performance ratings and pay determination, and
- distributive justice, which is defined as an employee's perceptions as to whether he or she gets adequate economic compensation for the performed job, often in comparison with other employees in similar job situations.

In general terms, organizational justice is the perception and employees' beliefs about the fairness of their social and economic exchanges with organizations (Blakely, Andrews, & Moorman, 2005). Moral understanding of the need for justice in reward allocation and the need for uncertainty reduction were the main reasons why people care more about justice and control it (Nadisic, 2006). According to theory, if employees think that they are treated unjustly either by the organization or their supervisor, they will believe that the social exchange with the organization is violated. This belief typically leads to withdrawal behaviors, which may include lower performance and increased absenteeism and turnover (Blakely, Andrews, & Moorman, 2005).

Perceived organizational support is defined by Eisenberger and colleagues (1986) as an employee's global belief that the organization cares for the employee and recognizes the employee's efforts. According to Eisenberger et al. (1986), perceived organizational support is based on two beliefs of employees that actions by agents (managers) are actions of the organization as a whole and rewards based on the organization's discretion. Perceived organizational support depends in part on employees' beliefs that organizational rewards a worker receives are based on discretionary choice indicating the organization's respect for employees as opposed to external pressures (Eisenberger, Cummings, Armeli, & Lynch, 1997). Perceived organizational support may act as mediator in the relationship between justice and organizational commitment (Loi, Hang-Yue, & Foley, 2006).

In one of the few previous studies in Eastern Europe, Alas and Edwards (2005) found in a study of Finnish and Estonian employees that even though the level of affective commitment was similar between these two countries, the antecedents of organizational commitment were different. In Estonia, pay and fringe benefits, competence of management, relationships with managers, promotion opportunities, and the extent to which work is interesting predicted commitment to the company. In Finland, only the extent to which work is found to be interesting predicted commitment (Alas & Edwards, 2005). The difference in antecedents of organizational commitment may reflect the difference in economic and political systems in Finland and Estonia. Estonia had been occupied for 50 years under a totalitarian regime with a planned economic system where people had to rely on the decisions of higher authority in all aspects of economic and political life and were subjected to coercive forms of political and economic control (Alas & Edwards, 2005). Because Lithuania has similar Soviet-rule experience as Estonia, it is likely that antecedents of the organizational commitment such as perception of fairness in pay distribution and organizational procedures will be significant antecedents of the three constructs of organizational commitment in Lithuania.

Study Methods

Data for this study were obtained from workers in research in a Lithuanian company which builds and repairs ships. In total, 135 questionnaires were distributed and 64 were returned (47% response rate). The sample of 64 respondents contained 74% men ($N = 48$) and 26% women ($N = 16$) employees. The average age of the respondents was 34 years. The average working tenure was 8.4 years. The average salary of the respondents was 1800 Litas (approximately 850 USD) per month. Three scales developed and validated by Meyer and Allen (1997) were used to measure the three constructs of organizational commitment. In this sample, the Cronbach's alpha for the affective commitment scale was .78; the normative commitment scale was .78; and the continuance commitment scale was .70. The three organizational commitment scales were measured with a 7-point Likert-type scale that ranges from 1 – strongly disagree to 7 – strongly agree (Fields, 2002).

Two multi-item scales developed by Sweeney and McFarlin (1997) were used to measure procedural and distributive justice. In this sample, the Cronbach's alpha for the procedural justice scale was .76, and the Cronbach's alpha for the distributive justice scale was .80. The procedural and distributive justice scales are measured with a 7-point Likert-type scale that ranges from 1 – strongly disagree to 7 – strongly agree. The scale for perceived organizational support (POS) was developed by Eisenberger and colleagues (1986). The Cronbach's alpha for the 9-item POS scale was .91 in this sample.

The scales making up the measure for each of the study variables (affective organizational commitment; normative organizational commitment; continuance organizational commitment; procedural justice; distributive justice; and perceived organizational support) were combined into a single questionnaire. The questionnaire was translated from English into Lithuanian by the first author and checked by a translator from a regional university. The translated scales and the original scales were back translated from Lithuanian to English by the Lithuanian language department at the regional university.

The anticipated relationships of the three types of organizational commitment, procedural justice, distributive justice, and perceived organizational support were assessed using hierarchical multiple regression. The control variables in each analysis were employee age, position, and income level.

Results

The purpose of this study was to investigate the extent to which procedural justice, distributive justice, and organizational support perceived by employees predict employee organizational commitment of three types. These results are summarized in Figure 1. We found the relationship between procedural justice and affective commitment was statistically significant (β = .41; p = .02), while the relationship between distributive justice and affective commitment was not. Of the control variables, only age had a significant relationship with affective commitment (β = .36; p < .01). The regression coefficient was positive, indicating that older workers tend to have higher levels of affective commitment. Procedural justice accounted for 15% of the variance in affective commitment. Neither procedural justice nor distributive justice were significantly related with normative commitment. The relationship between distributive justice and continuance commitment was significant (β = .49; p < .01), while the relationship between procedural justice and continuance commitment was not. Distributive justice accounted for 21% of the variation in continuance commitment.

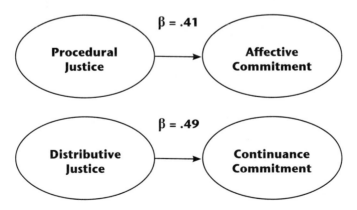

Figure 1. Relationship between Organizational Justice and Commitment.

As Figure 2 below illustrates, perceived organizational support (POS) mediates the relationship between procedural justice and affective commitment, but not the relationship between distributive justice and continuance commitment.

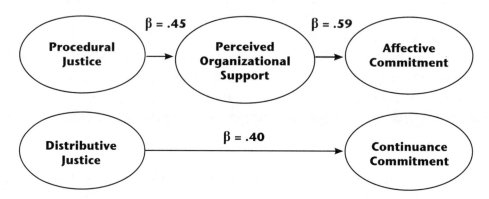

Figure 2. The Mediating Effect of POS.

Study 2: Servant Leadership and Employee Commitment

In this study, we explored the extent to which the leadership approach experienced by Lithuanian employees plays a significant role in organizational commitment. In studies of American employees, workers who receive valued rewards from an organization are motivated to provide something of a similar value back to the organization, for example loyalty and good performance. Because leaders are often perceived as the personification of the organization (Liden, Bauer, & Erdogan, 2004), subordinates may be motivated to return their leader's extra efforts, like helping the subordinates grow and succeed, with increased commitment to the organization. However, the applicability of this exchange perspective to Lithuanian settings has not been previously explored.

We focused on how a particular approach called servant leadership was related to the commitment of employees in two Lithuanian organizations. Servant leadership is a style of leadership that focuses on developing employees to their fullest potential in terms of task effectiveness, community stewardship, self-motivation, and future leadership capabilities (Greenleaf, 1977). The term *servant leadership* was first coined in 1970 by Robert K. Greenleaf, who was initially influenced by Hermann Hesse's short novel "Journey to the East" (Spears & Lawrence, 2002). Greenleaf (1977) suggested that the servant leader has a natural feeling to serve first, and, only after that, to aspire to lead. The best way to test this, according to Greenleaf, is to see whether those served grow as persons; while being served, moreover, the employees should become healthier, wiser, freer, more autonomous, more likely themselves to become servants (Greenleaf, 1977). To bring out the best in followers, servant leaders rely on one-on-one communication to understand the abilities, needs, desires, goals, and potential of followers and help the followers achieve that potential (Liden et al., 2005). A leader may help followers achieve their potential through building self-confidence (Lord, Brown, & Freiberg, 1999), serving as a role model, inspiring trust, as well as providing information, feedback, and resources (Liden et al., 2005). Servant leadership differs from traditional leadership approaches in that it stresses personal integrity and focuses on creating strong long-term relationships with employees. Also, it extends beyond the organization by servant leaders also serving their communities and society. Servant leadership shows promise as a way to build trust with employees, customers, and communities (Lord et al., 1999).

Robert Liden, Sandy Wayne, Hao Zhao, and David Henderson (2005) have proposed and empirically examined seven dimensions of the servant leadership construct. The seven dimensions are: (1) *conceptual skills,* possessing the knowledge of the organization and tasks at hand so as to be in a position to effectively support and assist others, especially immediate followers; (2) *empowering others,* encouraging and facilitating others, especially immediate followers, in identifying and solving problems, as well as determining when and how to complete work tasks; (3) *helping subordinates grow and succeed,* demonstrating genuine concern for others' career growth and development by providing support and mentoring; (4) *putting subordinates first,* using actions and words to make it clear to others (especially immediate followers) that satisfying their work needs is a priority; (5) *behaving ethically,* interacting openly, fairly, and honestly with others; (6) *emotional healing,* the act of showing sensitivity to others' personal concerns; and (7) *creating value for the community,* a conscious, genuine concern for helping the community (Liden et al., 2005). In a sample of American employees, servant leadership had a significant positive relationship with organizational commitment (Liden et al., 2005).

Contrary to the view that Lithuanian employees need highly directive and close supervision, it was anticipated that experiencing servant leadership would be positively related to employee organizational commitment. Since servant leadership might overlap with and not be distinguishable from transformational and transactional leadership, we included measures of two alternative approaches to leadership, transactional and transformational leadership, so that we could better understand the unique contribution of servant leadership to organizational commitment for modern Lithuanian employees.

Study Methods

We undertook this study to examine how the extent to which an employee experienced servant leadership was related to the employee's level of organizational commitment. Data for this study were obtained from the employees of two Lithuanian organizations. One company was a nationwide utilities provider and the other a public hospital. In the utility company, 40 usable questionnaires were collected. The employees of the utility company in the sample ranged in age from 26 to 57 with an average age of 40 years. Sixty percent of the respondents were female ($N =$ 24), while 40% ($N = 16$) were male. The average tenure with the organization was ten years. Seventy percent of the workers had university education and 33% held managerial positions. In the hospital, 23 usable questionnaires were collected; the hospital employees' ages ranged from 30 to 52 years with an average age of 39 years. One hundred percent of the employees responding ($N = 23$) were female. The average tenure with the organization was 17 years. One hundred percent of the workers had a college education, 78% of them were nurses, 17% were other hospital personnel, and 4% had a managerial position.

The Organizational Commitment Questionnaire (OCQ), originally developed by Mowday, Steers, and Porter (1979), was used to measure affective organizational commitment. Some example items include: "I am willing to put in a great deal of effort beyond that normally expected in order to help this organization be successful" and "I would accept almost any types of job assignment in order to keep working for this organization." Responses to these items were obtained using a 7-point Likert-type scale (Fields, 2002).

Servant leadership was measured using a scale developed by Liden and colleagues (Liden et al., 2005). The seven dimensions of the scale and the reliability of each in this sample are as follows: conceptual skills ($\alpha = .80$); empowerment ($\alpha = .79$); helping subordinates grow and succeed ($\alpha = .82$); putting subordinates first ($\alpha = .86$); behaving ethically ($\alpha = .83$); emotional healing ($\alpha = .76$); creating value for the community ($\alpha = .83$). Example items include: "My manager cares about my personal well-being"; "My manager is always interested in helping people in our community"; and "My manager gives me the freedom to handle difficult situations in the way that I feel is best." Responses to these items were obtained using a 7-point Likert-type scale.

In order to examine the unique effects of servant leadership on organizational commitment, we also measured the extent to which the employees also experienced two common forms of leadership, transformational and transactional leadership. Transformational leadership involves a series of behaviors directed at stimulating employees to perform at high levels in order to meet organizational goals. Transactional leadership involves a contingent reward interaction between the leader and employees. Transformational and transactional leadership were measured in our study with portions of the Multi-factor Leadership Questionnaire (MLQ) developed by Bass and Avolio (2000). Other variables controlled for in the study of servant leadership and organizational commitment were subordinate age, organizational tenure, position (distinguished between "managerial" and "nonmanagerial"), and type of organization (since the two organizations were considerably different in nature).

The items making up the scale measures for organizational commitment, servant leadership, transformational leadership, transactional leadership, and the demographic variables were combined into a single questionnaire. The questionnaire was translated from English into Lithuanian and retranslated back to English to check for consistency. It took the respondents approximately 20 minutes to fill out the questionnaire. Employees were asked to fill in the questionnaires directly at their workplaces. The relationships between servant leadership and organizational commitment were examined using hierarchical multiple regression.

Results

We found that the aggregated measure for servant leadership was positively related with employee organizational commitment after controlling for the effects of transformational and transactional leadership. Additionally, of the seven servant leadership dimensions, the dimensions "creating value for the community" ($\beta = .33$, $p = .008$) and "empowering employees" ($\beta = .36$, $p = .004$) were significantly related with organizational commitment.

Leadership Implications

Although limited by small samples of respondents, the results of our two studies clearly show that the nature of the justice, support, and leadership that Lithuanian employees experience at work are related to the levels of employee commitment to the organization. The evidence from these two studies could be of great interest to company investors and leaders in Lithuania because out-migration of qualified employees has led to decreasing supplies of reliable and qualified workers. Since joining the European Union in 2004, members of the Lithuanian labor force have been free to move without restrictions among seven other European Union member countries (Apribojimai, 2007). This freedom has resulted in the emigration of nearly fifty thousand workers (Oficiali, 2006). The lack of qualified employees in Lithuania is already a problem (A Disappearing Workforce, 2005). A recent human resource management study in Lithuania, conducted by one of the biggest Lithuanian market and society research companies, TNS Gallup, found that one of the most frequent problems in human resource management in Lithuanian organizations is employee retention (Tamošaitytė, 2006). According to the Lithuanian Statistical Bureau (Oficiali, 2006), more than 400,000 citizens have emigrated since 1990 (total population is 3.4 million in 2007). Since 2004, labor costs have been rising approximately 15% each year, whereas GDP growth has been approximately 6.5%; however, shortages in labor supply may lead to increases in labor costs which exceed gains in labor productivity.

While many skilled and educated workers leave Lithuania for jobs in Western Europe for higher pay levels, some migration out and/or reluctance to return to Lithuania may reflect employee anticipation of management or organizational practices that more skilled and educated employees find objectionable. One approach for leaders in Lithuanian organizations to improve retention is to focus on increasing the levels of organizational commitment among employees (Buck & Watson, 2002). Indeed, Petkeviciute & Kalinina (2004) have suggested that out-migration may be occurring in part because there may be a lack of commitment to organizations in Lithuania using authoritarian, directive, and manager-centered methods from the past Soviet system. The cost structure and relative labor productivity in Lithuania may not enable firms to compete with wages in Ireland and other Western European migration destinations. However, our study results suggest that leaders who provide a work environment perceived as just and employee-oriented may help retain skilled and experienced employees Lithuanian organizations need to succeed in the European (EU) markets.

❝ OUR STUDY RESULTS SUGGEST THAT LEADERS WHO PROVIDE A WORK ENVIRONMENT PERCEIVED AS JUST AND EMPLOYEE-ORIENTED MAY HELP RETAIN SKILLED AND EXPERIENCED EMPLOYEES LITHUANIAN ORGANIZATIONS NEED TO SUCCEED IN THE EUROPEAN MARKETS. ❞

Since Lithuania regained independence in 1991, the process of transformation from planned to market economy caused Lithuanian organizations to undergo numerous changes (Diskiene, 1997). Important changes have occurred in human resource management practices and perceptions. For example, employees who previously were viewed as simply "the means" to do the job, now are perceived as a significant part of the organizational system determining the efficiency of reaching organizational goals (Čiutienė, Sakalas, & Nevarauskas, 2006). The costs of acquiring, training, and socializing replacement employees may exceed twice the labor costs of a stable worker. Thus, greater requirements for employee replacement tend to increase a firm's overall labor costs and reduce productivity. The competitive position of Lithuanian firms clearly may depend on their abilities and willingness to implement approaches such as servant leadership, which increase employee confidence that their work organization will not only treat them fairly, but also support their development and achievements.

The concern with employees' welfare in some Lithuanian companies has increased considerably in the last 16 years. If indeed there has been a shift in managers' concern about subordinates' welfare in the workplace, our study results suggest that these approaches to leadership within Lithuanian companies may reduce employee departures and, consequently, improve Lithuanian organizations' cost efficiency and productivity. Not only are more committed employees less likely to change jobs, they are also less likely to be absent and more likely to be involved with their jobs and perform at higher levels (Krumm, 2001).

REFERENCES

Abbott, G., White, F., & Charles, M. (2005). Linking values and organizational commitment: A correlational and experimental investigation in two organizations. *Journal of Occupational and Organizational Psychology, 78,* 531–551.

A disappearing workforce. (2005). *Emerging Europe Monitor: Central Europe & Baltic States, 12*(4), 12.

Alas, R., & Edwards, V. (2005). Work-related attitudes: A comparison of Estonia and Finland. *Journal of Business Economics and Management, 4*(4), 207–217.

Allen, N., & Meyer, J. (1990). The measurement and antecedents of affective, continuance and normative commitment to the organization. *Journal of Occupational Psychology, 63,* 1–18.

Allen, N., & Meyer, J. (1991). A three-component conceptualization of organizational commitment. *Human Resource Management Review, 1,* 61–89.

Allen, N., & Meyer, J. (1997). *Commitment in the workplace.* Thousand Oaks, CA: Sage.

Apribojimai. (March 23, 2007). Retrieved April 4, 2007, from http://www.socmin.lt/index.php?-1215012452

Bagdanavicius, J., & Jodkonienė, Z. (2008). Brain drain from Lithuania: The attitude of civil servants. *Engineering Economics, 2,* 56–60.

Bass, B. M., & Avolio, B. (2000). *Multifactor leadership questionnaire: Technical report.* Redwood City, CA: Mind Garden.

Blakely, G., Andrews, M., & Moorman, R. (2005). The moderating effects of equity sensitivity on the relationship between organizational justice and organizational citizenship behaviors. *Journal of Business and Psychology, 20*(2), 259–273.

Buck, J. M., & Watson, J. L. (2002). Retaining staff employees: The relationship between human resources management strategies and organizational commitment. *Innovative Higher Education, 26*(3), 175–193.

Cotton, J. L., & Tuttle, J. M. (1986). Employee turnover: A meta-analysis and review with implications for research. *Academy of Management Review, 11,* 55–70.

Čiutienė, R., Sakalas, A., & Nevarauskas, B. (2006). Influence of personnel interests on formation of modern career. *Engineer Economics, 50*(5), 99–106, 8.

Diskiene, D. (1997). The influence of societal and cultural values on managerial behaviour in Lithuania. *Economics, 43,* 59–74.

Eisenberger, R., Cummings, J., Armeli, S., & Lynch, P. (1997). Perceived organizational support, discretionary treatment, and job satisfaction. *Journal of Applied Psychology, 82*(5), 812–820.

Eisenberger, R., Huntington, R., Hutchison, S., & Sowa, D. (1986). Perceived organizational support. *Journal of Applied Psychology, 71,* 500–507.

Fields, D. L. (2002). *Taking the measure of work: A guide to validated scales for organizational research and diagnosis.* Thousand Oaks, CA: Sage.

Folger, R., & Konovsky, M. (1989). Effects of procedural and distributive justice on reactions to pay raise decisions. *Academy of Management Journal, 32,* 115–130.

Greenleaf, R. K. (1977). *Servant leadership: A journey into the nature of legitimate power and greatness.* New York: Paulist Press.

Hale, J., & Fields, D. (2007). Exploring servant leadership across cultures: A study of followers in Ghana and the USA. *Leadership, 3*(4), 397–417.

Krumm, D. (2001). *Psychology at work.* New York: Worth Publishers.

Liden, R. C., Bauer, T. N., & Erdogan, B. (2004). The role of leader-member exchange in the dynamic relationship between employer and employee: Implications for employee socialization, leaders, and organizations. In J. Coyle-Shapiro, L. Shore, M. Taylor, & L. Tetrick (Eds.), *The employment relationship: Examining psychological and contextual perspectives* (pp. 226–250). Oxford, UK: Oxford University Press.

Liden, R. C., Wayne, S. J., Zhao, H., & Henderson, D. (2005). *Development of a multidimensional measure of servant leadership.* Paper presented at the Annual Meeting of the Southern Management Association, Charleston, SC.

Loi, R., Hang-yue, N., & Foley, S. (2006). Linking employees' justice perceptions to organizational commitment and intention to leave: The mediating role of perceived organizational support. *Journal of Occupational and Organizational Psychology, 79,* 101–120.

Lord, R. G., Brown, D. J., & Freiberg, S. J. (1999). Understanding the dynamics of leadership: The role of follower self-concepts in the leader/follower relationship. *Organizational Behavior and Human Decision Processes, 78,* 167–203.

Mathieu, J. E., & Zajac, D. (1990). A review and meta-analysis of the antecedents, correlates, and consequences of organizational commitment. *Psychological Bulletin, 108,* 171–194.

McFarlin, D., & Sweeney, P. (1992). Distributive and procedural justice as predictors of satisfaction with personal and organizational outcomes. *Academy of Management Journal, 35*(3), 626–637.

Meyer, J. P., & Allen, N. J. (1997). *Commitment in the workplace: Theory, research and application.* Thousand Oaks, CA: Sage.

Miskinis, A. (2008). Personal communication, April 20, 2008.

Mowday, R. T., Porter, L. W., & Steers, R. M. (1982). *Employee-organizational linkages: The psychology of commitment, absenteeism and turnover.* New York: Academic Press.

Mowday, R. T., Steers, R. M., & Porter, L. W. (1979). The measurement of organizational commitment. *Journal of Vocational Behavior, 14,* 224–247.

Nadisic, T. (2006). The motives of organizational justice. *Working Papers of HEC School of Management.* Retrieved December 21, 2006, from http://www.hec.fr/hec/eng/professeurs_recherche/index.html

Oficiali ir neoficiali emigracija 2001-2005 m. (October 16, 2006). Retrieved April 4, 2007, from http://www.stat.gov.lt/lt/pages/view/?id=1936

Petkeviciute, N., & Kalinina, I. (2004). Veiksniai didinantys darbuotojų organizacinį prisirišimą (Antecedents of organizational commitment). *Management of Organizations: Systematic Research, 31,* 179–193.

Spears C. L., & Lawrence, M. (Eds.). (2002). *Focus on leadership: Servant-leadership for the 21st century.* New York: John Wiley & Sons.

Sweeney, P., & McFarlin, D. (1997). Process and outcome: Gender differences in the assessment of justice. *Journal of Organizational Behavior, 18,* 83–98.

Tamošaitytė, A. (2006). Žmogiškųjų išteklių valdymo tyrimas. Retrieved March 20, 2007, from http://www.tns-gallup.lt/bin/ZI_TNS_ataskaita_06.ppt#262,1,Žmogiškųjų išteklių valdymo tyrimas.

United Nations Development Programme (UNDP). (2005). *Review of UNDP's partnership with Lithuania (1992–2005).* Vilnius: United Nations Development Programme.

DAIL FIELDS serves as a professor in the Regent University Ph.D. program in organizational leadership. He recently completed a one-year appointment as a Fulbright scholar in Klaipeda, Lithuania. He has presented seminars and research studies at annual meetings of the Academy of Management, the European Group on Organizational Studies, and the European Academy of Management. Dr. Fields has previously served on the faculties of George Washington University and the City University of Hong Kong. Prior to undertaking an academic career, he worked in business for over 20 years, starting a small business and holding management positions in such firms as Deloitte-Touche and MCI Communications Corporation. He holds a Ph.D. degree from Georgia Institute of Technology.

EVALDAS ANDZIUS has a bachelor's degree in business management and administration from LCC International University where he conducted organizational research analyzing the antecedents of organizational commitment. His professional career includes working as a business and industry analyst at the Euromonitor International in Vilnius, Lithuania. Evaldas is currently a master of science candidate in entrepreneurship and strategy economics at Erasmus University Rotterdam in the Netherlands.

RUTA KRISCIUNAITE graduated with a B.A. in business management and administration at LCC International University, where she conducted research on leadership and business performance. She started her professional career managing various business research and analysis projects in a business consultancy, later joining one of the leading UK banks as a management trainee in London, England. Ruta is currently a master of science candidate in business analytics and consulting at the University of Warwick in England.

The Impact of Culture on Chinese, Chinese-American, and American Women Working in China

By Joanne Barnes and Sharon Drury

CHINA HAS BECOME A PLACE OF HOST-COUNTRY OPERATIONS FOR many multinational corporations (MNCs). Women employees in China were aided overall by the founding of the All-China Women's Federation (ACWF) in 1949; however, its efforts remain concentrated in lower-level jobs in all sectors (Cooke, 2005). This article reveals what women say about their roles as leaders in four MNC locations in China.

As firms globalize and enter new markets, MNCs encounter new cultures, some of which may be less receptive to women in positions of authority than is present within their home-country operations. However, host-country cultures may also affect the MNCs' overall policies. Adler (1994, 2002) argues that managers of MNCs tend to rule out women as leaders[1] because of their perception that foreigners would resist women's leadership, an attitude that results in women being unequal to men in the areas of acceptability and effectiveness in the global arena. Similarly, Paik and Vance (2002) found that due to cultural expectations in host nations, women tend not to receive managerial positions in international assignments. In short, different cultures perceive women differently, and this often limits women's access to leadership positions in MNCs.

As corporations recognize the competitive value of doing business in China, more opportunities are opening up for Chinese women to hold the rank of manager or leader. However, studying this phenomenon of women as managers and leaders in China is considered uncharted waters by Korabik (1994):

> We have little direct knowledge about women managers in the People's Republic of China. There are several reasons for this. During the Cultural Revolution, social science research fell into disfavor, and China closed its doors to foreigners. Therefore, until recently, it was culturally unacceptable for Chinese scholars to carry out such research on women managers, and impossible for Westerners to obtain permission to do so. (p. 116)

Thus, for multinational corporations, placing Chinese women in managerial roles becomes a "trial and error" process (D. Deptowicz, personal communication, February 1, 2007). To address this problem, the authors sought published information on women in China, as well as access within MNCs to gather empirical evidence from women leaders in China.

GlobeSmart[2] suggests the influence of Confucianism still permeates the culture in China and the commonly-held belief that men handle the outside world and women maintain the home and internal family (Women in China, n.d.). This belief is additionally communicated through sayings in the culture, for example:

> Another famous common saying which could be attributed to Confucius' influence is "a woman's virtue relies on her lack of talent." A woman is thus held in high regard as long as she manages the household well (i.e., her husband and the in-laws are served, children are fed and the house is clean). At the same time, she is positively discouraged from pursuing any intellectual development. (Bowen, Wu, Hwang, & Scherer, 2007, p. 270)

Additionally, since the time of Confucius, women have been perceived as less intelligent than men. In the eighteenth century, a woman's brain was thought to be smaller and less capable of knowledge than a man's brain (Hayes, 1999). The influence of Confucianism appears to be strong in China's culture.[3]

Historical Look at Chinese Culture

The early history of China was steeped in the legacy of the Chinese philosopher Confucius, whose teachings had been associated with hierarchy and age along with having respect for those in authority. "Chinese behaviors are deeply rooted in the legacies left by the Chinese philosopher Confucius (551–479 B.C.) and for more than two thousand years, Confucius' disciples have worked to assure that his legacies have become an integral part of the Chinese social, economic and cultural inheritances" (O'Keefe & O'Keefe, 1997, p. 190). Pun, Chin, and Lau (2000) cite Chen (1995) describing the

Chinese management structure as being paternalistic and personalistic. Selmer, Kang, and Wright (1994) cite Redding (1990), Silin (1976), and WhiUey (1992) observing that "Chinese employees seem to prefer such a paternalistic authoritarian style, through which a benevolent and respected leader is not only considerate of his employees, but also takes skilled and decisive actions" (p. 51).

❝ CONFUCIANISM STILL PERMEATES THE CULTURE IN CHINA. ❞

Confucian principles and ideologies have permeated the Chinese culture and are well established in other countries such as Japan, Korea, and India (Wang, Wang, Ruona, & Rojewski, 2005). According to Wang et al. (2005), Confucian principles are twofold:

> One side of Confucianism is the affirmation of accepted values and norms of individual behavior in social institutions and human relations (Berling, 1982). As a moral system, Confucianism focuses on *wu lun*—five cardinal role relations between emperor-subject, father-son, husband-wife, elder-younger brothers and friend-friend. All these relationships involve a set of defined roles and mutual obligations. Each individual should conform to his or her proper role and act properly to perfect the society (Berling, 1982). With the exception of the last dyadic role relations, all the others are typically dominant-subservient in nature. (p. 314)

The *wu-lun* side of Confucianism set limitations for women in leadership due to the dominant-subservient relationships. Women had been secondary to men in all aspects of life, especially in the world of business. The values of Confucianism were segmented into five aspects: hierarchy and harmony, group orientation, *guanxi* networks (relationships), *mianzi* (face), and time orientation. In relation to hierarchy and harmony, Confucianism promoted predetermined positions in society (Wang et al., 2005). Renard (2002) also argued that "Confucian teaching envisioned male-female relations according to a political model" (p. 163). Confucianism suggests that women and younger individuals were to be obedient to men.

Benson and Yukongdi (2005) cite Ng and Chakarabarty (2003) from case studies conducted in 2003 that Chinese women managers felt they were treated unfairly because of the expectations given to them. Men in the organization felt women were not as capable as their male counterparts. Confucian culture had resulted in gender stereotyping and role expectations (positions are traditionally female, such as teaching and health care), allowing men to treat women as inferior in business and management settings. Therefore, the road leading to women in management and leadership positions has been slow and tedious.

All-China Women's Federation

One of the most significant changes aiding the roles of women in China was the founding of the All-China Women's Federation (ACWF). Established on April 3, 1949, it was the first official women's group which strived to create a social equality for all Chinese women. The ACWF, originally named All-China Democratic Women's Federation, changed names in 1957 to the Women's Federation of the People's Republic of China. However, in 1978 it converted back to its current name. The mission of the ACWF is "to represent and safeguard women's rights and interests and promote equality between women and men" ("ACWF Brochure," n.d.). The ACWF developed specific tasks to ensure they would remain focused. Today, the ACWF continues its foundation goal "to educate and offer guidance to women to strengthen their spirit of self-esteem, self-confidence, self-reliance and self-improvement, to improve their technical and professional skills and to enhance their overall competence" (All-China Women's Federation, n.d.). The National Congress of Chinese Women, the highest power of the ACWF, meets once every five years, discusses the major issues facing the national women's movement, and amends the constitution as required. Their most recent meeting took place in Beijing, August 22 through August 25, 2003. The focus included helping more women find employment and re-employment, increasing women's working opportunities and post, and better the distribution and variety of job opportunities. A major concern as stated by Gu Xiulian, vice president of the All-China Women's Federation, is the need to establish a legal system to protect the rights of women and children and social security for women (People's Daily Online, 2003).

Women Leaders and Culture

Perceptions of what a manager should be (male or female) substantially impact how others view a manager and the level of confidence they would have in that individual. Korabik (1994) states, "gender-role stereotypes were prevalent in China and hindered women's participation for managerial roles as well as their opportunities for promotion" (p. 117). More so, women in China had thousands of years of culture that had and would continue to have significant influence on their behavior both inside and outside of the office. Korabik (1994) contends that "women's self-confidence is also often undermined by their acceptance of the Confucian adage that 'it is a virtue if a woman has no ability'" (p. 117). Earlier studies conducted by Napier and Taylor (2002) and Mainiero (1994) also emphasize that American and Chinese-American women have also struggled to gain a significant standing as credible leaders in organizations, thus contributing to a level of low self-confidence.

According to Korabik (1994), the cultural influence of gender-role stereotypes in China has delayed women's ability to prepare for managerial roles. Korabik contends that as Chinese women enter into the workforce, they are characterized as shy and unassertive, which hinders their ability to be or become leaders (1994). Furthermore, Korabik refers to an article written in *Women in China*, which makes reference to how Chinese women seriously believe in the culture norms defining their sub-leadership ability and skills (Korabik, 1994).

Given the cultural history in China and the more recent initiatives to promote women as leaders in China, MNCs are hoping to expand and be able to use women in leadership positions of some of their operations in China.

66 UNTIL RECENTLY, IT WAS CULTURALLY UNACCEPTABLE FOR CHINESE SCHOLARS TO CARRY OUT RESEARCH ON WOMEN MANAGERS. 99

Method

To see how women leaders in MNCs are doing in their leadership roles, this research used a mixed-method approach to investigate the above problem. Two survey instruments were used to collect data on culture and managerial technique: the Women As Managers Scale (WAMS) and the Cultural Perspectives Questionnaire, version 8 (CPQ-8). In addition, observations of women leaders in China and interviews were used to collect data and then transcribed. Both data-collection processes were assisted by a Chinese-American translator. Only a small number of participants ($N = 33$) were found among the leader-manager ranks in four Chinese automotive plants. The interview participation was 100% across all three groups: Chinese, Chinese-American, and American women in China. The percentage of returned questionnaires was 51% for the WAMS and CPQ-8. The breakdown of groups participating in the survey were: Chinese-Americans – 6, Chinese Nationals – 8, and Americans – 19. Participation, along with the convenience sample of four automotive plants, is a limitation of the study and the ability to generalize the findings across a larger population.

Findings

Confucianism and values associated with Confucian beliefs were not specifically revealed through the survey data analysis, yet during observations of Chinese women leaders in China during social settings, it was evident that men were the predominant decision-makers in the organization and the home. Chinese women and Chinese-

American women respected the hierarchical positions associated with Confucianism. This was noted in interview results where three of three Chinese women and two of three Chinese-American women indicated they were influenced by male predecessors. Although two of three American women noted they were also influenced by men during the interview process, they also implied these men were used as mentors and they did not necessarily emulate their leadership style. Furthermore, a review of organizational charts for the multinational corporations that participated in this study illustrated women still had not moved into leadership ranks as often as men. In the four selected organizations, Chinese women in leadership positions were outnumbered by men 8 to 1. Therefore, Chinese women had little opportunity to have female predecessors or role models. However, Chinese-American and American women expatriates who had careers which began in the United States gained substantial ground due to the availability of female mentors and role models.

Chinese women as well as Chinese-American and American women expatriates who were interviewed for this study did not feel inferior to men. Chinese women did confirm during the interviews and casual conversations that they were not allowed to work as many years as their male counterparts, and women were forced to retire or end their careers five years earlier than men regardless of the position they held in the organization. One of the interviewees felt this contributed greatly as to why women were not promoted the same as men. It was also a reason that many Chinese women chose to work for multinational corporations rather than for Chinese-owned or government organizations.

In China, paternalism has historically been associated with male leaders (political and nonpolitical). Survey data and interviews show that this tendency continues today. Interestingly, contemporary Chinese women leaders demonstrate behaviors that can be perceived as paternalistic, including nurturing employees, practicing self-discipline, and being unselfish—all traits that Farh and Cheng (2000) link to the paternalist tradition of leadership in China. A key theme captured throughout the interviews and survey results of the CPQ-8 was the caring, nurturing, and development of followers, but always ensuring the right thing was done (morals) and maintaining respect for authority (male or female). Overall, Chinese women demonstrated some of the principles of Confucianism and paternalism.

China had been identified as a collective society where the group was considered to be more important than the individual (Hofstede, 2001). The CPQ-8 data had implied Chinese women and Chinese-American women expatriates believe collectivism was important to their leadership. However, younger Chinese women do not embrace the collectivist attitude and behavior, suggested one Chinese interviewee, due to their exposure to Western culture.

Chinese-American women expatriates who participated in this study demonstrated many of the same characteristics as their Chinese National counterparts. Men played a key role in influencing their leadership. However, results from the Women As Managers Scale contradicted responses from the interviews. During the interview process, Chinese-American women were nurturing and wanted to ensure their followers were trained; however, the responses from WAMS suggested that understanding the needs of the group was not as important as themselves being knowledgeable. Liang, Lee, and Ting (2002) suggested that Asian Americans were stereotyped as being "passive, unassertive, docile, and therefore lacking leadership skills" (p. 81); yet this study found that women in this demographic group were assertive and ready to take on leadership assignments.

The interview results were compared to the results of the WAMS and CPQ-8. Based on the comparative analysis of the interviews and questionnaire, there is a significant difference in the way women view themselves as leaders and how they have been influenced in their leadership characteristics. Chinese women and Chinese-American expatriates model their leadership after men and felt men offered them a strong foundation for leadership. Interestingly the literature suggests that China was a very paternalistic and hierarchical society (Farh & Cheng, 2000). The interviews support that women of Asian descent rely on men for direction, guidance, and leadership. A total of 21 dimensions were measured by WAMS to gain a better understanding of how women perceived themselves as leaders and managers. Women in all three categories of this study felt it was acceptable to compete with men for top management positions. For Chinese women, the mean was 6.125 where the maximum was 7.0 and the minimum was 5.0; Chinese-American women had a mean of 7.0, whereas the mean for American women was 6.941. Acceptance by the business community demonstrated a mean of 6.741, which indicated that women in all three populations believed acceptance by the business community was critical for their success as a leader. Contrary to this belief, women from all three groups did not necessarily feel accepted by the community or organizations in which they were working. American women had suggested that not being able to have long-term assignments, i.e., greater than one year in the host country, did not give them an opportunity to be accepted or prove they were good leaders.

An important component of this research is to understand the impact of culture on women. The CPQ-8 measured five primary dimensions which were closely linked to Hofstede's value dimensions (Maznevski et al., 2002). Within each dimension there are three sub-dimensions, with the exception of Nature of Humans which asked if people were basically good or evil. The research measured all dimensions and concluded with the following observations.

The first category analyzed was Relation to Environment (harmony, mastery, and subjugation). The data for Chinese women in this category realized a high probability that most women agreed harmony and subjugation have a cultural impact on them; however, there was statistically significant evidence ($p = 0.002$) that mastery constituted a strongly held belief within this demographic group.[4] Chinese-American women were similar to Chinese National women, while American women showed no significant indicator to this category. This implied "control" is not as important as "following."

The second category analyzed the Relationships among People (collective, hierarchical, and individual). The data illustrated Chinese and Chinese-American women felt the people and the group were more important than the individual. A p-value of 0.016 was realized for collectivism, while American women demonstrated a significantly high probability that most American women did not believe the group would come before the individual.

The third category measured by the CPQ-8 was Activity. Activity refers to the act of being, doing, or thinking. Across all three populations, there was little to no difference of perceptions in this category. The fourth category measured by the CPQ-8 was Nature of Humans. This category measures whether individuals view society as naturally good or evil. This question presented a statistically significant difference between Chinese (and Chinese-American) and non-Chinese women. Chinese and Chinese-American women view society as basically good, while non-Chinese American women are more likely to doubt this view. Perhaps this is a view embedded in American culture, or perhaps it is due to women's particular experiences of discrimination in American society.

The fifth and final category was Time (past, present, and future). Across all three groups in the category and subcategory, there was a statistically highly significant probability ($p = 0.014, 0.255$, and 0.309) that time is an important culture value. The past was a statistically significant contributor to how one's culture impacts leadership. Confucianism had suggested the past was foundational in its tenants, and respect for status and social order must be upheld. Based on the results of this category of the CPQ-8, Chinese and Chinese-American women respect the past and have a need to acknowledge the hierarchy within the corporation, thus indicating the influence of Chinese culture (Confucianism) on their leadership styles.

The interviews of Chinese women reveal that culture and status are instrumental for women's acceptance as leader. The Chinese women all felt the well-being of others was one of the most important characteristics of being a leader, thus confirming the earlier studies by Wang et al. (2005), and O'Keefe and O'Keefe (1997). Women in China are well educated and have a desire to move into leadership positions to set an example for followers; however, lines of demarcation that still exist in leadership positions are slowly being removed by multinational corporations but remain prevalent in Chinese-owned organizations and in government positions. For example, Chinese women are required to retire five years prior to men, so when working in Chinese- or Japanese-owned organizations in China, Chinese women felt they were not allowed to have the same and sometimes any power when compared to men. The Chinese government has many laws which impact the length of time a woman can work and how much a woman can be paid. Due to the difference in treatment of men and women, many of the younger Chinese women have adapted Western cultures and begun to seek employment in multinational organizations in order to advance into leadership positions.

66 THE INTERVIEWS OF CHINESE WOMEN REVEAL THAT CULTURE AND STATUS ARE INSTRUMENTAL FOR WOMEN'S ACCEPTANCE AS LEADER. 99

Conclusions

The three categories of women interviewed and surveyed for this study demonstrated little or no consistency across the sample size. The results revealed that American women who worked in China were not influenced by Chinese culture. It could be argued that the United States, being a young country in comparison to China and a very diverse country, has not established strong cultural beliefs and values which could be generalized across the total American population. The American women expatriates also did not spend a significant amount of time when working as an expatriate in China, therefore, according to Selmer and Leung (2003), they would not experience "much attitudinal change (psychological adjustment) of adult women" (p. 248) since most values are developed during adolescence.

China, by contrast with the United States, has a very ancient culture stretching back thousands of years. Throughout the years, China's dynasties each rendered beliefs and values which were passed from generation to generation. In addition, the government, especially during the early 1900s (O'Keefe & O'Keefe, 1997), began to develop different standards for men and women, and women took a subservient role to men (Wong, 2001). Implications of this study suggested Chinese women and Chinese-American women, due to the long history of instilled beliefs and values in China, are influenced more by the host culture than their American counterparts when working in multinational corporations.

Analysis of our findings suggests that American women tend to reflect the values of Americans and not necessarily the culture where they work. The triangulation of data implied American women were not influenced by host-country culture and regarded themselves as good leaders who were as capable as, or more capable than, their male counterparts. The American women's responses did not align with the values, beliefs, and leadership styles of Chinese and Chinese-American women. However, the Chinese and Chinese-American women leaders were strongly aligned in cultural influence and perception of self.

Multinational corporations who have placed American women in leadership positions in China may face challenges of acceptance unless they are willing to allow for an extended international service assignment. The data imply American women will not necessarily adapt to the culture of the host country, whereas Chinese-American women are more likely to adapt due to already having similar beliefs and values as the host country.

Recommendations for Multinational Corporations

Based on the results of this research, leaders of multinational corporations need to understand the impact history and culture have on how women leaders are perceived and how they will lead. When MNCs select women for expatriate leadership assignments in China, they need to consider if the expatriate will be capable of closing the gap of past perceptions of women and overcome the paternalistic culture. Additionally, the women placed in leadership positions who come from a country where individualism is high must be able to become more of a participative leader and focus on the group rather than her accomplishments, ideas, and plans.

When MNCs select Chinese National women to lead, there should be an in-depth evaluation of their followers. If the followers are men, will they show respect to the woman leader and will she have the authority to accomplish goals and objectives? The foundation for women being successful as leaders in China lies in the preparation of the women as well as the employees they will be leading.

In these ways, it is hoped that leaders of MNCs can balance sensitivity to the host-country culture and the organization's legal and ethical obligations to equality and diversity, including leadership by women.

NOTES

1. Throughout this study, the words *leader* and *manager* are used interchangeably since that is a common practice in China. Other related research, as reported by Cooke (2005), Adler (1997), and Robinson and Lipman-Blumen (2003), have also interchanged the words leader and manager in their writings and data summaries.

2. *GlobeSmart* is a Web-based tool providing business personnel with quick and easy access to extensive knowledge on how to conduct business effectively with people from countries around the world. GlobeSmart uses Aperian Global's editorial team, which first conducts a literature review of recent publications for each

country in *GlobeSmart*. The reviewers search for books, articles, and newsletters that have been written in the last three years that contain useful information on the specific business topics that are covered in *GlobeSmart*.

3. According to Chen (2002, p. 11), "The concept of culture can be defined as values and ways of life specific of a specific society, which are transmitted from generation to generation through childhood socialization (Hu, 1995, p. 48)."

4. Mastery is defined as where "our purpose and natural role is to control nature and the environment around us" (Understand CPQ, n.d.).

REFERENCES

Adler, N. (1994). Competitive frontiers: Women managing across borders. In N. J. Adler & D. Izraeli (Eds.), *Competitive frontiers: Women managers in a global economy* (pp. 22–40). Cambridge, MA: Blackwell.

Adler, N. (1997). *International dimensions of organizational behavior* (3rd ed.). Cincinnati, OH: South-Western College Publishing

Adler, N. (2002). Global managers: No longer men alone [Electronic version]. *International Journal of Human Resource Management, 13*(5), 743–760.

Benson, J., & Yukongdi, V. (2005). Asian women managers: Participation, barriers and future prospects [Electronic version]. *Asia Pacific Business Review, 11*(2), 283–291.

Berling, J. A. (1982). Confucianism. *Asian Religions, 2*(1), 5–7.

Bowen, C. C., Wu, Y., Hwang, C., & Scherer, R. F. (2007, February). Holding up half of the sky? Attitudes toward women as managers in the People's Republic of China. *International Journal of Human Resource Management, 18*(2), 268–283.

Chen, W. C. (2002). Analysis of cultural factors in leadership and succession practices in Taiwan businesses. *Dissertation Abstracts International* (UMI No. 9315947)

Cooke, F. L. (2005, June). Women's managerial careers in China in a period of reform [Electronic version]. *Asia-Pacific Business Review, 11*(2), 149–162.

Farh, J. L., & Cheng, B. S. (2000). A cultural analysis of paternalistic leadership in Chinese organizations. In J. T. Li, A. S. Tsui, & E. Weldon (Eds.), *Management and organizations in the Chinese context* (pp. 84–127). London: Basingstoke.

Hayes, A. (1999). The new presence of women leaders [Electronic version]. *The Journal of Leadership Studies, 6,* 10.

Hofstede, G. (2001). *Culture's consequences: Comparing values, behaviors, institutions, and organizations across nations* (2nd ed.). Thousand Oaks, CA: Sage.

Korabik, K. (1994). Managerial women in the People's Republic of China: The long march continues. In N. J. Adler & D. N. Izraeli (Eds.), *Competitive frontiers: Women managers in a global economy* (pp. 115–126). Cambridge, MA: Blackwell Publishers.

Liang, C. T. H., Lee, S., & Ting, M. P. (2002). Developing Asian American leaders [Electronic version]. *New Directions for Student Services, 97,* 81–89.

Mainiero, L. A. (1994). Getting anointed for advancement: The case of executive women [Electronic version]. *Academy of Management Executive, 9*(2), 52–67.

Maznevski, M. L., Gomez, C. B., DiStefano, J. J., Noordenhaven, N. G., & Wu, P. C. (2002). Cultural dimensions at the individual level of analysis: The cultural orientations framework [Electronic version]. *International Journal of Cross Cultural Management, 2,* 275–295.

Napier, N. K., & Taylor, S. (2002, August). Experiences of women professionals abroad: Comparisons across Japan, China and Turkey [Electronic version]. *International Journal of Human Resource Management, 13*(5), 837–851.

O'Keefe, H., & O'Keefe, W. M. (1997). Chinese and Western behavioural differences: Understanding the gaps [Electronic version]. *International Journal of Social Economics, 24*, 190–197.

Paik, Y., & Vance, C. M. (2002). Evidence of backhome selection bias against US female expatriates [Electronic version]. *Women in Management Review, 17*(2), 68–79.

People's Daily Online. (August, 22, 2003). Retrieved from http://english.peopledaily.com. cn/200308/22/eng20030822_122847.shtml

Pun, K., Chin, K., & Lau, H. (2000). A review of the Chinese cultural influences on Chinese enterprise management [Electronic version]. *International Journal of Management Reviews, 2*(4), 14.

Renard, J. (2002). *101 questions and answers on Confucianism, Daoism, and Shinto.* New York: Paulist Press.

Robinson, J. L., & Lipman-Blumen, J. (2003, September/October). Leadership behavior of male and female managers, 1984–2002 [Electronic version]. *Journal of Education for Business*, pp. 28–33.

Selmer, J., Kang, I. L., & Wright, R. P. (1994). Managerial behavior of expatriate versus local bosses [Electronic version]. *International Studies of Management & Organization, 24*(3) 48–63.

Selmer, J., & Leung, A. S. M. (2003). Expatriate career intentions of women on foreign assignments and their adjustments [Electronic version]. *Journal of Managerial Psychology, 18*(3), 244–258.

Wang, J., Wang, G. G., Ruona, W. E. A., & Rojewski, J. W. (2005). Confucian values and implications for international HRD [Electronic version]. *Human Resource Development International, 8*(3), 311–326.

Women in China. (n.d.). Retrieved December 12, 2006, from http://www.globesmart.com

Wong, K. C. (2001). Chinese culture and leadership [Electronic version]. *International Journal of Leadership in Education, 4*(4), 309–319.

JOANNE BARNES has been with Delphi Electronics and Safety for 36 years. In her position as Global Quality Systems Manager, she travels widely across America and overseas, including China. Joanne has presented at various conferences on global issues and earned her Ed.D. in organizational leadership from Indiana Wesleyan University in 2007.

SHARON DRURY has been the Dean of the College of Adult and Professional Studies at Indiana Wesleyan University and now teaches full-time as professor of organizational leadership in the doctoral program at IWU. She earned her Ph.D. at Regent University, has presented at numerous conferences on adult learning and leadership research, and is the author of *Systems of Excellence in Adult Higher Education.*

Global Leadership Portraits and Visions for the Future

The Poet's Vision and the Promise of World Peace

By Suheil Bushrui

> Without high virtues by poetry laid down
> No glorious deed by man can be achieved.
>
> —Abu Tammam
> *Translated by the author from the original Arabic*

Poets are the hierophants of an unapprehended inspiration; the mirrors of the gigantic shadows which futurity casts upon the present; the words which express what they understand not; the trumpets which sing to battle and feel not what they inspire; the influence which is moved not, but moves. Poets are the unacknowledged legislators of the world.

> —Percy Bysshe Shelly
> From *A Defense of Poetry*

> I said the poets hung
> Images of the life that was in Eden
> About the child-bed of the world, that it,
> Looking upon those images, might bear
> Triumphant children
>
> —William Butler Yeats
> From *The King's Threshold*

I

The great poets, for as long as we remember, have been true leaders of humanity. Their vision was always the inspiration for the great spiritual conquests of the human race, the triumph of the spirit before which all other values are nonexistent. The poet's leadership is vindicated against what one poet calls "the reasoners and merchants" and of the "unmitigated exercise of the calculating faculty." How true in today's social and political climate is this claim of the poet, for the greatest poetry can never compromise the Truth.

Political discourse has dominated for too long all discussion, both national and international—emphasizing the so-called "realities of time and place," and employing in research the quantitative and empirical methods that have not yielded many positive results. The power of the *word*, the power of poetry and the power of literature, survive both time and place. Emphasizing this fact, Yeats, one of the great poets of the twentieth century, expressed his belief that

> . . . literature is the principal voice of the conscience, and it is its duty age after age to affirm its morality against the special moralities of clergymen and churches, and of kings and parliaments and peoples. But I do not expect this opinion to be the opinion of the majority of any country for generations, and it may always be the opinion of a very small minority.[1]

In a world overwhelmed by "the politics of time," the poet provides that leadership that can reconcile it with the "politics of eternity." The eminent Irish poet and mystic, AE (George Russell), explains this aspect of the poet's leadership in his book entitled *The Interpreters*, published in 1922, as follows:

> Those who begin to live consciously in the spirit must be guided by an ethic based on the nature of the ancestral self or heavenly man. In that being . . . all human life is reflected, so that none can be our enemies, and we can overcome only by the fierce and tender breath of love, if love be the heavenly name of that which yearns in us to be intimate with the innermost of all life. Once that spiritual awakening has begun for any the old life should be over, and they should no longer be concerned in the politics of time, and should leave the life of conflict and passion and fit themselves for the politics of eternity.[2]

II

The great poets of humanity were, above all, universalists and believers in an unknowable essence that was one, indivisible, and permanent. Muhyi'ddín ibn al-'Arabí and Abu al-ala' al-Ma'ari of Arabia, Jalaluddin Rumi and Hafiz of Persia, Kabir and Tagore of India, Li Bai of China, Homer of Greece, Virgil of Rome, and the Hebrew poet-prophets—just to mention a few—received their inspiration from the same source. It has been said that when poetry dies, language dies—and when language dies, civilization dies. Indeed Western civilization, it has been said, endures in large part in the works of three great poets: Dante, Shakespeare, and Goethe. Islamic culture owes an immense debt to Muhyi'ddín ibn al-'Arabí, the great Sufi poet of Islam, who was able to reconcile all opposites and allow his heart to accept even Islam's greatest enemy, the idol. In his *Tarjumán al-Ashwáq*, he thus sings:

> My heart is capable of every form:
> A pasture for gazelles,
> A monastery for monks,
> An abode for idols,
> And a place where the votaries of the Kaaba come.
> In my heart, both the Tablets of the Torah and the Holy Qur'an
>   are to be found.
> My faith and religion is love: wherever it beckons me, I follow.[3]

In a world split apart by religious strife and dissension, such a quest for unity, love, and reconciliation may seem an act not merely of blind faith but of the highest folly, and those who insist on pursuing it, or inciting others to follow their own vision of a world where true unity transcends all such divisions, may indeed seem to be empty dreamers or no more than idle singers of an empty day which can never exist. Yet, as we read the works of the great poets of every age and language, from Dante, Goethe, and Shakespeare to Browning and Tennyson, Shelley and Blake, the more unmistakably apparent it becomes that, even when unaware of one another's existence, still less their writings, they have in common a luminous vision of a future which is not only achievable but the sole possibility for mankind to survive and go forward into an age of light rather than darkness—and which can only be attained by facing the darkness which at present appears well-nigh impenetrable.

Nothing could be further from the truth than the idea that poets are impractical dreamers with no concern for the realization of their visions or their consequences for mankind. From what follows it will become clear that poets are not only the unacknowledged legislators of the world, in Shelley's phrase, but also reflect in their works the great virtues that sustain humanity.

Shelley, the author of that notorious pamphlet "The Necessity of Atheism" which ruined his university career, was one of the most eloquent poets of his age. In his denunciation of the spiritual corruption of the time, as evoked in "England in 1819," he attacked "Religion Christless, Godless—a book sealed" and boldly proclaimed a future in which the human spirit would triumph over ignorance and apathy. He also expressed the hope that mankind would be bound by universal ties of kinship and zeal to bring a new world into being. In his unfavorable comparison of the drabness and materialism of his own times with the radiance and intellectual beauty of ancient Greece, he shared the outlook of other poets of that era: Goethe, Hölderlin, and Schiller in Germany, André Chenier in France, and, in his own country, Wordsworth, who deplored the contemporary tendency to lose sight of the values of the spirit in the pursuit of wealth:

> The world is too much with us; late and soon,
> Getting and spending, we lay waste our powers:
> Little we see in Nature that is ours;
> We have given our hearts away, a sordid boon![4]

Wordsworth was no atheist, but despite this shared with Shelley a profound sense of dislocation from a society whose nominally Christian people were becoming increasingly out of touch with the natural world and thus losing any awareness of those forces which underpinned the whole of creation and united the peoples of the world with one another and with their natural surroundings, inspiring in them a sense not only of wonderment but of mutual responsibility.

III

This deep dissociation between the outward practice of religion and a lack of reverence for creation and for fellow human beings, especially as the pace of industrialization and the exploitation of the natural world and its resources gathered speed during the nineteenth century, can be perceived through the works of many of that century's greatest poets. This is by no means to say that Matthew Arnold or Tennyson were atheists, despite the doubts and anxieties which these reflections necessarily evoked in poets of highly developed sensitivity and intelligence. Rather, their awareness of the schisms and shortcomings of the society in which they lived led them to look beyond the immediate present in a search for a resolution of these conflicts, and to voice not merely a pallid hope but a vehement conviction that such a resolution could and should be attained. These poets faced the inevitability of industrial progress, with its enormous cost in human suffering and environmental damage. They were also aware of the much-vaunted benefits of so-called progress as an irreversible fact, which only confirmed their passionate belief that such advances must be accompanied by a corresponding expansion in human sympathies and an understanding of the price to be paid if further disaster was not to ensue.

William Blake emphasizes the responsibility of those people of vision—prophets, poets, and seers—to arouse the Spirit of Truth, the God in all men. He therefore announces in his great poem, "Jerusalem":

> . . . I rest not from my great task!
> To open the Eternal Worlds,
>   to open the Immortal Eyes
> Of Man inwards into the Worlds of Thought,
>   into Eternity
> Ever expanding in the Bosom of God,
>   the Human Imagination.[5]

This responsibility, however, did not preclude, for example, William Butler Yeats's passionate involvement in the creation of an independent Irish state, but was a potent instrument in determining what form it should take by a direct appeal to the informed sensibilities of those who would inhabit and shape it. Poetry could, without relapsing into nationalistic bombast, rouse them to think what it meant to be not only truly Irish but fully human, and to reflect on their responsibilities to their country and beyond, whether as citizens of Ireland or of the world.

Yeats's ideas, though applicable to and arising from a particular set of political circumstances, attained a wider validity comparable with the statements of many of his great predecessors. As early as the sixteenth century Thomas More had, in his *Utopia*, developed the concept of an ideal state in which equity and harmony would prevail between its citizens and those of other countries. The theme of unity had evolved still further in the poetry of William Blake, whose horror at the building of "dark Satanic mills" with the coming of the Industrial Revolution led him to proclaim his vision of the New Jerusalem, the true city of peace, which must be built with unremitting effort and fierceness of purpose to achieve the abolition of the human misery and injustice which they symbolized.

To move against the trends of the times, as it were, suggested a degree of what almost seemed like lunacy. Industrialization was not only an established fact but one whose significance could only increase as mechanization came to dominate production in every area from mining to textiles; however, the child laborers such as the chimney-sweep given a voice by Blake and the young boys and girls set to work among the dangerous machinery of the cotton mills or to be harnessed to pull carts along subterranean passages too narrow for adults were eventually afforded some degree of protection by the legislation initiated by Lord Shaftesbury: More's "utopian" vision, after long years, eventually bearing fruit.

IV

Yet as well as the exploitation of the earth's resources and those whose lives were sacrificed to win profit from them, the growth of the British Empire also depended on the colonization and development of territories all over the world, frequently at the expense of conflict with those already inhabiting them. There was one author who did more than any other to capture the public's imagination through his poetry and his prose works, such as his account of encounters between Britain and India entitled *Plain Tales from the Hills*, where he blended trenchant observation with dry wit and an awareness of the sacrifices which the service of the Empire demanded. In his stories Rudyard Kipling viewed with a sympathetic but unsentimental eye the vicissitudes of soldiers, Indian Civil Service officials, memsahibs, and camp-followers. Kipling recognized the fact that, in a wider sense, Indians and Britons were all brothers. To assume "the white man's burden" was not an act of arrogance but the assumption of a grave responsibility for one's fellow human beings, and it must be done in full consciousness of the sacrifices which might be required. In general terms, Kipling's poetry emphasizes the responsibility of the ruling class for those in their charge, the officer for his men and the governor for those entrusted to him, from the eponymous hero of "The Roman Centurion's Song" to the tough practical "Sons of Martha" in the poem of that name, whose hard work laid the roads and built the physical structures of the Empire. Without romanticizing them, he offers a vision of the courage and fortitude needed to hold that Empire together, and not least of the essential need for a mutual respect for one's fellow men.

Kipling's inevitable identification with a particular period of history which he evokes so vividly should not blind us to the fact that the truth which he declares here is timeless and universal, and is essentially the same as the message so resonantly proclaimed by Goethe when speaking of his "West-Eastern Divan":

> He who knows himself and others
> Here will also see,
> That the East and West, like brothers,
> Parted ne'er shall be.

> Thoughtfully to float for ever
> Tween two worlds, be man's endeavour!
> So between the East and West
> To revolve, be my behest![6]

and by Victor Hugo:

The glorious banner of us all,
The flag that rises ne'er to fall,
Republic of the World.[7]

This future state is described as a "republic" in that it dispenses with any notion of human supremacy or attempts by one individual to lord it over mankind, but in universal terms it is a world ruled by a Power far greater than any human agency, whose empire is one of unity in its truest sense under one law and one God. Yeats, in "The Second Coming," written in 1919 in the aftermath of the First World War, foresees a new horizon and a new future for humanity. In this famous poem, Yeats faces unflinchingly the current condition of the world, whose desperate loss of harmony and control cries out for and even heralds a resolution:

Surely some revelation is at hand;
Surely the Second Coming is at hand.[8]

What, in turn, unifies all the poets whom we consider here, from Kipling and Yeats to Matthew Arnold, Goethe, Dante, and Shakespeare, is their common conviction that a deeper unity binds mankind together, transcending all boundaries of birth, culture, class, creed, or politics, and that it is the poet's duty to give this expression. To do so with honesty and integrity may and frequently does require the poets to speak in harsh and unsparing terms of the darkness and delusion in which the world finds itself before its peoples are gathered together under one banner and become united.

V

The poet, unlike the scientist, the philosopher, and the psychologist, seeks not to explain our existence but to take us, through the synthesis of reason and emotion in the deepest recesses of the soul, to the essential truth of life itself. For poetry is nothing less than the meeting of the human soul with truth. Of all the senses, it is hearing, the ability to assimilate and respond to the spoken word, which is the last to be lost as consciousness dissolves with the departing of the soul. As we seek to fathom the power of the word, arching from one generation to another to make *Beowulf* or *The Waste Land* or *The Thousand and One Nights* as relevant now as when they were first composed, we may find an answer in Coleridge's "Kubla Khan" and his account of the singular circumstances of its genesis, conceived in a dream.

In Xanadu did Kubla Khan
A stately pleasure-dome decree:
Where Alph, the sacred river, ran

Through caverns measureless to man
Down to a sunless sea.[9]

As we read through the poem, we gradually fall under the spell of its rhythm, its alliteration, which conjures up the surge of the sea and the dreamy wandering of the sacred river Alph, and not least to the power of its symbols and images—towers, woods, caves, a river, and a fountain—which speak to us through the collective unconscious, cutting through the accretions of centuries of rationality which led humankind to undervalue the imaginative and intuitive and lose touch with the profound insights which they alone provide. The final lines describe the poet's own magic and awesome power:

A damsel with a dulcimer
In a vision once I saw:
It was an Abyssinian maid,
And on her dulcimer she played,
Singing of Mount Abora.
Could I revive within me
Her symphony and song,
To such a deep delight 'twould win me,
That with music loud and long,
I would build that dome in air,
That sunny dome! those caves of ice!
And all who heard should see them there,
And all should cry, Beware! Beware!
His flashing eyes, his floating hair!
Weave a circle round him thrice,
And close your eyes with holy dread,
For he on honeydew hath fed,
And drunk the milk of Paradise.[10]

VI

The poet's ability to speak to his hearers through the inner language of the word, playing on the mysterious strings of an instrument tuned to evoke the most subtle and inexplicable responses, enables him to address the profound concerns of an age and to face bleakness and despair while seeing beyond them to a landscape of hope and fulfilment. While acknowledging the trials of this present world, he does not merely palliate his audience's sufferings with vague promises of nebulous rewards in the distant future, but fires their spirits with a conviction that that future is attainable, and with the courage to work toward its achievement. It was not in vain that Andrew

Fletcher of Saltoun, the eighteenth-century Scottish patriot who staunchly resisted the Act of Union with England in 1707, declared, "Give us the poets. Anyone can make the laws."[11] He understood that once the true spirit is present, the letter of the law follows and is imbued with it, and it is that spirit, that unity of being and purpose, which the poets embody and enshrine.

It is striking that many of the greatest such proclamations date from the nineteenth century, an age of growing nationalism that, on the surface of things, might have been expected to act as a divisive force. Side by side with the determination to cast off foreign domination, however, there existed a sense of kinship among the smaller nations, the oppressed, and those who shared a consciousness of their past suppression and future potential.

VII

Yet the wider the gulf which opened between rich and poor, industrialist and labourer, conqueror and conquered, the more acute became the poets' awareness of the overarching forces which united these divided cultures and classes and the urgent need to make mankind aware of them and of the potential which it afforded for peace and reconciliation. Centuries before, the prophet Isaiah had foretold the coming of just such a peaceable kingdom, where the lion would lie down with the lamb and a little child play fearlessly among the haunts of cockatrice and adder and lead savage beasts in docile company, and Virgil had likewise sung in his Fourth Eclogue of the coming of a wondrous child whose birth would herald a new golden age where nature and man would be in perfect accord and the wild creatures would gather round the infant to marvel at him. This poem was responsible for the view among the early Christians of Virgil as a righteous pagan who, though not able to receive the sacrament of baptism, had been blessed with a presentiment of the coming of Christ Himself, and for Dante's choice of Virgil as his guide through the Inferno and Purgatory in his *Divina Commedia*, only leaving Dante at the entrance to Paradise which, as an unbaptized person, he could not enter, relinquishing him to the guidance of his beloved Beatrice.

Whether or not the critic accepts this interpretation (and much ink has been spilt in efforts to prove a "rational," historical identity for the baby whose advent Virgil so joyfully anticipates), it is undeniable that beyond all attempts to fix such utterances and limit them to a specific time and place, there resounds the poets' prophetic certainty of a future untainted by the present miseries of the world, and of a divine guidance which is eternally present to make it not merely a pious hope but a firm and radiant goal. Moving from the first century of our era to the nineteenth, we find Tennyson, in the concluding lines of "In Memoriam," expressing precisely that belief in:

That God, which ever lives and loves,
    One God, one law, one element,
    And one far-off divine event,
To which the whole creation moves.[12]

Elsewhere in the same poem he warns against neglecting the intuitions of poetry in favour of sole reliance on "reason" and philosophy:

Hold thou the good: define it well;
    For fear divine Philosophy
    Should push beyond her mark, and be
Procuress to the Lords of Hell.[13]

These glimpses of truth are vouchsafed so that we may cleave to them in spite of all who might use prosaic arguments to seek to persuade us that they are insubstantial or deluded.

In one of the most famous sections of the poem, often extracted to be read alone, the poet prophesies, as the bells ring out the old year, its death to usher in a new era of justice, peace, and unity:

Ring out old shapes of foul disease;
    Ring out the narrowing lust of gold;
    Ring out the thousand wars of old,
Ring in the thousand years of peace.

Ring in the valiant man and free,
    The larger heart, the kindlier hand;
    Ring out the darkness of the land,
Ring in the Christ that is to be.[14]

Incorporated into this vision is the renewal of the poet himself:

Ring out the want, the care, the sin,
    The faithless coldness of the times;
    Ring out, ring out my mournful rhymes,
But ring the fuller minstrel in.[15]

Tennyson foresees the emergence of a new way of life "with sweeter manners, purer laws,"[16] proceeding from the entire transforming and regeneration of humanity in accordance with a supreme and universal Law of love and equity and the spontaneous choice to follow it.

This sense of the right and necessary ending, even of what may seem good so that it may be succeeded by the Supreme Good, recurs throughout Tennyson's writing, from those famous words from "Morte d'Arthur":

> The old order changeth, yielding place to new,
> And God fulfils himself in many ways,
> Lest one good custom should corrupt the world.[17]

to "Locksley Hall," with its terrible vision of aerial warfare following the young man's optimistic excitement at the achievements of mankind:

> Men, my brothers, men the workers, ever reaping something new;
> That which they have done but earnest of the things that they shall do.[18]

This, however, gives place to a new age of peace-making:

> Till the war-drum throbb'd no longer, and the battle-flags were furl'd
> In the Parliament of man, the Federation of the world.
>
> Then the common sense of most shall hold a fretful realm in awe,
> And the kindly earth shall slumber, lapt in universal law.[19]

Thus Tennyson faces squarely the dreadful possibilities of a future which must be lived through and transcended if the new world order which he welcomes is ever to come into being; humanity must confront the responsibility for what has been done in the past and its own potential for destruction if that regeneration is to be a genuine one, capable of atoning for the horrors of history and making reparation. This unflinchingly realistic appraisal of humanity's position in an age of declining faith is shared by Matthew Arnold, as he states in "Dover Beach," appealing to human love and constancy in the face of the delusive hollowness of the world's attractions:

> Ah, love, let us be true
> To one another! for the world, which seems
> To lie before us like a land of dreams,
> So various, so beautiful, so new,
> Hath really neither joy, nor love, nor light,
> Nor certitude, nor peace, nor help for pain;
> And we are here as on a darkling plain
> Swept with confused alarms of struggle and flight,
> Where ignorant armies clash by night.[20]

VIII

We have already seen how Yeats viewed the Second Coming in his poem of that name; he was not, however, the only Irishman to write of those whom Arthur O'Shaughnessy had referred to as follows:

> . . . scorning the dream of to-morrow,
> Are bringing to pass, as they may,
> In the world, for its joy or its sorrow,
> The dream that was scorned yesterday.[21]

These "music-makers . . . the dreamers of dreams" appear to be unworldly visionaries with little influence on the outcome of human affairs, and yet they are the movers and shakers "Of the world for ever, it seems."

O'Shaughnessy continues, in the second verse,

> With wonderful deathless ditties
> We build up the world's great cities,
> And out of a fabulous story
> We fashion an empire's glory:
> One man with a dream, at pleasure,
> Shall go forth and conquer a crown;
> And three with a new song's measure
> Can trample a kingdom down.[22]

The poets and singers are compelled to keep "a little apart" from their fellows to preserve their vision:

> How, spite of your human scorning,
> Once more God's future draws nigh,
> And already goes forth the warning
> That ye of the past must die.[23]

He sums up the calling of the poet as a visionary who inspires his fellow-mortals to press forward into a future beyond their imaginings, drawing not only on the strength of their own dreams and insights but on the vocabulary of spirituality throughout the ages, from Thomas Carlyle's conclusion in *Sartor Resartus* that "the Universe is one vast Symbol of God" to Gerard Manley Hopkins's proclamation of man as the symbol of Christ.

To do so entails a vast leap of faith on the part of the poet which he might well be unable to undertake were it not for the absolute conviction which his calling gives him in his ability, as Shakespeare puts it in *A Midsummer Night's Dream*:

The lunatic, the lover and the poet
Are of imagination all compact:
One sees more devils than vast hell can hold;
That is the madman: the lover, all as frantic,
Sees Helen's beauty in a brow of Egypt;
The poet's eye, in a fine frenzy rolling,
Doth from heaven to earth, from earth to heaven;
And as imagination bodies forth
The forms of things unknown, the poet's pen
Turns them to shapes, and gives to airy nothing
A local habitation and a name.[24]

Charles Lamb, indeed, states the "the true poet dreams, being awake"; but these statements point to the suspension of a rational way of thinking and willed choice of words to allow free play to the force of that true inspiration defined by Aristotle in his *Poetics,* where he suggested that poetry of this kind proceeded from "either a strain of madness or a happy gift of nature." Wordsworth himself, one of the prime examples of a poet who not only experienced inspiration but was able to speak of its workings, explained:

One moment now may give us more
Than years of toiling reason.[25]

in attempts to reach out toward the essence of truth and express it in words which all could understand. Elsewhere, in "The Excursion," he wrote:

Oh! many are the Poets that are sown
By Nature; men endowed with highest gifts,
The vision and the faculty divine;
Yet wanting the accomplishment of verse—[26]

those who may lack the polish acquired by those who frequent Yeats's "singing-school," but nevertheless, like John Clare, the ploughman turned poet, find the means to utter the words vouchsafed to them:

Poetry is indeed a thing of God;
He made His prophets poets: and the more
We feel of poesie do we become
Like God in love and power.[27]

To achieve this blessed state, however, requires an ability to be still and to contemplate sadly lacking in the busy striving of everyday life, as Matthew Arnold acknowledged:

Too fast we live, too much are tried,
Too harassed, to attain
Wordsworth's sweet calm, or Goethe's wide
And luminous view to gain.[28]

Nor was it only poets writing in the English language who looked forward to an age in which singers and seers would lead the peoples of the world toward reconciliation with one another and with themselves. The Austrian dramatist Grillparzer spent long periods during the 1840s working on his play *Libussa*, based on the ancient Bohemian legend of a princess who, unlike her two reclusive and withdrawn sisters, actively seeks involvement in the world. The princess actively rules her people, chooses as her consort the wise ploughman Primislaus, and works for justice and peace. Exhausted by her efforts, she is near to death when her sisters reappear and reproach her for, as they see it, betraying herself and squandering her gifts. She replies that human beings are fundamentally good, but too easily preoccupied with the business of striving for earthly achievements at the expense of their inner life, and will eventually feel the emptiness in which they live and listen once again to the voice of the poet, the voice of the heart, of love, and awareness of their own powerlessness which is also an awareness of the great spiritual powers latent in every human heart:

Then will the age return that's passing now,
The age of seers and of gifted ones.
When knowledge and expediency part,
Feeling they take to join them, their third fellow,
And then they make their way to heaven itself.
The earth will climb once more to her own place,
And in our hearts the gods will dwell again:
Humility herself rules and unites them.[29]

NOTES

1. *The Letters of W. B. Yeats*, ed. Alan Wade (London: R. Hart-Davis, 1954), p. 356.

2. AE (George Russell), *The Interpreters* (London: Macmillan, 1922).

3. Based on the translation of R. A. Nicholson in M. Ibn al-'Arabi, *Tarjuman Al-Ashwaq: A Collection of Mystical Odes*, ed. and tr. R. A. Nicholson (London: Theosophical Publishing House, Ltd., 1978), p. 67.

4. William Wordsworth, "The World Is Too Much with Us," in *The Complete Poetical Works of Wordsworth*, ed. Andrew J. George (Boston: Houghton, Mifflin and Co., 1904), p. 349.

5. William Blake, "Jerusalem," in *The Complete Writings of William Blake*, ed. G. Keynes (London: Oxford University Press, 1972), p. 623.

6. Johann Wolfgang von Goethe, "On the Divan," in *The Poems of Goethe*, ed. and tr. Edgar Alfred Bowring (New York: John B. Alden, 1883), p. 208.

7. Victor Hugo, "Temps Futurs," in *The Universal Republic*, December 16–20, 1853.

8. William Butler Yeats, "The Second Coming," in *W. B. Yeats: Selected Poetry*, ed. A. Norman Jeffares (London: Macmillan, 1968), p. 100.

9. Samuel Taylor Coleridge, "Kubla Khan," in *Samuel Taylor Coleridge: The Complete Poems*, ed. William Keach (London: Penguin Books, 1997), p. 259.

10. Ibid., p. 251.

11. Quoted in A. J. Stewart, *Died 1513–Born 1929: The autobiography of A. J. Stewart* (London: Macmillan, 1978), p. 269.

12. Alfred Tennyson, "In Memoriam," in *The Complete Poetical Works of Tennyson*, ed. W. J. Rolfe (Boston: Houghton, Mifflin and Co., 1898), p. 198.

13. Ibid., p. 175.

14. Ibid., p. 190.

15. Ibid.

16. Ibid.

17. "Morte d'Arthur," in *The Complete Poetical Works of Tennyson*, p. 67.

18. "Locksley Hall," in *The Complete Poetical Works of Tennyson*, p. 93.

19. Ibid.

20. Matthew Arnold, "Dover Beach," in *The Poems of Matthew Arnold*, ed. Kenneth Allott (New York: Barnes & Noble, Inc., 1965), pp. 242–243.

21. Arthur O'Shaughnessy, "Ode," in *The Golden Treasury*, selected and arranged by Francis Turner Palgrave (London: Oxford University Press, 1963), pp. 474–476.

22. Ibid.

23. Ibid.

24. V.i., 7–17.

25. William Wordsworth, "To My Sister," in *The Complete Poetical Works of Wordsworth*, p. 82.

26. "The Excursion," in *The Complete Poetical Works of Wordsworth*, p. 412.

27. Philip James Bailey, *Festus: A Poem* (London: William Pickering, 1852), p. 338.

28. Matthew Arnold, "Stanzas in Memory of the author of *Obermann*," in *The Poems of Matthew Arnold*, p. 133.

29. Grillparzer, *Libussa*, V., 2482–2489 (tr. Susan Reynolds).

SUHEIL BADI BUSHRUI is a distinguished author, poet, critic, translator, and media personality, well known in the United States, Europe, and the Arab world. Widely recognized for his seminal studies in English of the works of W. B. Yeats and for his translations of Yeats's poetry into Arabic, Professor Bushrui is also the foremost authority on the works of Kahlil Gibran. At present, he is the Director of the Kahlil Gibran Chair for Values and Peace in the Center for Heritage Resource Studies at the University of Maryland. The Chair is the first academic forum in the world devoted to the preservation of Gibran's legacy and the promotion of East-West intercultural relations.